NEVER SURRENDER

NEVER SURRENDER

Confederate Memory and Conservatism in the South Carolina Upcountry

W. SCOTT POOLE

The University of Georgia Press
Athens & London

© 2004 by the University of Georgia Press
Athens, Georgia 30602
All rights reserved
Designed by Walton Harris
Set in 10/13 Sabon by Bookcomp, Inc.
Printed and bound by Maple-Vail
The paper in this book meets the guidelines for
permanence and durability of the Committee on
Production Guidelines for Book Longevity of the
Council on Library Resources.

Printed in the United States of America

03   04   05   06   07   C   5   4   3   2   1
03   04   05   06   07   P   5   4   3   2   1

Library of Congress Cataloging-in-Publication Data

Poole, W. Scott, 1971–
Never surrender : Confederate memory and conservatism
in the South Carolina upcountry / W. Scott Poole.
    p.   cm.
Includes bibliographical references and index.
ISBN 0-8203-2507-4 (hardcover : alk. paper) —
ISBN 0-8203-2508-2 (pbk. : alk. paper)
1. South Carolina—Politics and government—1865–1950.
2. South Carolina—Politics and government—1775–1865.
3. South Carolina—Intellectual life—19th century.
4. Conservatism—South Carolina—History—19th century.
5. Memory—Social aspects—South Carolina—History—
19th century.   6. Political culture—South Carolina—
History—19th century.   7. United States—History—
Civil War, 1861–1865—Influence.   I. Title.
F274 .P66 2004
320.52'09757'09034—dc21   2003012361

British Library Cataloging-in-Publication Data available

CONTENTS

ACKNOWLEDGMENTS

A mealtime blessing from the Buddhist monastic tradition gives thanks for "the thousand hands that gave us this bread." Like the making of bread, the making of a book is a cooperative enterprise. It simply would not have reached completion had it not been for "a thousand hands."

First, I want to thank Charles Reagan Wilson, whose work *Baptized in Blood: The Religion of the Lost Cause, 1865–1920* (University of Georgia Press, 1980) opened to me the world of southern history. Though I use his work critically in this volume, I continue to find his pathbreaking research a joy to learn from, as well as a joy to teach. Charles continues to serve as my ideal of both a scholar and a gentleman, my greatest teacher in a life full of wonderful teachers.

Susan Edwards's continued interest in and encouragement of my work means more to me than she probably realizes. The dedication of a future work belongs to her, for reasons only we two are able to understand. In a college cafeteria, a long time ago, she told her friends I "looked like a writer." I hope that she has been able to see even more important things in me in recent years.

The wonders of the South Caroliniana Library have made possible the deluge of titles in southern history over the past several decades. I want to especially thank Robin Cox and Beth Bilderback for helping me track down sources and photographs. A number of archives proved very helpful, including the Special Collections at Clemson University, the Newberry College archives, and the Baptist Historical Collections at Furman University, where Carolyn Lancaster always proved willing to lend a hand. I would also like to thank John Boles and the *Journal of Southern History*. Chapter 6 of this book first made an appearance in the August 2003 issue of that fine journal. Derek Krissoff at the University of Georgia Press helped shepherd this project through and answered all my questions along the way, as did my copyeditors, Madelaine Cooke and Jennifer Reichlin.

A number of individuals provided encouragement and criticism along the way. Special mention should be made of Alan Richard, who has graced me with his lifelong friendship. Our frequent discussion of the meaning of South Carolina history, the history of the place "where we were born and raised," continues to open up new doors of understanding for me and sharpen my perceptions when they become a bit hazy with the details. His own forthcoming work on *Briggs v. Elliott* and the civil rights era in South Carolina will do much to illuminate and, it is to be hoped, effect change in a place that changes only slowly and unwillingly. Danny Varat and Benjamin Wynn are by turns encouraging voices and sparring partners. Edward Blum, my Yankee friend, has been a wonderful conference companion. His own scholarship, soon to make quite a splash, has provided a worthy model to emulate. Other friends and companions must be mentioned—Gina Varat, Christophe Boucher, Jessica Dorman, Patrick and Jennifer Speelman, Alice Lauchessee, Minoa Uffelman-Evans, Rebecca Click, Rosemary Brana-Shute, George Hopkins, Bruce Baker, and lots more that I am undoubtedly, and ungratefully, forgetting.

Several colleagues have given encouragement and criticism, reading drafts, listening to ideas, and making suggestions. My friend David Gleeson, undoubtedly my favorite Irishman, has been an important source of both wisdom and comic relief, all shared over a Guinness or two. As I think of all the other colleagues, mentors, and role models in my professional life, I'm struck by how blessed I am to know such amazing personalities and intellects, including Gaines Foster, Bernard Powers, Jack Bass, Cleveland Sellers, Lee Drago, James Farmer, Valdis Lumans, Elaine Lacy, Tom Brown, and Marvin Dulaney. All have offered, in different ways, something of themselves to my life and work.

My students at the College of Charleston deserve some mention. By turns exasperating, inspiring, and even illuminating, they are one of my life's chief joys. I especially want to mention the students of my South Carolina history lectures from the fall of 2002 and the spring of 2003. No assistant professor, fresh from graduate school and nervous about the demands of the tenure track, could be given a finer group of young women and men with whom to spend the first year of his career. Amy Sottile and Nakia White have been special joys, with their commitment and enthusiasm for the study of southern history. My graduate student Catherine Fitzgerald took time from her own important work on women and the Lost Cause to help clarify my thinking on gender and Confederate memory. She also graciously looked up a citation or two, a grand favor much appreciated. Her own scholarship will soon surprise, challenge, and impress us all.

Finally, my parents, Clarence and Joan Poole. If my heart did not belong to the ghosts of the past, the dedication of this book would, by rights, go to them. What would have become of me if they were not the people they are? I would not wish to know.

NEVER SURRENDER

INTRODUCTION

South Carolinians Never Surrender

South Carolina and the
Roots of Southern Conservatism

Thomas Nelson Page, the 1880s author of "Old South" romance, liked to tell the story of a Confederate soldier making his way home following the surrender at Appomattox. Along the way he encountered disaffected southerners tired of the war, many of whom articulated less-than-patriotic sentiments. One jovial young lad, undoubtedly glad to have missed Antietam and Gettysburg, called out to the veteran from a tavern door. "Hey Johnny, have you had enough? Don't you think them Yankees will come looking for you?" Scowling, the veteran turned to his nemesis. "If they do," he growled, "I reckon I'll just whip 'em again." [1]

Page's tale captures the ethos of southern conservatism in postbellum South Carolina. The hotspur Palmetto State, described by Eugene Genovese as "having made fewer concessions than any other state to the democratic ideology and practice," fashioned a conservative response to Confederate defeat—in fact, conservatives used defeat itself to configure a stance of inveterate defiance against the larger world of the late nineteenth century. [2] Confederate South Carolinians, at least on a cultural level, refused to go gently into the good night of surrender, refused to yield to modernity and the world the Yankee made. For a brief time, southern conservatism transformed the postbellum landscape into a theater of resistance, showcasing alternative worlds that seem exotic growths in the garden of American mass democracy. Rallying around the fallen banner of the Confederacy and celebrating the Lost Cause, southern conservatism sought to find a voice of provincial dissent and to create an oppositional culture. The Lost Cause, elaborated in intellectual life, public performances, religious experience, and cultural production, became the crux of the culture of southern conservatism.

This book reopens debate on what has come to be known as "the Lost Cause movement," an omnibus term that describes how southern-

ers across the region celebrated the defeated Confederacy in the waning years of the nineteenth century. Public memorial monuments, Confederate memorial days, and even southern religious life focused on the
"Confederate War," its heroes, its victories, and, of course, its ultimate
defeat. Two divergent interpretations of this movement have appeared in
the last two decades. Charles Reagan Wilson's *Baptized in Blood* views
the work of Confederate memory as "a cultural revitalization movement"
in which a religious interpretation of southern identity played a central
role. Postwar southerners, Wilson argues, created a "sacred society" out
of the ruins of the defeated Confederacy, a society whose values acted
as a prophetic challenge to the proponents of the New South world of
railroads and factories. Wilson uses the concept of "civil religion" to explain the southern attempt to fashion a sacred society in the aftermath of
war and Emancipation. Wilson borrows this term from Robert Bellah and
Will Herberg, suggesting that just as the broadly American civil religion
provided people from different traditions "a sense of belonging" so did
the Lost Cause offer postwar southerners "a sense of meaning, an identity
in a precarious and distinct culture."[3]

The second influential interpretation of the Lost Cause movement appears in Gaines M. Foster's *Ghosts of the Confederacy: Defeat, the Lost
Cause and the Emergence of the New South* (1987). Foster views the Lost
Cause not so much as an attempt to construct cultural myth and a civil
religion, but as an effort to overcome the psychological anxiety attendant upon defeat and an attempt by the newborn southern bourgeoisie
to legitimize the values of the New South. Religion had little to do with
this commemoration, since the churches had little to do with shaping the
tradition. The leadership of the Confederate veterans' organizations, in
Foster's interpretation, came from the rising commercial class that discovered in the memory of the Confederate experience a legitimization for
their entrepreneurial values. Foster disdained the notion of civil religion
and explained the Lost Cause with the term "Confederate tradition," a
term that suggests malleability and elastic change over time in response
to social tension and upheaval."[4]

The notion of Confederate commemoration as cultural revitalization
seems truer to the experience of most southerners in the period immediately following the Civil War. Much of Foster's evidence that Confederate
memory acted as a gloss on New South materialism comes from the period following the 1890s. Unfortunately, neither side of the debate has
engaged in much local study, and, stranger still, neither focused much on
South Carolina, the heartland of southern radicalism and secession. Both

Wilson and Foster spend much time on commemoration in Virginia, along with Tennessee and Georgia. Furthermore, the role of the Lost Cause in the upheaval of Reconstruction and Redemption plays little to no role in either account.

A number of problems inhere in both interpretations of this important movement. Wilson's use of Robert Bellah and Will Herberg's contested concept ignores that a civil religion, acts, by its very nature, as an inclusive phenomenon. Wilson himself notes that what he calls the "southern civil religion" does not function like Herberg's welcoming haven of liberalism and democratic values.[5] The religion of the Lost Cause, instead, celebrated personal and corporate virtue and drew strict lines of demarcation between the blessed and the damned—a sharp dichotomy not allowed by civil religion. Foster's Confederate tradition, meanwhile, does not do justice to the profoundly religious character of this movement and its tendency to immerse itself in the language and ethos of evangelical Christianity. Clearly, new conceptual tools are needed to fully explain the importance of the Lost Cause in the waning years of the nineteenth century.

This study makes use of the phrase "Confederate religion" to describe the relationship of the Lost Cause and religion and, as a more general category, the "aesthetic of the Lost Cause" to describe how conservatives fashioned a variety of cultural materials into a public articulation of an ordered and organic society, a society that worked harmoniously guided by a patriarchal ethos. Devotion to the Confederacy became a religious value for South Carolinians who sought to shape a southern sacred world. The experience of conversion in particular provided a paradigm for regenerative change amid the ruins of the Old South. South Carolina's romantic conservatism shared its cultural roots with an explosive evangelical revivalism that the sanctified the ideal of social hierarchy and prescriptive tradition.

Scholars who have examined southern conservatism have assumed that the antebellum era was its golden age. My own study takes a different approach. The Old South contained a number of inherent contradictions that, ironically, could find resolution and catharsis in Confederate defeat. South Carolina conservatives could then deal with the paradoxes of their society by creating a public aesthetic, a dream of the world. Shaping these contradictory themes into a public aesthetic solved some of the difficulties for conservatives, since, as Susanne Langer and Walker Percy have argued, metaphors are always a kind of mistake. Aesthetics seems especially promising for southern historians seeking to understand "the mind of the South," since, as G. W. F. Hegel wrote, aesthetic expression represents a society's "intuition of the world." In postbellum South Carolina, conservatives used the Lost Cause to express their intuition of the world, a meditation and an appeal that called white Carolinians to defiance and defined the effort of white conservatives to create a narrative out of defeat, a tale of rupture and redemption.[6]

The use of an aesthetic model for understanding southern conservative ideology is in part inspired by European expressions of conservatism. The southern conservative tradition shows some resemblance to continental romantic conservatism that looked to the classical and medieval past as a guide for a society more deeply human than the turbulent world created by the political and economic revolutions of the eighteenth and nineteenth centuries. Romantic conservatism saw the political good embodied in an ordered society that drew its *raison d'être* from tradition and custom. The liberty of the aristocratic elite rested on their ancestral claims to property. The idea of "natural rights," rights abstracted from the tissue of custom and tradition rooted in a glorious past, had no meaning for the romantic conservatives. Rejecting Rousseau's, Hobbes's, and Locke's understanding of the contractual state, the romantic conservatives viewed human society as a living, breathing organism, and heartily rejected notions of civil polity as contract. Edmund Burke, whose writings against the French Revolution are considered the fountain of modern conservative thought, writes, "The state ought not to be considered as nothing better than a partnership agreement in a trade of pepper and coffee, calico or tobacco, or some other such low concern. . . . It is a partnership in all science; a partnership in all art; a partnership in every virtue, and in all perfection. As the ends of such a partnership cannot be obtained in many generations, it becomes a partnership not only between those who are living, but between those who are living, those who are dead, and those who are to be born."[7]

Southern intellectuals found in European conservatism a framework that seemed to explain their region's plight, paradigms of their ongoing struggle with modernity. The richness of German romantic conservatism in particular made its way to the American South through the writings of Thomas Carlyle. This cranky English thinker had imbibed from German romantic conservatives a hatred for radical democracy, seeing it as an unnatural mechanism that unhinged the divine order. Referring to the antislavery movements in England and America as "twaddle," he gave instinctive support to the Confederacy in 1861, calling the abolitionist north "shot through with atheism, decadence and self-indulgence."

European roots

Carlyle's often unpopular opinions set him strongly in the tradition of cultural alienation, a centerpiece of romantic conservatism. Rather than truly seeking to conserve the established order in their respective societies, romantic conservatives sought a radical return to earlier times and social relations. In the words of Lord Acton, another British supporter of the Confederacy, they are "partisans of sinking ships."[8]

My examination argues that intellectual influences like these, while important, played a lesser role in the making of southern conservatism than the public symbolisms shaped by celebrants of the Lost Cause. South Carolina at the end of the American Civil War became a platform upon which romantic conservatives acted out their drama of history. A look at how they fashioned a cultural aesthetic offers a window on the much-debated meaning of conservatism, and of southern conservatism in particular. In method, this study follows the lead of the new cultural history in arguing that we cannot analyze political ideology with simple reference to underlying social structures, finding in those configurations a raison d'être for political rhetoric.[9] In fact, this work assumes that ideology loses its contextual meaning if separated from the cultural products of those who believe in it. Ideology and culture have an unbreakable bond, although ideology and social, and economic structures are often deeply alienated. Culture, on the other hand, acts as the handmaiden of ideology, the crucial element without which an ideology becomes the private vision of cranks. This examination does not, then, simply present an intellectual history of individual conservative thinkers, though it does include some discussion of those important matters. Neither does it examine the economic and social structures of the South Carolina upcountry and then seek to explain how these structures conform to an abstract paradigm of conservatism. This is, instead, an examination of cultural trends, an examination of *mentalities*. Examining the cultural efflorescence of an ideology in South Carolina, at a particular historical moment, allows us to consider the animal on a run, rather than simply the animal at rest. I hope this study helps define the animal.

"Civilizations, vast or otherwise," wrote Fernand Braudel, "can always be located on a map." Making sense of southern conservatism, understanding the civilization shaped by it in the postbellum period, requires an understanding of the complex web of land and people that brought it to birth. Most social historians would not consider this work a local study; it is preeminently a cultural history. However, we will never gain an understanding of conservatism, or of any ideology, if we abstract it from its social context.

In this work, I focus on the South Carolina upcountry. Though the state often displayed a unified political ethos, its cultural ethos tended to be multivalent. In fact, even a look at a map of South Carolina shows that the Palmetto State never displayed a geographical unity concomitant with its tendency toward outward political unity. Stretching from the Atlantic coast into the sandy midlands, the so-called low country, with its heavy rainfall, well-drained soil, and fertile swampland crisscrossed by numerous blackwater rivers, offered wealth and political power to the slaveholding rice planters who dominated South Carolina politics from the imperial period into the nineteenth century. The backcountry, or upcountry, defined here as both the sandhills along the fall line, and the piedmont region that fingers its way into the edge of the southern Appalachians, acted as the boisterous younger brother to the low country, coming of age in the nineteenth-century cotton boom and working in tandem with its older, wealthier sibling to create the state's peculiar cultural and political system. Cut by numerous rivers that intersect the low country's complex river system and bounded by the Blue Ridge mountains to the north, rolling hills, red clay, and long-leaf pine are the region's most prominent topographical features, although in the colonial and antebellum periods, the ubiquitous red clay had a ten- to twelve-inch layer of verdant topsoil, now worn by erosion and poor farming practices. This rich topsoil had helped make the upcountry the center of the South's cotton boom before the settling of Alabama and Mississippi.[10]

In the earliest records, the upcountry appears as a theater of constant change, a frontier that provided a backdrop for colliding cultures and value systems. The protean nature of this region makes an appearance in the earliest contacts between settlers and native peoples. The cultural clash between entrepreneurial Europeans and the Cherokee, Creek, and Catawba not only rerouted the course of native economic life but also profoundly affected the Indian's mythopoeic world, introducing apocalyptic themes into their religious experience. In the late seventeenth and early eighteenth centuries, the smattering of Englishmen who made their way from coastal Carolina's Oyster Point into the blue hills of the southern Appalachians heard tales from their Cherokee trading partners of a "time of trouble" that had recently overshadowed them. Their religious apocalypse had led to a transformation of traditional Cherokee religious practice in response to the withering hand of disease touching the backlands through the presence of French and Spanish explorers and commercial agents. The traditional ties of Cherokee to their land, to their deer, and to their gods suffered the fate that would follow so many who inherited

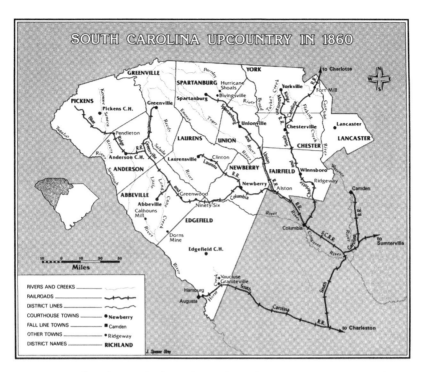

From *Origins of Southern Radicalism: The South Carolina Upcountry, 1800–1860* by Lacy K. Ford Jr., copyright © 1991 by Lacy K. Ford Jr. Used by permission of Oxford University Press, Inc.

the stands of pine and rich soil—a Götterdämerung brought by strangers in search of fortune.[11]

The reach of the whites expanded quickly in the early eighteenth century. Following the quelling of the Spanish threat on the frontier, entrepreneurs eager to profit from the deerskin trade with the Cherokee and Creek trickled into the backcountry. Thomas Hatley describes how these traders, who often made their homes in the lower Cherokee towns, occupied a liminal space, a netherworld between the English pretensions of the coast and the "native" wilderness.[12] Interestingly, Hatley's anthropological construction of the early white experience in the backcountry seems to have been widely shared by many eighteenth-century observers, who also saw whites in the region as living on a borderland between savagery and civilization. Even after the massive eighteenth-century infusion of Scotch-Irish into the Carolina backlands, most observers viewed the region as tottering on the edge of barbarism. Charles Woodmason's narrative of his struggles as an Anglican emissary to the backcountry seems the very incarnation of what has been called "the imperial gaze," the construction of an arena of savagery by a self-conscious representative of "civilization."[13] Woodmason viewed the Scotch-Irish yeoman and English merchants and settlers of 1766 as a people "of abandoned morals and profligate principles . . . rude ignorant and void of manners." Woodmason, understandably piqued by the Scotch-Irish Presbyterian's tendency to upset the proprieties of Anglican worship by firing off squirrel guns and loosing hunting dogs on his communicants, described the lifestyle of the upcountry as "a state of nature as irregular and unchaste as Indians."[14]

Late-eighteenth-century travelers in the upcountry often carried away an impression similar to that of the Anglican missionary. "They . . . reside in log houses isolated in the woods which are left open in the night as well as the day," wrote the French botanist François Michaux, who concluded that the "moral character" of the backcountry had "received the vices and the defects" of the Scotch-Irish who "come every year in great numbers." An attempt at a more balanced view came from Lucius Bierce, a northern schoolteacher who wrote that those who lived in the land of "barren sand and pitch pine timber" had the virtues of "Love of Liberty, hospitality, charity and a nice sense of honor" while exhibiting the vices of "indolence and drunkenness." Life in the Carolina upcountry, in large part because of conflict with the Cherokee and the struggles inherent in frontier life, remained a marginal region in western culture. South Carolina was regarded as "the world's end" by many eighteenth-century low-country planters, and even one modern historian has anachronistically referred to the region as "dysfunctional."[15]

The raw newness of the region allows us to watch the emergence of a new cultural ideology in South Carolina, a cultural ideology born in violence and the search for order. Many of the emerging planters in the backcountry who would soon challenge British rule cut their teeth as leaders of South Carolina's Regulator movement of the late 1760s. Intent on bringing order to the frontier and defending the rights of the propertied, slaveholding men of means led armed bands against, "rogues, and other idle worthless and vagrant people." The backcountry did play unwilling host to a number of vicious outlaw gangs, but the Regulator cavalry also went after drifters and hunters who owned no property and represented a danger to the planter's ideal. Women who had taken up with the outlaw gangs after being captured as children, or who lived lives of ill repute, faced the wrath of the vigilante. Not only, remembered one contemporary, was "the country purged of all villains" but also "the whores were whipped & drove off . . . tranquility reigned, industry was restor'd." Many of these same leaders simultaneously squelched the last resistance of the native peoples in the bloody Cherokee War of 1760–61.[16]

Their struggle to bring order to the backcountry, and their willingness to use violence to achieve order and defend property, would become a defining characteristic of upcountry conservative leaders as would, sometimes paradoxically, a gnawing distrust of "the people," whose appetites and passions could lead to disorder. Less than twenty years after the Regulator movement, South Carolina's revolutionary fathers would express admiration for the most conservative versions of ancient republicanism because of their ability "to check and restrain democracy." The state's 1790 constitution attempted to embody this conservative republicanism by limiting the franchise to white men who owned at least a fifty-acre freehold, a requirement that excluded one-third of South Carolina white men from the political process. Property represented power, and the South Carolina elite sought to marginalize those who did not own property, whether they were native people, outlaws, or down-at-the-heels white men.[17]

The defense of property as a basic individual right has become the sine qua non of modern American conservatism. In the Age of Revolution, however, this idea found its defenders among bourgeois liberals assaulting the allied forces of throne and altar. Eugene Genovese and Elizabeth Fox-Genovese have attempted to combine respect for tradition and historic institutions with the concern for personal liberty in the southern context by writing of the South's "social bond individualism." This assertion, on its face, represents question-begging of the highest order. First, social bond individualism functioned only for free white men in the South, forcing a rather tortured definition of "liberty." Moreover, can white southern males exhibit personal liberty when they are compelled to live according to prescribed social roles involving duty, honor, and the ability to command? In sum, social bond individualism seems to be little more than an elegantly stated contradiction.[18]

Landownership for white South Carolinians does seem, however, to have carried both personal independence and membership in the social order. Whatever ideological label best suits the impulse to personal independence, it is nevertheless true that the theme of centralized power as a danger to liberty and property emerged early in the polemics of Carolina against the world, an idea shaped both by the heritage of Revolutionary republicanism and by the emerging economic milieu. While backcountry farmers feared that a consolidated national government would force them to pay their overwhelming debts, the rising planter class feared a powerful central government that might emancipate slaves. Aedanus Burke, an upcountry representative to the first meeting of the U.S. Congress, spoke out against attempts by Pennsylvania Quakers to submit antislavery petitions for the consideration, calling himself "an advocate for the protection of property." The homespun philosopher caused great embarrassment among the genteel Carolina delegation, made up mostly of low-country nabobs. Burke's tenure at the convention almost ended in a duel with Alexander Hamilton. At home his upcountry constituents had greeted the new U.S. Constitution by parading "a coffin painted black . . . as an emblem of the dissolution and internment of publick liberty." The fear that personal liberty might fall victim to various conglomerations of power would remain a central theme in upcountry life. In the 1830s, upcountryman John C. Calhoun's own hatred of consolidated power found expression in his fear of "turbulent majorities" that could be controlled by consolidated and centralized power. Such a view of the deadly nature of centralized power combined with a dour view of human nature grew out of what one of his biographers describes as a "political skepticism" learned from Aristotle and Machiavelli. Reflecting Calhoun's fear of the unsettled masses directed by the controlling hand of tyrannical government, his view perfectly expressed the sense of Carolinians that liberty must be rooted in land lest outside influences, political and cultural, corrupt, weaken, and destroy.[19]

Calhoun described as much as he prescribed for the upcountry, because land and economic power, as well as political power, had become interlinked by the early nineteenth century. The cotton boom transformed its political system and solidified the upcountry's devotion to slavery, the "peculiar institution." Meanwhile, the low country, with its vast plantations ruled by the rice lords of Charleston, had passed its prime by the coming of the American Revolution. The invention of Whitney's gin made possible a short-staple cotton culture in the lands above the fall line, transforming the hunting grounds of the dispossessed Cherokee into a cradle region of the Old South. Slavery in South Carolina no longer hugged the coast, and the entire state took on the qualities of southern black-belt regions. This development strengthened backcountry people's concerns for property, the ownership and protection of which they invariably linked to the maintenance of their liberties and of their social order.[20] A recent study of South Carolina's antebellum political culture has concluded that the state represented "a unified slave economy and society virtually unique in the South."

The tendency toward consensus with regard to slavery resulted from a broad distribution of slave ownership in the upcountry. Though only one-fourth of upcountry households held slaves in 1800, by 1820 almost one-half had entered the slaveholding class. Many of the most prominent slaveholders lived in the southernmost part of the upcountry, often called the midlands. Richland District's Wade Hampton represented this group, becoming one of the wealthiest men in the South from his Carolina cotton plantations. However, the western region of the upcountry, often referred to as the piedmont, also contained a powerful and growing class of slaveholding planters and farmers by 1860. Even in the mountainous Pickens District, enslaved black Carolinians made up 10–20 percent of the population. Those who did not own slaves at least could hope to one day enter the planter class. Calhoun, for example, had his plantation in mountainous Pickens District and was but one generation away from Scotch-Irish settlers who had lived in rough-hewn cabins and fought with the Cherokee.[21]

United with the coastal planters by the institution of slavery, upcountry yeoman and planters nevertheless perceived themselves as a distinct cultural region in South Carolina. The spread of slaveholding among the white yeomen, combined with the frontier nature of upcountry society, made upcountry planters much less inclined to style themselves as lordly aristocrats, and from the period of the Revolution on, these planters tended to view themselves as spokesmen for the common man. The oratorical strategy for upcountry legislative representatives centered on the pose of "republican simplicity" set against the "opulent decadence" of Charleston.[22] This contrast would become a recurring theme in South Carolina politics and culture. Having grown up in a yeoman home in Pickens District, Ben Robertson remembered that his "kinfolks" had "believed in plain clothes, plain cooking, plain houses, plain churches to attend on Sunday. . . . Charleston was a symbol to us—it represented luxury and easy soft living and all the evils of Egypt." The people of the upcountry evinced republican fears of "luxury" and the degenerating corruption of easy living on both white men and women. "Do not teach your daughters French before they can weed a flowerbed at sunrise," opined one upcountry editor, warning that simple living and hard work adorned an upcountry Carolina woman more than "a simpering tongue and fashionable accomplishments."[23]

Fears of corruption in relation to gendered identities would not end with fears of "simpering tongues." The fear of corruption of the household, corruption that came from outside forces that weakened hierarchy, ultimately expressed an anxiety about the ability of white men to defend the world they created. Conservatism imagines society as an organic whole, a living being. As such, Carolinians believed, the social order could sicken and die if social bonds were not grounded in ordered households and the economic production necessary to sustain the household. Those social bonds held taut partly from affective sentiment—and partly from oppressive patriarchal power. Even the relatively liberal-minded David Ramsay, one of South Carolina's first historians, praised his wife primarily for her "submissiveness." White South Carolina men would not go to the wall to defend a Lockean notion of absolute property rights, but they would die in defense of their control of the household. Maintenance of property meant the maintenance of the patriarchal order.[24]

This book attempts to integrate several recent, influential works on the nature of southern gender, ideology, and economics. The seeming contradiction at the heart of the ideology of South Carolina white men, the dichotomy between modern notions of political individualism and premodern conceptions of mastery of the household, has been defined by Stephanie McCurry as "the two faces of republicanism." McCurry uses this phrase to explain the South Carolina yeomen's belief in their right to act as citizens in the egalitarian realm of the public sphere, a right they simultaneously grounded in their control of dependents within the household. Proslavery spokesmen, she writes, "returned repeatedly to gender relations, exploiting assumptions about the 'natural' relations of men and women." The allegedly "natural" oppression of women became a metaphor for all relationships of power, giving white South Carolina men a vested interest in maintaining the institution of slavery.[25]

A different view of the influence of republican ideology in South Carolina appears in the work of historian Manisha Sinha. Sinha rejects the entire framework of what she calls "the burgeoning republican neoconsensus of American history." A number of proslavery theorists, ministers, and politicians sought to shape a conservative, antidemocratic ideology in the antebellum period. Antebellum South Carolina, she argues, did not simply choose one of the more conservative varieties of republicanism to adopt as its own. Instead, it rejected republican ideology in favor of their defense of slavery in the abstract.[26]

This work follows Sinha's willingness to reject a simple equation of the ideology developed in South Carolina and American republicanism. South Carolina created its own conservative tradition that borrowed from a number of influences. It does, however, challenge Sinha, in that it recognizes the flowering of southern conservatism in the years following the war rather than in the nullification crisis or even secession itself. Nor does it assume that conservatism in South Carolina meant a simple rejection of republicanism. Sinha's study of proslavery apologists certainly shows them attempting to cobble together a conservative consensus, but it also clearly shows them using materials borrowed from disparate sources—including republicanism. Sinha also fails to note the crucial role played by imagery and symbol in the shaping of ideology. Much of the imagery deployed by conservatives, as McCurry argued, centered on the household. The defense of the household, intertwined with the defense of slavery, became a common theme in South Carolina's proslavery polemics. Civil war and emancipation would suggest the household's fragility and would make the creation of gendered symbolism an integral part of postbellum conservatives' aesthetic project. Southern conservatism existed in the realm of public symbolism, not simply in the politician's turn of phrase.

Political rhetoric does not constitute the gravamen of South Carolina conservatism; neither do economics and social structure. This book joins a growing literature that seeks to bypass the debate over whether southern slaveholders were either "premodern patriarchs" or "bourgeois entrepreneurs." Evidence from the upcountry clearly shows that, as one recent historian has put it, "ideals of organic reciprocity" and "market capitalism" worked in tandem to produce South Carolina's social and economic world. McCurry's emphasis on concern for the defense of the household underscores why some of the traditional dichotomies used by historians—capitalists versus aristocrats, for example—simply do not apply in the South Carolina upcountry in the early nineteenth century. Upcountry slaveholders combined these roles and could best be described as entrepreneurial patriarchs, men who actively sought economic power in which to ground their identity as white members of the polis and their control of their households. Their independence rested on the ownership of productive property that often allowed them to become quite prosperous, at least by the standards of a frontier subsistence region. Nonslaveholder Henry Hortman of Pickens, for example, willed to his wife and children "a cow and a calf, one hundred dollars in money, too hogs, crop, household and kitchen furniture," all productive property with which to work their freehold.[27] John P. Poole, though living in the isolated "Dark Corner" of northwestern Greenville District, accumulated a significant degree of wealth in "cattle, hogs, sheep" and had, by the late 1840s, managed to substantially enter the planter class by becoming master to "fourteen likely negros." Sinha rightly concluded after her study of South Carolina that we should hesitate to use "the terms capitalist, noncapitalist, or precapitalist to describe a hybrid conservative ideology that defended bound labor with as much vigor as the notion of property."[28]

Upcountry Carolinians exulted in the economic possibilities of the cotton boom and pondered the profitability of sheep-raising and even wine culture on their upland farms.[29] Though not an entrepreneur on a large scale, the upcountry farmer certainly sought to better his position as much as possible, often to accomplish closely intertwined goals: to stay out of debt, to ensure independence, and to exercise mastery. A Spartanburg farmer, David G. Harris, told his journal with seeming exultation in 1859, "I have almost enough money to pay my debts" and reflected, "I know that when a man is in debt he has a hard taskmaster; *out of debt out of trouble.*" The short-staple cotton economy and the possibility of entering into the slaveholding class made it possible for the poor man to both make his fortune and secure the liberties that belonged to the ruling class.[30]

Though proudly agrarian, the entrepreneurial patriarchs of the upcountry made every effort to diversify their productive property. Land, what Charles Sellers rightly calls "the most conservative force in history,"[31] did not act as a barrier to entrepreneurial attitudes. Even before the Revolution, upcountrymen like Camden's Moses Kirkland engaged in several business ventures, including a sawmill, a gristmill, a brewery, a tavern, and an illegal rum trade with the Catawba Indians.[32] Traveler's Rest planter S. S. Crittendon not only planted cotton with the labor of twelve chattels, but also, along with his father-in-law, ran a local inn and operated a stagecoach and a stagecoach shop.[33] Greenvillian Vardry McBee's Reedy River Factory represented an early attempt to combine the South's cotton culture with textile culture, although he only employed about ten workers.[34] Yeomen also tried their hand at various enterprises. David Harris operated a local icehouse and made brandy for sale. Cotton farmer George Feagle, of Lexington County, sold crossties to the railroads during the 1850s, clearing a profit of nine hundred dollars, which he promptly took to Greenville to purchase a slave.[35]

Clear evidence of the profit-seeking schemes of upcountrymen suggests that South Carolina, though attempting to isolate itself from northern abolitionism, never wanted isolation from the rewards of the market revolution. The case of Spartanburg County and its proposed railroad line serves as one example of this attitude. The *Carolina Spartan*, which saw itself both as a booster of development and the sworn enemy of northern abolitionism, insisted in the late 1840s that without a railroad line Spartanburg would fall into "agricultural decay and ruin." The *Carolina Spartan's* ongoing defense of the railroad line reveals that there were many critics of the proposed railroad but none who opposed it on the basis of simon-pure agrarianism. Opponents charged instead that the proposed line would not be profitable. Certain of the economic bounty that would run along the iron veins, the *Spartan* crowed that some denied the profitability of a railroad just as "some deny the existence of a Supreme Being."[36]

Economic profit and the intrusion of market forces did not make organic social relations impossible. Proslavery ideologues who wanted to see antebellum South Carolina as a conservative society on the model of slaveholding Athens—or some of the aristocratic republics of the early Renaissance—could find some evidence for their hopes. Certainly many of the basic materials for the making of a conservative society existed in antebellum South Carolina, slavery itself being the most obvious. The growing economic strength of the region does, however, show that a number of forces pushed this young society in an utterly different direction. Even slave ownership could make for increased independence free of the social bonds of an organic society. What historian James Oakes calls, "a culture of upward mobility" rather than a society made up of traditional organic bonds best describes the Carolina upcountry. Such a society made for a radical individualism that often refused to accept aristocratic class pretensions. Controversy frequently erupted between yeoman farmers and planters over questions of trespass, right-of-way, and customary use—all questions related to, and energized by, the ownership of property.[37]

Religion became an arena of contest between cultural ideas in nineteenth-century South Carolina. Separate Baptists, better known as New Light Baptists, trumpeted a spiritual autonomy that went so far as to free the converted from the constraints of the social order. Women occasionally preached in highly unrestrained worship services, and men took part in the ritual foot-washing that replicated the humility of Christ at the Last Supper. Such rituals of subordination, undertaken by white men, represented the sum of all fears to the men who had tamed the backcountry, fought the British and the Cherokee, and ruled their patriarchal households with lordly consequence. Prominent backcountry Baptist Richard Furman effected an organizational alliance between the Separates and the much more conservative General, or Regular, Baptists. As slavery closed its grip on upcountry culture, some of the Separates more egalitarian practices would disappear. Nevertheless, despite the best efforts of Furman and others, the disjuncture between individual freedom in the world of the spirit and the expectations of a hierarchical social order would remain to the time of the Civil War. On the one hand, the church fellowship suggested the ideal of an organic society, a world interlinked by Christian duty and fellowship, social bonds sanctified by Word and Spirit. On the other hand, it focused sacred experience on the individual in a society in which the individual autonomy of white men already played a central and, some planters would add, disruptive, role.[38]

The emerging conservatism of the South Carolina backcountry thus thrived in a world of contest and conflict. The planters of South Carolina may have been, as a European observer called them, "the Nobility of the American states." Nevertheless, they were young nobility with, primarily, the institution of slavery, and the wealth slavery created, to prop up their pretensions to hegemony. Slavery has, therefore, rightly received enormous attention from historians hoping to explicate the nature of southern conservatism. Drew Gilpin Faust, for example, found in the South's proslavery argument the intellectual and cultural production of southern thinkers seeking to shape a definable social role within their society. Rather than suffering from an "intellectual blockade," southern proslavery writers engaged basic questions regarding the meaning of the Industrial Revolution, the validity of natural rights, and the shape and scope of allegedly universal values. Their reflections issued forth in a profound critique of nineteenth-century western civilization, answering claims of "liberty, equality, and fraternity" with an ideology of social organicism rooted in scripture and the classical tradition. These ideas, disseminated by members of the slaveholding class, or those attached by familial or ideological ties to the slaveholding class, allegedly shaped the antebellum South into a conservative society.[39]

Bundled with the idea that the antebellum South developed into a conservative society is the assumption that the Civil War, by destroying slavery, destroyed the material basis of southern conservatism. The destruction of slavery, historians such as Eugene Genovese, Elizabeth Fox-Genovese, and Barbara Fields have argued, snapped the social bonds necessary to the existence of an organic society. Studies of the postbellum world have explored postwar conservatism solely in relationship to politics and economics. Only recently have cultural studies of this crucial period in southern history emerged, although they have not always challenged C. Vann Woodward's use of the terms "sterility," "cultural famine," and "intellectual malnutrition" to describe life in the southern states following Confederate defeat.[40]

In this book I challenge the view that southern conservatism died with the social relations of slavery. In fact, in the antebellum period, self-conscious conservatives faced a number of oppositional forces that prevented them from shaping South Carolina into the web of social organicism they had read about in Carlyle and Burke. The defeat of the Confederacy, and the reimagination of the society that had been defeated, laid the foundation for the creation of a conservative culture. Southern conservatism flourished in South Carolina through the medium of the Lost Cause, an aesthetic representation of memory and yearning. Confederate memory provided southerners with an ideology of historical declension, the notion that Confederate loss meant the triumph of materialism, irreligion, and social anarchy.

South Carolina conservatives accepted historical declension as an inevitable outcome of living in history. Holding to this position, they rejected modernity outright. This attitude defines the most basic difference between South Carolina conservatives and their opponents. Modernity, for southern conservatism, had its clearest representation in the radically autonomous self, abstracted from paternalist and hierarchical relationships. Southern conservative resistance to modernity became especially acute after Appomattox, the defeat of the Confederacy becoming a symbol of declension. The emancipation of slaves opened a Pandora's box that released all types of radical autonomy. The Lost Cause, then, legitimized southern conservative defiance to modernity, rendered a narrative of its most noble struggles against its growing power.[41]

Despairing over the emergence of this brave new world of suddenly emancipated dependents, South Carolina conservatives sought to awaken the imagined glories of the past. Irony became the preferred mode of historical memory as white South Carolinians attached themselves to the past by mourning its irretrievable loss. Historical declension constituted a center of gravity for the world the South Carolina conservative created after the Civil War. Like many conservatives, defeated Carolinians viewed the decay of civilization through time as a constituent principle of fragile human community, decay that usually results from some explosive event that unleashes the forces of chaos and disrupts social harmony.

The Civil War did radically transform the world of South Carolina slaveholders. Laura Edwards has written that civil war and emancipation "shook the antebellum household to its foundations."[42] Such a profound disruption inevitably ensured, as I have already argued, that symbols of gender and household haunted the cultural production of southern conservatives as they attempted to deal with this particularly terrifying aspect of modernity. The freeing of the slaves, after all, raised questions about an entire range of paternalistic systems of control in marriage and family life. This crisis in the household seemed to challenge more than a political ideology, raising fears of the loss of manhood and mastery. Such concerns explain why the world of symbols white conservatives deployed included the frequent use of feminine bodies, allegories, and energies as part of the aesthetic of the Lost Cause, highlighting how southern white conservatives linked the crisis of the south with the crisis of masculinity created by Confederate defeat. Effeminacy may have been a constant threat, but the sacred supports of a divinized southern womanhood shored up southern masculinity against this crisis.

The experience of South Carolina thus explicitly challenges an older generation of southern historians who assumed that southern conservative ideology following the Civil War constituted a thin veneer of superstructure over essentially economic concerns. In contradiction to this view, postbellum South Carolina provides a perfect illustration of how ideology survives and flourishes in cultural representation.[43] A focus on the making of a culture suggests that the conservative ethos emerged from the death of slavery and the southern ancien régime. Acting as a response to crisis, to the rupture in history created by Confederate defeat, allowed southern conservatives to weave the vision of an organic society from the scattered threads of antebellum materials. Conservative South Carolinians shaped a culture of dissent during the years following their war for independence. Unable to secede from the Union politically, southern conservatives led South Carolina's attempt at a cultural secession from the optimistic, nationalist, and bourgeois experience of the modernized West.

Brigadier General Martin W. Gary did not take the tidings of Confederate defeat with reconciliation on his mind. Hearing the news of Appomattox, he encouraged his cavalry troopers to ride away without turning their arms over to Grant's triumphant blue tide. "South Carolinians," he reminded his cheering troopers, "never surrender." Gary's attitude of defiance epitomizes the attitude of many South Carolinians of the postbellum era, men and women who never surrendered to the imposition of Reconstruction and who, in fact, shaped a cultural omnibus that glorified defeat and continued resistance to the rising tide of modernity.

Nevertheless, South Carolina conservatives never solved some of the contradictions of their social order nor of their conservative ideology. In the 1870s, conservatives used the aesthetic of the Lost Cause to appeal for mass political participation to overthrow the Reconstruction regime. Conservatives thus found themselves in the most ironic of positions—convinced of the dangers of Calhoun's turbulent majorities, they attempted to create just such a raucous movement in the 1876 Red Shirt campaign.

Hoping to fashion an organic society, Carolina conservatives unleashed generations of deadly racial violence. By the turn of the century, much of South Carolina would surrender, would yield to the blandishments of the new bourgeois world and of Benjamin Ryan Tillman who knew how to ride the wild horse of turbulent majorities to the governor's mansion and beyond. The Lost Cause would remain but would cease to become a yearning for lost worlds, subtly changing its ethos and meaning in a new, bourgeois South Carolina. Taught by the Lost Cause to expect defeat, conservatives saw in this new loss more proof that the truth lives among ruins.

CHAPTER ONE

A Spirit amongst These Hills

Confederate Defeat and Conservative Cultural Triumph

The aesthetic of the Lost Cause did not emerge in a historical vacuum. The threads of the Lost Cause narrative weave through the concerns of antebellum South Carolinians who believed themselves engaged in a running battle with the North, a battle to protect their mastery over their households from outside intrusions. Moreover, conservative leaders in antebellum South Carolina hoped to create an organic society out of the short and raucous past of the Carolina frontier. Gendered constructions and performances provided symbolic representations of this organic world. However, other cultural forces were at work in the antebellum Palmetto State. Countervailing cultural moods caused structural stresses in South Carolina society that were never resolved in the antebellum period. The crisis of the Civil War itself exposed this breach and left the upcountry world in ruins, ruins that ironically provided the materials for the creation of a new world, an aesthetic world of images centered on the Lost Cause.

Antebellum South Carolina, ironically, seems an unlikely place for the emergence of a romantic conservatism. The characteristics we have already seen in upcountry society—personal independence, economic development, open markets, diversification of production for profit—suggest that by the antebellum period the white male inhabitants of the region were little more than Lockean liberals in backlands buckskin. Secessionist leaders, however, sought to make this newborn social order a site of construction for a peculiarly southern conservatism. Labor and familial relationships made possible an ersatz hierarchy on the Carolina frontier, though one undergoing constant redefinition. Husbands and wives, masters and slaves, fathers and children exhibited affective ties, yet embodied in their relationships were assumptions regarding the meaning of patriarchal authority. South Carolina households did not, as did households in the North, represent a retreat from the world of profit-taking. Instead they functioned as centers for economic production and provided an exhibition of cultural ideals regarding hierarchy, subordination, and the proper use of power by masters and patriarchs.[1]

The marriage of Unionist slaveholder Benjamin F. Perry, of Greenville District, highlights some of these themes. Liza and Benjamin Perry evince *household* in their correspondence a profound sense of affective partnership, even as Benjamin Perry reminded his wife of her subordinate position, and she acquiesced in often ritualistic fashion. Meanwhile, both Perrys show little evidence that they had accepted the northern bourgeoisie ideal of separate spheres. Perry regularly took time off from his law practice and political activities to can strawberry preserves and to care for his children. Indeed, the Perry's relationship suggests that many households in the upcountry could be regarded as experiments in organic social bonds. Perry's wholehearted participation in the public world of politics and law and in the allegedly private world of the home suggests that he saw himself as the master of both worlds, with no dividing line raised by the dichotomy of home and commerce. Unlike men in the bourgeois north, the men of South Carolina sought to exercise mastery over dependents, rather than to exhibit competency in the emerging commercial culture. Instead of drawing hard lines between economic production and sentiment, as was customary in the American north and much of western Europe, Carolinians shaped that ideology around a language of mastery and dependency draped in affective sentiments.[2]

Upcountry elites used their wealth and influence to exercise a paternalistic hegemony over middling farmers. These relations continued even as the antebellum world reached its crisis in the Civil War. Local notable James Earle Hagood of Pickens had his time taken up not only with serving as clerk of court and operating a resort hotel on Caesars Head but also with answering requests from a Mary and William Rider of Table Mountain for help getting "a horse or a mule." Returning Confederate soldiers like Samuel Roper beset Hagood with requests for "some arrangements to get us a small place so that we can make out to live in these hard times." These relationships provided a means of attaining or maintaining productive property for those whose ill-fortune had caused them to slip outside the upcountry's social system.[3] Other examples of attempts at shaping an organic society through the creation of patron-client relationships between white men abound. Economic production, and control of the modes of production, enabled elite planters to begin shaping networks of power, patronage, and mastery. One common example relates to the ownership of cotton gins and grist mills in the upcountry, almost all of which belonged to individual planters in the antebellum period. Planters sometimes developed these into small-scale entrepreneurial enterprises. As often, and sometimes in tandem, they allowed their neighbors to use the gins and mills either for free or for a nominal fee. Thus, economic production had the same hybrid character of much of antebellum South Carolina's social milieu; planters strengthened the hand of the elite while providing economic services for the entrepreneurial backcountry farmers who saw in ginned cotton the promise of upward mobility.[4]

These examples show that the entrepreneurial spirit of the antebellum Carolina frontier did not lead to the creation of a modern bourgeois society. The prospects for a bourgeois society developing in the upcountry withered in the face of the hierarchical world of a slave society, bounded by the fierce insistence on the maintenance of white men's liberty. In an effort to ensure this liberty, upcountrymen insisted that their version of economic development move along lines different from those of their northern and English cousins. In 1849, the *Spartan*, eager for the fruits of the industrial revolution in the form of a railroad line, warily warned that manufacturing should not come to the South "as a system." Such an intrusion, the coming of the full complexity of industry and finance, would "disastrously affect our institutions." Carolina's identity as a slave society came first and foremost. The ownership of productive property meant independence for individual farmers and planters; a healthy growth of manufacturing meant independence for South Carolina herself. In 1850, and again during the crisis of 1860, calls for secession would join calls for increased manufacturing meant to ensure South Carolina's independence from the North. "Is there any better way of resisting the Yankee than by encouraging our own mechanics and manufactures," wondered one editorial writer in Greenville County.[5] Conservatives sought not an industrial society, but a conservative republic in which limited manufacturing served as handmaiden to agriculture, and iron rails connected South Carolina to a world of merchant capital. This linkage would aid them toward their true end: mastery. Productive property and economic success, grounded in a slave economy, made their mastery of those around them a social reality rather than simply the rhetoric of the hopeful elite.

The entrepreneurial patriarchs of the upcountry clearly sought economic independence for the sake of essentially premodern values—the mastery over dependents and the liberties of white men within a context of a hierarchical society. This underscores the important point that an interest in manufacturing and internal improvements does not signal the emergence of either modern or liberal values. In their study of Bismarck's Germany, David Blackbourne and Geoff Eley have noted that historians too quickly equate economic and moral progress, liberalism, and industrial development. A newly unified Germany in the late nineteenth century, they point out, managed to combine a commitment to industrial capitalism with a culture solidly committed to a profoundly conservative ethos. If this is true of post-1870 Germany, which experienced a revolution in heavy industry, it certainly was the case in the antebellum South, in which about thirty-five hundred white males engaged in nonagricultural occupations, and only several hundred of those worked in occupations even remotely industrial. The antebellum political economy assumed the absolute priority of agriculture and saw increased manufacturing as a tool for promoting independence for free white men grounded in mastery over dependents rather than in the path of ill-defined progress.[6]

When examining the yeoman-planter propensity for entrepreneurial schemes, historians should examine not only what they did but also why they did it. The evidence suggests that the term "capitalist" hardly applied to the young society of the South Carolina upcountry. Historians who seek to prove the capitalist nature of southern society in general must define capitalism simply as a desire for profit-taking, transforming Marx's analytical scalpel into a blunt instrument. Elizabeth Fox-Genovese has persuasively argued that such a definition makes the term "capitalism" applicable to all societies in all places at all times. It is therefore useless as a means of categorization. Fox-Genovese rightly views southern social relations as shaped preeminently by slavery and certainly not by the contractual wage labor characteristic of a capitalist society. At the same time, slavery does not represent the only problem for those who would find a simple "slaveholding liberalism" in the Old South.[7] The theme that runs through the slaveholders' attempts at profit-taking and the development of manufacturing is the maintenance of property and independence, particularly as sectional conflicts heated up in the late 1850s. In December 1859, the *Keowee Courier* praised John Bowen's opening of "a first class powder mill" in Pickens District, since it forwarded the cause, not of industrial development, but of "home manufactures." The editor noted that this had become especially important because of "the present conditions with our northern 'brethren'." In 1859 Bowen received a subsidy from the State Agricultural Society to continue his enterprise.[8] South Carolinians sought to ensure their productive property against all comers in their desire for mastery. Neither yeomen nor planters dreamed of centralizing resources and capital, but instead sought to make a little cash to purchase a field hand, more land, or perhaps simply a hunting dog with which to, as the saying went, "ra'er around."[9]

The Carolina upcountry, therefore, had a profoundly complex relationship with modernity. The upcountry functioned as a hybrid society; its conservatism did not grow from an American-born feudalism. South Carolina, and much of the Old South, embodied the Janus face of modernity. Chattel slavery, undergirding the most profitable sector of the upcountry economy, did not come hobbling into modernity as a sickly creature, but strode forward as a strapping new creation of the modern world. The very fact that southerners regarded slaves as chattel and absolute property, suggests that the institution drew its strength from new definitions of ownership and conditions created by what Genovese and Fox-Genovese call "the rise of merchant capital." Carolinians of the backcountry, though perhaps not exhibiting many of the characteristics of capitalist social relations, lived in a world that capitalism had shaped.[10]

Antebellum South Carolina presents us with a set of entrepreneurs willing to use slave labor to make profits, combined with a political leadership interested in tapping into new technologies that would link the upcountry with modern markets.[11] Furthermore, if we define a conservative society as one that roots itself in a prescriptive tradition, upcountry South Carolina does not qualify. A significant white population had lived in the region for only two generations by the time of the Missouri Compromise. Calling the upcountry "conservative" more accurately describes its attitudes if we mean something resembling the stubbornness in the face of change common to agricultural societies throughout time. In this attitude, its people did not evince characteristics very different from those in rural New England or eighteenth-century France, or from the yeomen farmers of the classical Greek polis. The description of the upcountry as conservative serves only if we use the term in the sense that Braudel saw the *longue dureé* as conservative—an agrarian unwillingness to demand change, because property and independence rest on stability and recurrence.[12]

South Carolina behaved as a conservative society only in this limited sense, but that did not prevent Carolina ministers, intellectuals, and political ideologues from attempting to shape the state along the lines of romantic conservatism, an example of what Eric Hobsbawm has called "an invented tradition." These men of mind, generally tied closely to the planter class, sought to shape a public culture that would exhibit the values of hierarchy, prescriptive tradition, and liberty tied to traditional respect for land and mastery. Public rituals such as the antebellum militia muster, and political movements such as the drive for secession, became opportunities to elaborate an ideology of romantic conservatism. Slavery itself acted as the generative ground for this cultural ideology.

The South Carolina upcountry had, by 1850, clearly passed over the barrier that separated a society that holds slaves from that of a slave-holding society. Slavery wove religion, social custom, the economy, and law into a tight web of social relations. A commitment to defend these social relations by force of arms further strengthened this increasingly self-conscious social order. Since the early nineteenth century, the state had featured an elaborate military apparatus in the form of a locally organized militia. Each year, state law required the state adjutant general to call up, or muster, the South Carolina militia, ostensibly to ensure that it had learned proper discipline and the manual of arms. These annual musters proved both less practical and less important than the company musters that could occur in local townships as often as four times a year. South Carolina's militia system, probably the most elaborate in antebellum America, paraded an increasingly self-conscious ideology that healed the tension between imagined hierarchies and personal autonomy.[13] The state's use of the militia system mirrored Niccolò Machiavelli's prescription for the maintenance of conservative republics. Machiavelli, in his discussion of the meaning of conservative republicanism, had insisted on the importance of a citizen militia in the preservation of both order and independence.[14]

Gendered hierarchies, in this case the assertion of planter manhood coincident with the assertion of yeoman manhood, allowed everyone in this cultural system a sphere of gender performance. The muster provided a ritual site where Carolinians melded the seemingly contradictory values of liberty and hierarchy into a conservative ethos. Militia musters became theaters for the performance of yeoman and planter masculinity, with the style of performance varied according to class location. Upper-class Carolinians used the militia meetings as opportunities to display military finery and oratorical power, attributes they hoped would confirm them as the ruling class of southern society. In Pickens County, the *Keowee Courier* recorded the antebellum musters as not only opportunities for units such as the Walhalla Riflemen to "go through the performance of a few evolutions" but also the chance for wealthy planter, lawyer, and conservative ideologue William King Easley to show what one contemporary called his "mesmerizing" ability to sway crowds. Dressed in military finery and flanked by his "well-equipped staff," Easley would give hot-blooded speeches for southern rights and then review the troops as they "performed several difficult evolutions." Even the practice of the manual of arms for the Carolina militia included a ritual celebration of hierarchy. Governor John Lide Wilson's manual for Carolina militiamen called upon them to engage in an elegant ritual of subordination to the planter commanders that went far beyond the rough-and-tumble style of other state militias: "direct the eyes to the sword hilt, bringing the right hand with a brisk action across the body and seize the hilt. . . . wait in that position for the next word of command." Wilson also wrote a guide for affairs of honor that put heavy emphasis on rituals of deference, elaborate etiquette, and a strong sense of class position. The uniform worn by the militia officer would have further strengthened his performance as a member of the upcountry elite. The 1839 state general assembly had prescribed for officers of militia units an elaborate set of regalia that included "a cocked hat . . . ornamented with a gold embroidered shield . . . a black silk cravat. Long boots reaching as high as the knee worn over the trousers . . . a plume of single white ostrich feather." [15] Public displays such as these profoundly shaped the planter class's understanding of society and of themselves as the ruling class.

South Carolina denied the yeoman farmer, the militia private, the power of command. He would not, however, be denied the opportunity to display masculine prowess. Instead of evincing the right of command, his attempts to display Carolina manhood were marked by rituals of violence and consumption. Ladies who came to watch the militia work its way through the manual of arms just as likely witnessed violent brawls induced by heavy drinking. In August 1855, militiaman Thomas Bates stabbed seven men with the constant companion of the rural Carolinian, a bowie knife. His rampage ended with Bates being knocked unconscious by the butt of a musket. All the combatants, reported the *Greenville Southern Enterprise,* had been drinking "mountain dew." [16] Thus the masculine rituals of the planter class and the yeoman reinforced one another. The ability to drink and willingness to fight on the part of the yeoman expressed their devotion to a hell-for-leather sense of personal independence. These outbursts of drunken frenzy and injured honor worked in tandem with the planters' sense of authority over the masses and provided an opportunity for local notables to step forward, complete with epaulets and ceremonial sword, to assert their right of command.

Reformers in the 1850s attempted to end the militia musters' reputation as drinking sprees. Evidence suggests that these attempted reforms were less than successful. We can explain at least part of the allegedly

Ciceronian power of southern orators by noting their tendency to provide liberal quantities of alcoholic beverages to their auditors. One Greenville County militia private concluded his description of an 1854 muster by issuing thanks "to all those who furnished the critter in any quantity."[17]

The political turmoil of the 1850s transformed these companies from slave patrols and opportunities for masculine performance into political cells. Increasingly, calls for reform in the militia system came forth from the thin ranks of upcountry Unionists who rightly saw the musters as hotbeds of secessionist sympathy.[18] The oratorical efforts of Carolina secessionists reached their heights at these annual gatherings, speeches that often defended the militia system, slavery, and the southern way of life against the attacks of Unionists and Yankees.[19]

Mustering for defense of the Palmetto State, specifically for the institution of slavery, functioned much the same as political ritual in other societies. The open celebration of political ritual encourages what Lynn Hunt has called "the impulse to invest politics everywhere." Public spectacles such as marches, parades, uniforms, banners, and cockades are vehicles for the exercise of power, creating a drama of power in which the practice of ritual becomes the justification for, and the explanation of, a culture's ideology. Greenville County's Minute Man organization marched on the grounds of Furman University wearing blue cockades that symbolically linked them with the Carolina patriots of the Revolutionary War. Speeches made at these public spectacles excoriated "the dangers of black republicanism" to the Constitution and made specific calls for secession. Another Greenville County militia unit, the University Riflemen, drew on the student body of Furman University, an institution that acted as a seedbed of secessionist sentiment in the upcountry. On the Fourth of July, in 1859, the University Riflemen paraded with another prosecessionist militia known as the Butler Guards, complete with secessionist minister James C. Furman offering prayers.[20]

The politicization of South Carolina society grew out of ritual evocations of masculinity, the accompanying anxieties regarding gender, and the strengthened commitment to slavery at all levels of the social order. David Harris, a small slaveholding yeoman from Spartanburg District who often participated in militia musters and slave patrols, registered in his journals a commitment to opposing the abolitionist threat and to attending political meetings after Lincoln's election, "a fever heat for the state to secede." The antebellum upcountry's equivalent of an urban working class shared the same stolid commitment. A stonemason in Columbia who spoke too openly of his doubts about slavery found himself dunked in a pond by his fellow workers, stripped naked, and covered with tar and feathers.[21]

Slavery and its defense became the linchpin for secessionist political activity. In contrast to the modern apologetics of neo-Confederates that Tony Horowitz discovered, most South Carolina secessionists in the 1850s clearly apprehended the meaning of their quarrel with the North. Speaking to a militia gathering in Columbia in the fall of 1851, O. M. Dantzler asked, "where then does the issue lie between South Carolina and the Federal government? . . . Is it not inscribed in blazing and ineffable characters on the broad expanse of heaven? . . . all proclaim that [the issue] is the abolition of the institution of African slavery." Dantzler went on to describe all other points of contention between North and South as merely "collateral" to slavery, which was, he said, "the leading and paramount issue."[22]

Secession provided the moment of profound contest within the South Carolina upcountry in which political and religious leaders attempted to birth a fully formed conservative ethos. William King Easley serves as a fitting example of the more colorful secessionist orators of the 1850s. A little-known South Carolina intellectual, signer of the Ordinance of Secession, and the organizer of the Third South Carolina Cavalry, Easley defined the most extreme boundary of secession sentiment and of the ideology of southern conservatism.[23]

Born in tiny Pickens Courthouse, Easley became a successful lawyer and local notable in the near-frontier region. Apparently a powerful speaker, he had, according to a contemporary, a "mesmeric influence" on the people of the upcountry. An autodidact, Easley often wore his learning quite heavily. His political opponent, Benjamin F. Perry, called him "a laborious student of history and science, as well as poetry and general literature." Easley's intellectual obsessions, which echo through his secession speeches in the 1850s, are examples of struggles for independence drawn from the classical era, the English Civil War, and Easley's own interpretation of the American and French revolutions. Easley drew his understanding of the latter from his reading of Burke.[24]

Easley evoked these past struggles to do two things. First, he sought to valorize South Carolina's struggle with the North by placing it in a long line of heroic struggles for republican liberty. In this tendency, he places himself in the tradition of Aedanus Burke, who saw the English Commonwealthmen as the inspiration for shaping a conservative republican world in the seventeenth century. Similarly, in Easley's oratorical world, the Kansas-Nebraska controversy of 1854 merged with Parliament's struggle with Charles I over republican liberties, and both fit into a narrative of republicanism stretching back to the stand of the immortal three hundred at Thermopylae. All these struggles he compared to the American Revolution. Easley clearly evinced the tendency of romantic conservatives to construct mythical worlds in the past and to use them as the basis for jeremiads against the present.[25]

Second, Easley sought to show that the heroes of the past gained their liberty only through a performance of masculine combativeness. In speeches delivered to militia musters and on court days all over the upcountry, Easley equated liberty with manhood, and slavery with effeminacy. Speaking in Pickens County in 1854, Easley refers to a willingness to submit to the North as "the argument of slaves and cowards."[26] Romantic conservatism, in other words, became more than a celebration of ordered republics in the past. Easley made it into a tradition worth fighting for, indeed a tradition that became meaningful only in the midst of battle.

If the struggle that Easley called for drew on the image of republicanism, it surely represented the most conservative face of the ideology. One of the most revealing of his speeches occurred at a Fourth of July celebration in the flash-point year 1854. Such celebrations had, during the nullification crisis of the 1830s, represented opportunities for upcountry leaders like Benjamin Perry to declare their loyalty to the Union and, in public pageantry and spectacle, invoke the image of the Revolutionary past to portray nullifiers as treasonous rebels. In the 1850s secessionists managed to lay claim to the celebrations as Unionist numbers and sentiment dwindled.[27]

Easley used the celebration of the Fourth to describe the American Revolution, perhaps paradoxically to modern ears, as "a conservative revolution." The struggle of the Founding Fathers for republican principles, to Easley's Burkean mind, "did not disturb the peace and good order of society. . . . there was nothing like anarchy among the people." Easley compared the American struggle favorably with the French Revolution and with the more recent revolutionary struggles in Europe. These upheavals, Easley asserted, had a decidedly different result than the struggle of the colonies. The French Revolution "made a slaughterhouse of Europe"; the continuing revolutionary turmoil in Europe meant, not republican liberty, but to Easley's mind, "rapine and violence."[28] The principles of the American Revolution, born of a republicanism of liberty tied to property ordered by prescriptive relationships between independent white men and their dependents, had created the American Union.

Such sentiments point to a primary theme, not only of southern conservatism but also of the modern ideology of conservatism broadly considered. Easley and his secessionist comrades lived in an age of revolutionary sentiment, where, perhaps for the first time in the history of the West, social revolution had replaced dynastic struggle as the impetus for internal conflict within human societies. The Paris crowds midwifed modernity in the storming of the Bastille and in the October Days march on Versailles, ushering in an age in which the cry of natural rights would join with the celebration of the centralized nation-state seen as a repository of those rights. Thus the French Revolution became a womb for all kinds of modern ideologies of the left and right, from liberal republicanism to the fascist state.

Easley, along with most romantic southern conservatives, turned to Carlyle as well as to Burke's *Reflections* with much approval. Burke's praise of hierarchy, balance, organicism, and order founded upon prescription and tradition made the Whig an important thinker for those who sought to transform the frontier South into a prescriptive society with a ruling class organized around the disposition of enslaved labor.[29] At the same time, thinkers such as Easley recognized the relative youth of southern society, knowing that in spite of all their invocations of "the southron chivalry" that their infant aristocracy had only to go back a generation or two to find overseers, peddlers, merchants, and impoverished schoolteachers. Thus they reached back not only to the American Revolution but into the English and classical past to find precedence for their rule in a constructed history of conservative republicanism. Evocations of classical Greece, republican Rome, the English civil war, and the American Revolution provided Carolina conservatives with a usable past. Ritual expressions of hierarchy, deference and local autonomy in militia musters, hot-blooded oratory, and even the power relationships of the household all represented attempts to construct an organic society on the South Carolina frontier.

Sentiments similar to these emerge not only in the speeches and personal reflections of self-conscious intellectuals like Easley. Country newspaper editors evinced similar concerns. During the late 1840s, as news of increased abolitionist fervor came from the North, and the unsettling tales of revolutionaries on the barricades drifted from Europe, Carolina conservatives became convinced that they saw a pattern of subversive radicalism in these events, and that they, the Christian republic of South Carolina, had become a besieged minority. France, the editor of Spartanburg County's *Carolina Spartan* reminded his readers, had tried all forms of government from "the imperial bayonet" to the "ferocious mob and its master of the moment, the ruling demagogue." Like the abolitionists, the revolutionary party in Europe screamed of liberty and equality, "high-sounding words," grumbled the *Spartan,* that "meant the right to claim any man's property."[30]

The effect of John Brown's raid on Harpers Ferry, the election of Abraham Lincoln, the quick secession of South Carolina, and the military action against Sumter has been characterized by one modern historian as a "crisis of fear."[31] Anxiety over slave rebellion, and fears that the world that slavery had made would come crashing down, certainly played a central role in the secession crisis. This view ignores the slow but steady drumbeat of southern nationalism that had been building since the 1830s only to explode when optimistic prosperity made Carolinians certain that they could strike for independence, creating a slaveholding polis safe from meddling abolitionists. Moreover, slavery and anxiety over its fate cannot be disentangled from other fears felt by the conservative revolutionaries of South Carolina. Slavery functioned as the root of the Carolina conservative vision, branching out into a commitment to hierarchy, deference, and liberty linked to property. However, many of the most avid of secessionists hoped not only to save slavery but also to *use* slavery to shape a social order grounded in their own vision of traditional society.

Columbia secessionist Maxcy Gregg embodied the desire to shape a new order based on slaveholding and independence for South Carolina. As described by contemporaries, he was as "stern as Brutus," and had an avowed personal and political commitment to slavery and to the independence of South Carolina. Gregg even felt that a new southern Confederacy would hamper the free exercise of republican liberties, saying that "consolidation with Georgia and Tennessee" was "only not quite so great an evil as consolidation with New York and Ohio." Gregg's commitment to slavery did not, however, prevent him from openly challenging the Declaration of Causes at the South Carolina secession convention, an apologia that made the institution of slavery the centerpiece of the state's unraveling of the Union. Gregg hoped that the convention would challenge not only the North for its alleged abolitionist fervor but also the unjust tariff that subsidized Yankee manufacturing interests. Gregg managed to whip together only 31 votes in his effort to table the declaration; a landslide of 124 votes buried his minor insurgency. However, this should be viewed as significant when juxtaposed with the South Carolina Convention's mania for uniformity.[32]

Gregg's understanding of events does not represent an eccentric view of how the matter stood. William King Easley stumped the upcountry with the same theme after Lincoln's election. Easley warned the upcountry yeomen that the North planned to tax them "for the support of northern manufactures and northern commerce." He raised the specter of northern society amassing both political and economic power that would be guided not by a virtuous elite but by "a fierce and turbulent majority" who would not cease their meddling until Carolinians had lost "every right and every liberty that belongs to free men."[33] Other secessionists reminded their yeomen listeners that the North had long benefited from "an unjust system of taxation" that had allowed them to enjoy all the fruits of the industrial age.[34] An 1860 muster of militia companies in Pickens District heard Dr. Benjamin Rhett declare that the issue at hand was not so much slavery as the long struggle of Carolina against the protective tariff. "The object of the North," Rhett insisted, "is to get the reigns of government in their hands and impoverish us."[35]

The alleged "object of the North" embodied South Carolina conservative fears regarding the larger crisis of western civilization. The dangers of ideological fanaticism, the untrammeled franchise directed by "interested" politicians and fundamental inequities in a centralized economic system, worried conservative thinkers from Burke to Disraeli to Calhoun and the upcountry politicians and ministers who followed him. In the social arrangements of the northern states, a society shaped by the market revolution and free labor, the upcountry of South Carolina thought it saw the abomination of desolation, a blasphemous image of evil erected in the very temple of the republic. How could the republic of yeomen—linked in networks of patronage with local notables, struggling to exert mastery over dependents and to create an organic society—survive the assaults of the mechanized North? More and more, secessionist leaders emphasized deep cultural differences between North and South, drawing the conflict in terms larger than economics and slavery. A prosecession stump speech delivered in Greenwood, South Carolina, constructed the North as an "unmanly antagonist" who troubled the South out of the "cupidity and fanaticism" that the speaker believed endemic to Yankeedom.[36]

The secession of South Carolina on December 20, 1860, destroyed what little upcountry Unionism had survived the 1850s. The rhetoric of upcountry Carolina then became one of unyielding defiance. J. G. Sloan of Pendleton exulted in how "warlike" the news had grown by February 1861 and hoped for a "chance to display southern courage and chivalry."[37]

The long and sometimes bitter cultural split between Charleston and the upcountry surfaced in the early months of the struggle. Some doubt seems to have been felt among many in the state concerning whether the upcountry, especially the extreme northwestern part of the state, would have the same commitment to the southern cause as the slave-majority counties of the low country. Some low-country planters even seem to have doubted the southern patriotism of the upcountrymen. They should not have been concerned. Easley told a crowd in Pickens that "though our district is thinly populated, there is a spirit amongst these hills and mountains, a spirit of freedom and hatred of tyrants." A letter to Greenville's *Southern Enterprise* from a self-described "mountain maiden" sought to assure the newspaper's readers that the people of upper Greenville District, Pickens District, and other isolated hill hamlets would make their contribution to the Confederate effort. When the mountain maiden referred to the "nutmeg peddlers" of the North seeking to spread their fanatical ideas by force of arms, she expressed the same sense of the North's cultural otherness that could be found on the manorial rice plantations near Charleston or in the cotton kingdoms of the midlands.[38]

Carolinians of the upcountry displayed a strong commitment to the institution of slavery as well. John Crusy, a Confederate soldier from Pickens District, believed the war to be a struggle for "self-government" against a northern populace intent on meddling with slavery. "I now believe," he wrote in the first year of the war, "our mountain boys more staunch on the question than any set of men and that they will be an honor to their mountains."[39]

M. E. Bradford has described the Confederate army as something more like "the gathering of a Highland Clan" than a "modern military juggernaut," and such seems to have been the case in upcountry regiments. The Confederate government certainly hoped to fashion the rebel armies into a professional instrument of destruction, but the instrument continually proved to have ideas of its own. Soldiers from the upper counties sent to aid the ongoing defense of Charleston resented their treatment by low-country officers, one insisting, "they treat us like their niggers."[40] One upcountry Confederate filled his regimental history with disdain for officers who put on aristocratic airs. He also insisted that an upcountry militia tradition persisted during the brief period of drill instruction his regiment had in the Carolina low country. Instead of learning the manual of arms, the boys of the Fourth South Carolina spent their time "drinking popskull [grain alcohol], frying pancakes and bruising around generally."[41]

Bradford's description of the Confederate army as "an armed extension of the community" also applies to the upcountry regiments. Regi-

ments often maintained close connections to their home front, so much
so that local politicians eagerly sought their support when running for
office. James Hagood, in his 1864 attempt to reclaim his seat as clerk of
court for Pickens District, eagerly wrote to his supporter J. B. Sanders,
encamped in the Petersburg trenches in August 1864. Hagood hoped to
discover how Sanders's South Carolina regiment had voted. Much to his
dismay, he heard back from Sanders that "the boys all went again you"
and had voted for his rival, a Mr. Boykin. The reason? "They are all
Bowkins kin and nabors," wrote Sanders, suggesting that community ties
and the bounds of kin and neighborhood remained strong even after four
years of war in Virginia. Moreover, Sanders also testified to the continuing strength of the republican spirit in these upcountry soldiers when
he told Hagood of how one Pickens Confederate had said he "would be
damned" if he voted for Hagood, since the politician had told him he
would not run again.[42]

Stories such as this one, along with numerous instances of soldiers writing home complaining that they were not receiving their mail or worrying
over how their military reputation affected their standing in the community, suggest continuing close attachments to their counties, to their
poleis. Four years of hard fighting in the army of their new nation had
not sundered their commitments to kin, neighbors, and homeplace. The
rhetoric of personal liberty associated with the cause of secession itself
served to strengthen their local attachments, even as Jefferson Davis and
elements of his administration attempted to transform the South into a
modern, centralized nation-state through persuasion and coercion. Soldiers such as J. W. Reid of Anderson used the rhetoric of secession against
the government that supposedly represented secession, referring to the
Conscription Act of 1862 as evidence of Davis's desire to become "a
dictator" more malevolent than Lincoln. P. E. Maxwell, a Confederate
cavalryman from Pendleton, saw in the conscription act an attempt to
"legislate patriotism out of existence." Captain John R. Jefferies, whose
father had signed the Ordinance of Secession, wrote home in April 1862,
referring to the "Executive Council" that had been appointed to put South
Carolina on a war footing, as "our masters." Jefferies wrote that that he
would gladly vote to "abolish" this effort to centralize Carolina's military
and economic resources, since even this strengthening of state power in
wartime represented a threat to liberty.[43]

Carolinians' concern over the direction of the Davis administration
points out the profound contradictions at the heart of Confederate identity, contradictions that arise from the paradoxical yearnings of romantic

conservatism. South Carolinians found themselves attempting a conservative revolution that would use the upheaval of war to defend their ideal of a settled society. The Confederate effort shattered the possibility that Old South would become a static society, a "thick" society along the lines of the Tory dream of England. The Faustian pact of southern secessionists with nationalism had yielded a paradox: the use of the weapons of modernity against modernity. Conservatives had turned to the nation-state, that most modern of political mechanisms, in an effort to preserve traditional mores. A number of South Carolinians rightly came to believe that the Confederacy did not represent the embodiment of southern conservative ideals but rather represented their betrayal. Had Lee taken Washington and dictated terms of surrender to Lincoln on the White House steps, southern conservatism would have died aborning. The men of the South Carolina regiments who groaned under the Conscription Act would have found a centralized modern state on their hands, with a chief executive constitutionally weak but strengthened enormously by the prosecution of a successful war. The nation that had levied an income tax, confiscated its people's property in the form of slave labor, centralized control of manufacturing and railroads, and transformed the South into a nation-in-arms would have surely followed other newly created national polities of the late nineteenth century in the continuing consolidation of national power to the detriment of personal and local autonomy. South Carolinians had been willing to use modernity against modernity, but modernity had the deck stacked either way. Had the Confederate war effort proved successful, their romantic conservatism would have gone the route of so many European conservatisms after 1848 and dissolved into a full-throated modern nationalism.[44]

The South Carolina backcountry at the coming of the Civil War represented a social order *in foetus*. Frontier characteristics remained an important part of its identity, even as the Cherokee passed from the scene. Meanwhile cotton made it a new frontier, making possible tremendous economic prosperity. The profoundly agrarian character of this society, shaped and bounded by slavery, did little to rein in a drive for economic development. However, upcountry Carolina had also been profoundly shaped by unfree labor, and concern for "our institutions" colored South Carolinians' view of a world that, by the mid nineteenth century, regularly flung down institutions and erected new ones on the charred rubble. Both yeomen and planters anxiously wrung their hands over the safety of property, the very basis of independence and manhood, in a world with a revolutionary consciousness. Men of mind, such as William King

Easley and Maxcy Gregg, hoped that South Carolina would take its place among other great conservative republics in history, resisting the tides of change by grounding their social relations in organic custom. The romantic conservatism of Easley, Gregg, and innumerable newspaper editors and prosecession firebrands failed, not at Appomattox, but in the Davis administration's attempt to meld local liberties and folk customs into a new national state.

The war itself did not dim these hopes, despite the overwhelming defeat of the Confederacy. An aesthetic of the Lost Cause emerged from the chasm of war and defeat even as the institution of slavery disappeared. Indeed, with the ruins of southern society to contemplate, men influenced by romantic conservatism were very much in their element. The drive to fashion a conservative republic lived on, nurtured by Carolina's faith in evangelical religion. This faith, with its emphasis on cataclysmic personal conversion solidifying traditional relationships of hierarchy, perfectly matched the conditions of the South Carolina upcountry and the efforts of politicians, preachers and men of mind to sculpture a conservative commonwealth out of the land of the Cherokee. The evangelical faith, nurtured primarily in the Baptist and Methodist congregations, provided transcendent legitimation for the customs and culture of antebellum South Carolina. The mechanics of congregational life helped shape the upcountry into a cohesive community dedicated to a common ideology. The emphasis on transformation of the self, the possibility of a new birth that overcame the chaos of sin and brought individuals into the realm of proper, prescriptive relationships with God, superiors, inferiors, and the entire social order, perfectly reflected the needs and hopes of the upcountry—changing, wary of change, caught up irrevocably in the terrors of history. Southern conservatives turned to the common symbols of faith to help construct their aesthetic of the Lost Cause.

The importance of evangelicalism to the making of southern conservatism requires a separate analysis because of the issues it raises regarding the contest that conservatives faced. The historiography of southern evangelicalism emphasizes how, at least after the 1820s, the churches provided a means of solidifying southern culture. Evidence in South Carolina suggests otherwise, the records of upcountry churches suggesting continuing points of contest between the desire of ministers to create an organic and ordered world and the continuing insistence of personal independence by yeoman and slaves. Only in the turmoil of war, when the churches linked themselves with the Confederate cause, did the means of shaping a sacred order present themselves.

CHAPTER TWO

We Have No Head but Christ

The Struggle to Shape a Sacred World

In November 1861, almost a year after her state seceded from the Union, Mary Kelly seceded from Big Creek Baptist church in Anderson County, South Carolina. The church fellowship had presented an unexplained charge of "unchristian conduct" against "Abby (colored) and the property of Mary Kelly," a charge in itself not unusual in the records of antebellum southern churches. What does make this a peculiar case is the response of Kelly to her fellowship's decision to discipline her slave. Not only did she apparently dispute the church's findings, they seemed to so enrage her that Kelly herself left the church, taking with her two other slaves, Easter and Cumby. Slaveholder Mary Kelly chose to disregard a decision of her minister and her congregation, leaving the church and taking her movable property with her.[1]

The story of Mary Kelly illustrates how upcountry conservatism owed many of its deepest contradictions to this evangelical ethos. During the antebellum era, evangelical churches acted as cradles for the emerging ideology of southern conservatism, even as they became sites of contest within the allegedly organic nature of South Carolina social order. Church leadership, like the state's political leadership, hoped to shape a sacred order concomitant with their slave system. Evangelical doctrinal discourse concerned with human sin, the explosive experience of conversion, and the nature of the Christian community intertwined with romantic conservatism's concern for social hierarchy and prescriptive order to shape a sacred world in the South Carolina upcountry. At the same time, the congregational nature and informality of evangelical worship made it a preservative of folk mores that allowed evangelical men, and women like Mary Kelly, a sphere of personal independence. Historians who have examined evangelical religion in the South have argued that it brought white southerners into ideological unity by 1860. The evidence from South Carolina suggests that the antebellum churches never accomplished this goal

of unity. Ironically, war and defeat strengthened the ties that bound this
sacred world. The churches played a crucial role in shaping a Confederate
identity, conjoining this identity with the peculiar institution, southern
honor, manhood, and evangelicalism. At the same time, evangelicalism
provided, first, the Confederate effort and, later, the celebration of the
Lost Cause with a sense of transcendence, fashioning a Confederate religion in the Carolina upcountry.[2]

    Evangelicals worshiped in the South Carolina upcountry as Baptists,
Methodists, Presbyterians, and, often, even Episcopalians. Though often divided on issues such as church polity or the sacramental nature of
church ritual, all found agreement on a common view of human nature
shaped by the doctrine of original sin. David E. Frierson, a prominent
Presbyterian minister in Anderson County, referred to "the sinful and
deformed heart" of the unregenerate insisting, in an age that increasingly
idealized the experience of childhood, that the young "are distorted with
a monstrous depravity." Rejecting the optimistic nineteenth-century's assertion that scientific improvement would lead to the uplift of the entire
human race, Frierson refused to see a correlation between moral improvement and an increase in scientific knowledge. Attacking postrevolutionary
France, a favorite target for southern conservatives, Frierson grumbled
that "the eminence of the French in physical research is notorious." The
minister added, uncharitably, "They are to nature what vermin are to an
old mansion: acquainted with every nook and recess of the building but
know not the possessor."[3]

    Samuel Hill accurately describes conversion as the central tenet of
southern evangelicals. They were, above all, people who had experienced
regeneration by water and the Spirit. The upcountry of South Carolina
seems to have lived an ongoing conversion narrative in 1802, when revival fires first burned brightly in the Carolina backcountry. The period
between 1802 and 1805 marked the "charismatic" period of revival, in
which large camp meetings transformed tiny supply-store towns into massive encampments of five thousand or more. The emphasis in these early
revivals centered on the experience of the Spirit, often exhibited in highly
individualistic and emotional revivalism. An observer of one upcountry
revival, whose own Lutheran tradition had divided views on the spiritual
efficacy of the movement, wrote that the revival's participants looked
"as though they were struck by lightning, speechless and motionless; and
when they somewhat recovered, they could be heard shrieking bitterly
and supplicating God for mercy and grace."[4] These meetings, especially
in the beginning of the period of revivalism, exhibited significant cooper-

ation between Baptists, Methodists, and the doctrinally fastidious Presbyterians. The theology of this movement rooted the unity of disparate
religious groups in the experience of conversion: the turning from sin and
the reception of grace.[5]

Lacy Ford has noted that the revivals begin during the upcountry's
greatest demographic growth, which provided impetus for the growth
of the social order. The polity of the upcountry grew into its adulthood
entangled with the experience of evangelical religion. Denominational
leadership, especially among the Presbyterians and Baptists, managed
to channel the charisma of the revival encampments into organizational
structures and to transform grace-filled converts into dutiful church members. Padgett's Creek Baptist Church grew directly out of the "Great Revival" period among South Carolina evangelicals, adding 420 members
between 1802 and 1803.[6] Later revivals, in the 1830s, also led to the
creation of organized communities of faith. Conversion became the entry
point, not only into the life of the Spirit but into the sacred order of the
upcountry. The inner frontier fell under the control of Christ, even as the
outer frontier fell under the sway of cotton plantations and courthouse
squares.

Historian of southern religion Samuel Hill has noted that conversion
became, above all, an experience of the individual—an enclosed arena of
transformation where only the human soul and God could interact. The
individual soul had been warped by personal sins; evangelicalism offered a
personal salvation. One upcountry minister, speaking in Richland County
in 1861, called conversion "a second life . . . with which the stranger may
not intermeddle and that he [the convert] shares only with God."[7]

Such a heavy emphasis on individual experience, particularly one that
theoretically remained open to all people, offered inherent difficulties for
a slave society. The egalitarian tendencies of evangelical thought are obvious and have been well explicated by scholars such as Rhys Isaac, Donald
Matthews, and, most recently, Christine Heyrman.[8] Could not women,
slaves, and other dependents have their own private interchange with the
divine, sealed off from the interference of white men in search of mastery?

The nature of evangelical conversion did sometimes raise uneasy questions about the slaveholders' conservative order. So highly did evangelicals value personal experience with the divine that moments of great
irony break out in church records when the matter at hand relates to the
conversion of slave property. In August 1858, at Milford Creek Church,
of Greenville District, the church conference notes record that "Brother
Washington Taylor's black boy Phillip came forward and related a Chris-

tian experience and was received." Though Brother Taylor clearly plays
the master, asserting mastery even in the records of the church possession
of his chattel, the "black boy Philip" leaves his own imprint, a personal
experience of the sacred that makes him a member of the upcountry sacred world. Certainly unrecognized by the good elders of Milford Creek
Church, the metaphor of fellowship in this case trumped the reality of
enslavement. The evangelical sacred world never found a way to rein
in these profound contradictions. The evangelical ethos of the upcountry ignored the Carolina legal code's insistence that the enslaved African
American be regarded as chattel while simultaneously linking slaves with
their masters.[9]

The incident concerning Mary Kelly suggests that the difficulties faced
by upcountry churches appear most vividly in the efforts of fellowships
of faith to discipline their members. The effort to shape a conservative
order occurred within the confines of the "church conference," or "the
session," as church leaders attempted to squelch the anarchies of the Carolinian soul. The theory and practice of church discipline made it clear to
congregants that the Christian faith restricted individualism in significant
ways. Moreover, interpretations that view the influence of church discipline waning after 1820 fail to see the crucial role of the church conference
in upcountry churches throughout the antebellum period and beyond.[10]

The style of church discipline in the evangelical churches of the upcountry reflected the rural, prebourgeois nature of the land and people.
Church discipline seldom passed over instances of sexual misconduct in
their quest to root out human sin. No bourgeois delicacy kept upcountry
congregations from confronting what they saw as evidence of rebellion
against God—a much more serious matter than simply a lapse in bourgeois respectability. Sexual misconduct did not represent a betrayal of
middle-class decorum but rather a refusal to obey the commands of the
Word and a refusal of the gift of the Spirit—it had to be dealt with quickly,
harshly, and publicly. Church proceedings are filled with instances of children born out of wedlock and women being "taken" in adultery. Big
Creek Baptist Church, in Anderson County, went so far as to openly cen-
sure two girls for engaging in "twistification," a teenager's dance with
sexual overtones.[11]

Evangelical churches showed substantial concern with the maintenance of good order, sometimes acting as arbiters in matters of personal
conflict. Milford Creek Baptist Church, of Greenville County, had to
deal with the troublesome Mr. William Pennington, who, in 1856, "related a difficulty" between himself and another church member and asked

for arbitration. In 1860 Pennington again came before the congregation "asking pardon" for the fisticuffs he had engaged in with yet another member of "the brethren."[12]

Maintaining an ordered polity in the antebellum upcountry included the paternalistic oversight of slaves. Churches sought to maintain good order between slaves, masters, and the larger social order. In this fashion, the churches interlinked with the militia system and the familial hierarchy on individual farms and plantations to create this slave society. The coming of secession increased concerns over the activity of African Americans. In December 1864 Padgett's Creek Church expressed anxiety over "a cake walk at Sister Cornelia Rays," where there had been "a considerable collection of negros."[13]

Discussion over the meaning of slavery further reveals some of the profound contradictions in upcountry life. Eugene Genovese has argued that many proslavery ministers in the late antebellum period hoped to shape the paternalistic Abrahamic household and move away from the commodification of slaves into absolute property. This organic ideal of servitude influenced South Carolina Judge John Belton O'Neal's argument that slaves should become a nonalienable peasant class, attached to freehold. James Henly Thornwell, a South Carolina Presbyterian minister and one of the most influential southern theologians, defined slavery as the use of another's labor "independently of the provisions of a contract" and called for the humane treatment of slaves that followed the provisions of New Testament household codes.[14]

Thornwell and other honest conservatives understood that the inherent contradictions of South Carolina's social order could not be kept at the church door, and congregations clearly recognized the a priori right of masters over their chattel, even at times disregarding spiritual concerns in their efforts to ensure property rights. In Chester County, the Hopewell Presbyterian Church, for example, had "a number of black persons" apply for membership in the summer of 1851. The fellowship of the brethren proceeded cautiously: "The session not being acquainted with the blacks were desirous of seeking their owners before they would be admitted."[15] The fellowship of the brethren sought to shape a southern sacred world in which, as Saint Paul put it, "all was done decently and in order," both in and outside the congregational walls.

Nevertheless, slaveholding Christianity never settled the conflict between its desire to shape an organic order and its doctrinal emphasis on the power of conversion. Collisions between themes of dependency, the desire for mastery, and the distribution of power occurred constantly in this unsettled sacred world. The crucible of war only heightened these tensions, as Mary Kelly's rebellion against the sacred order in Anderson County shows. The connection between property ownership and independence gave this woman an interstice through which to slip. This incident suggests that the upcountry congregations often failed to herd the independent people of the upcountry into a social order based on "the fellowship of the brethren." Slave property, sometimes viewed as the bedrock of the Old South's allegedly organic social order, could also produce enormous strain within that social order, pushing slaveholding individualists and entrepreneurs in the direction of personal autonomy grounded in ownership of both slaves and the land they worked.[16]

If the fellowship of the brethren failed to exercise control over slaveholding women like Kelly, they certainly faced fierce resistance from white men protective of their own liberties and insistent on the right to personal experience with the Divine. This especially proved to be the case when congregations attempted to discipline members with regard to contested moral issues. Consumption of alcohol seems to have been such an issue in nineteenth-century South Carolina. The temperance movement that played such an important role in the formation of a northern evangelical bourgeoisie had made few inroads into South Carolina by the time of the war. A protemperance historian of Spartanburg County, writing at the end of the nineteenth century, admitted that the state's few temperance organizations in the antebellum period had died by 1860. The first state temperance society, founded in 1829, quickly collapsed. The society reorganized in 1838 and had a skeletal existence until 1851, when it disappeared again until 1856. In 1856 one Baptist seminarian in Greenville District who attempted to sell the society's paper was told by one of the upcountry's "sturdy yeoman" that he would "be run out on a rail" if he came around again.[17]

Most nineteenth-century evangelicals in South Carolina, and throughout the South, seem to have viewed the consumption of alcohol as a risky but not iniquitous pastime. Richard R. Michaux, a minister in western North Carolina, remembered of the antebellum period that "in past years it was not uncommon for prominent church members to run a distillery; and they made whisky and brandy and drank it too. The good old deacon or class leader would set out the bottle to his preacher when he visited him, who did not scruple to take a drink." A practice deeply embedded in upcountry culture, drinking alcohol appeared to most evangelicals as a matter for the individual conscience, and churches sought to restrain and discipline only when good order seemed endangered. In

1866 Neals Creek Church, in Anderson County, brought charges against Brother D. H. Watson for "hauling fruit to the still." Significantly, the charge seems to have been allowed to die. Moreover, the record leaves it unclear whether this was a Sabbath violation (the hauling was performed "on the Sabbath") or specifically directed against the production of alcoholic beverages. David G. Harris, a slaveholder in Spartanburg, writes of his attempt at brandy-making without taking the time to justify his behavior by evangelical standards. Harris would have been expected to write such an apologia, since he often pondered religious questions in his journal. The son of a minister, Harris lived on property conjoined to his father's. He frequented both the Baptist and Methodist churches, and his journal betrays a tender evangelical conscience.[18]

A changing ethos regarding the production and consumption of alcohol can be seen in the antebellum sources. Padgett's Creek Baptist Church, for example, challenged Brother John Bishop's running of a still. Bishop responded by asserting that he had been distilling for many years and, in his words, "felt clear and would continue." It is, of course, noteworthy that Bishop responded to the fellowship of the brethren with a declaration of personal experience, the very basis of an evangelical's salvation. No action seems to have been taken against Bishop, and his demand to be left alone with his conscience stands in the records of the congregation who sought to discipline him.[19] Such recalcitrance also emerged in the Presbyterian Church of Hopewell. In November 1866 the church charged upcountry farmer David McWilliams with "using ardent spirits too freely and also distilling the same." McWilliams would have none of it. He was "requested to attend a meeting of the Session but declined."[20]

Much of this evidence suggests that the evangelical churches of South Carolina had less than overwhelming success in shaping the southern social order. Two powerful social and cultural forces, slaveholding and evangelicalism's own insistence on the power of personal experience, weakened the church's hold on these stubbornly feisty people. South Carolina ministers attempted to shape a sacred order, knowing that from the human soul came the chaos of sin that could wreck the supposed harmonies of a slaveholding society. The spiritual discipline of repentance represented, in the words of one upcountry minister, "the plain course of duty." Meanwhile, lack of penitence became "the violation of a known duty." Jealous of their liberties, upcountrymen, and sometimes women, resisted, believing their church covenants that often asserted that they "had no head but Christ."[21]

If the desire to shape a sacred order foundered on this evangelical individualism, the creation of Confederate religion provided an answer, to the evangelical dilemma. The language and rhetoric of evangelicalism shaped the secession movement and then supported the Confederate effort to Appomattox and beyond. Antebellum evangelicals could not agree on disputed subjects such as the distilling of spirits or the tricky issue of disciplining someone else's property. They could agree that their southern sacred world, with all its inherent contradictions, was being threatened by a powerful enemy in the form of the northern abolitionists, alleged fanatics who twisted the grammar of the sacred to their own dark ends. The war for South Carolina's independence became a holy war against demonic foes, and after Appomattox, evangelicalism provided a sacred patina for the Lost Cause, lifting both its memory and its claims into a transcendent realm. The vehicle of the Lost Cause would combine with the pervasive evangelical ethos to create a deeply southern conservatism. The devotion to liberty, so often a thorn in the side of the effort to construct an organic society, became associated with the communal effort of the sacred cause. Confederate religion became a cultural ideal that melded the Carolina upcountry, bringing its disassociated themes into a recognizable pattern. Drawing on aesthetic representations of the Confederate war effort provided southern conservatives with a platform from which to speak.

The Reverend T. L. McBryde, of Pendleton, elaborated on many of the themes of Confederate religion in January 1861, telling his congregation that the North had decided to engage in "an unrighteous and unchristian war" against slavery. This effort, McBryde proclaimed, represented only the most obvious blemish on the perverted Yankee soul. The North had become a modern-day Sodom in which all the evils of modernity paraded themselves shamelessly. "Abolition," the minister proclaimed, "is but one of the fruits of the evil tree that grows so luxuriantly in the North." McBryde believed that abolitionism was merely the vanguard of a host of ideologies that would unloose the bonds of society, bringing down what he imagined to be the beautiful harmonies of the traditional South. Religious purification became the only option, purification achieved by the act of secession. "Come out and be separate from them"; cried McBryde, "touch not the unclean thing." [22]

Church leaders in South Carolina viewed the North as much more than a political threat. Northern abolitionism represented heresy, a betrayal of the evangelical ethos that made the North not only a cultural, but also a spiritual other. The *Confederate Baptist* insisted that the Confederacy's foes had "chosen Lucifer for their patron divinity, and are seeking to reinstate him to his lost dignity and honor." In the Confederate religion of the upcountry, the blue flood tide from the North represented the hosts of darkness, bent on the destruction of a sacred South. Not only religious newspapers but also local newspapers reflected this theme. The *Keowee Courier* made reference to Satan as "the first abolitionist" and supported their exegesis by arguing that Satan had been the first being who attempted to upset the divine order by appealing to a "higher law."[23]

The effort to create an ordered polity through Confederate evangelicalism received immeasurable aid from the work of a number of South Carolina religious colleges that had their roots in the antebellum period. These schools, such as Wofford College, in Spartanburg District (Methodist), Furman College, of Greenville (Baptist), and Newberry College (Lutheran), sought to train a generation of southerners in a peculiarly southern conservatism through a combined curriculum of the classics, a rigidly orthodox Christianity, and the apologetics of the proslavery argument.

John Bachman, a proslavery writer and accomplished natural scientist who served as the minister of Charleston's Saint Matthew's Lutheran Church, spoke at a ceremony for the laying of Newberry's cornerstone in the summer of 1857. Bachman set an agenda for the young academy that included a set of professors who embodied both "sound learning" and an attachment to "the peculiar institutions of our southern country." Newberry College would, Bachman hoped, "become the mother of many sons . . . who when duty shall require it, will become defenders of the time-honored institutions of our southern land." Bachman saw in Newberry the chance to create a "well-educated yeomanry" who would combine their practical agricultural experience with classical and biblical training, making them free of "the wild and speculative theories" of modernity. Bachman had his wish. In 1860 B. M. Zettler, a student from Savannah, remembered taking part in nightly patrols looking for "abolition emissaries." The Newberry College faithful succeeded only in waylaying two apple and tobacco peddlers from North Carolina, caught sharing apple brandy with "two negros." The town urged the peddlers to move on. The head of the theological department, "said to be an abolitionist because he employed white servants," also faced difficulty at the young Lutheran academy. "He was advised to leave and did so," dryly commented Zettler.[24]

Furman College grew directly from the split between northern and southern Baptists, owing its founding in Greenville to James C. Furman, who vociferously advocated both political and ecclesiastical secession

from the North. Supporters of the founding of the college in Greenville
District included P. E. Duncan, a Greenville secession convention delegate, and a future colonel of the Sixteenth South Carolina, Charles J.
Elford. Furman's learned professor of theology, James P. Boyce, perhaps
the most important Baptist theologian of the nineteenth century, served
as a chaplain to Confederate regiments in Charleston and James Island.[25]

The ritual beginnings of Confederate regiments drew on the symbolism
and emotive power of evangelical religion. Efforts at shaping the Confederate religion continued for South Carolinians at the front. John R.
Jefferies wrote home about a "fine sermon" he attended in May 1861 in
which the Fifteenth South Carolina heard the minister assert, "we are not
fighting through malice or envy, but for principle and liberty." Such sentiments mirrored evangelical sermons on the home front, knitting soldiers
and congregations into a common effort. The Reverend T. L. McBryde,
during a dark period for the Confederacy in the spring of 1862, told his
upcountry congregation that the southern war effort embodied "eternal
truth and right." "Liberty—especially at the hands of unprincipled and
ferocious tyrants," McBryde reminded his congregation, "comes only at
the price of blood and treasure."[26]

The events of the war entered into the very heart of the fellowship
of the brethren—congregational life. Upcountry churches provide evidence that the Confederate army became an extension of the community
and that individual congregations became celebrants of Confederate religion. Milford Creek Baptist Church, of Greenville, accepted members
who joined "by experience" while still in the ranks of the Confederate
armies. The state Baptist newspaper, aptly named the *Confederate Baptist*
during the war, kept up a steady stream of reporting on revivalism in the
army, the spiritual nature of the struggle, and often fairly secular accounts
of military matters and anecdotes from the Confederate ranks. One upcountry church even went so far as to use the power of church discipline against a member who had failed the standard of Confederate honor
and courage. Big Creek Baptist Church, in Williamston, brought charges
against J. B. Turner in January 1865 "for acting the torey and deserting
our army and going over to the yankee army." The Confederate Baptists
of Big Creek "excluded" Turner from the fellowship of the brethren for
this act, even as he had excluded himself from the southern war effort.[27]

The Confederate religion of the upcountry undergirded the war effort
by making defense of the homeland against a demonic force of evil a basic
Christian duty. The *Confederate Baptist* called on South Carolina evangelicals to "devote all their energies to strengthening, clothing and feeding

our self-sacrificing and gallant armies." Since Confederate religion viewed this as a spiritual struggle, the Confederate army must become an "army of the Lord" through the purification of sin and the sanctification that evangelicals believed came through the experience of the Spirit. "Every kind of excess and impurity," wrote one Confederate evangelical, "should be consumed and disappear before the intense flame of patriotism that should burn in every bosom and make every heart an altar."[28]

[*handwritten margin note:* want to make the Confederate army an "army of the Lord"]

The congregations of the upcountry, though often depleted of membership by the Confederate war effort, experienced what the upcountry faithful called "a season of revival" during the war years. This explosive revivalism drew on the perennial need to explain crisis in transcendental terms and to weave meaning, especially theological meanings, from the disparate threads of human experience. Grace Brown Elmore, a Columbia child of the planter class, pondered, "How very desolate those must be to have no God on whom to lean at a time like the present."[29] Late in 1864, as the war turned decisively against the South, Beaver Dam Baptist Church, of Laurens District, experienced a revival that according to one observer served as an example of "God giving victory over the hosts of sin and Satan," even as "our political clouds are still dark with war."[30] Observers noted that "not a few of the converts were leading members of the community" and that the power of Confederate religion appealed especially to "the tender and loving youth of both sexes." Wounded Confederate soldiers returning home played a prominent role in these revivals. One veteran who "had lost a limb in his country's services" now "gladly enlisted under the banner of the cross."[31]

Confederate religion, the taut connection drawn during the war between the experience of conversion and the mythic struggle for southern independence, provided a way to knit together a region fundamentally fragmented. Confederate religion became an instrument of order and the unifying theme of the aesthetic of the Lost Cause. The experience of conversion, open to all ages, genders, and classes provided a common experience of religious transformation during a time of profound social and political transformation. Former Confederates "gladly enlisted under the banner of the cross," becoming holy warriors for the ideals of ordered liberty, a freehold for white men, and a prescribed order of gendered and racial relations, even as this sacred order went down in flames around them.

The women of the South Carolina upcountry both acceded to and supported the shaping of this southern conservative order out of the Confederate religion. Evangelicalism and gendered spectacles conjoined to create rituals of devotion to the Confederacy. Mary Montague White personally committed a regimental flag to a company of the Fourteenth South Carolina in a ceremony in Anderson County. A local Baptist minister then passed down the line of men and "presented each member with a Bible."[32] Lucy Holcombe Pickens, the wife of Governor Francis W. Pickens, presented a regimental banner to the Holcombe Legion, a brigade of cavalry, infantry, and artillery named in her honor. In an accompanying letter that Pickens presented to the regimental officers she promised to keep the men in her prayers, certain that God would make the men "a legion of heroes." Many similar accounts suggest that this type of ritual beginning for upcountry regiments became common. For example, the women of Lexington County customarily gave their departing men New Testaments as they entrained for Virginia or embattled Charleston.[33] In this way, the role of women expanded in the aesthetic constructions of upcountry conservatism. At the antebellum militia musters, women had merely watched and cheered the display of arms in defense of the slaveholding order. The crisis of the war transformed Carolina women into symbols of Confederate religion, conferring upon the upcountry regiments the status of chivalrous defenders of feminine virtues and of a South constructed as feminine. Following the war, the role of women, especially young and beautiful Carolina women, would become central to the aesthetic of the Lost Cause and South Carolina's romantic conservatism.

A theme that would enter deeply into Lost Cause mythology concerned the allegedly undying loyalty of women to the Confederacy. The women of the planter class did much to strengthen this view. Planter women in Columbia, for example, held a bazaar to raise money for the war effort as late as February 1865. A banner that pictured a Palmetto tree, the state's proudest symbol of its revolutionary war heritage, flew above eleven tables of cakes, pies, and pastries, each table representing a state of the Confederacy. The women of Columbia took this symbolism very seriously, one commenting that an observer would have no doubt that "the doctrine of state's rights and state's sovereignty . . . could never be eradicated."[34]

Religious experience often has at its core a sentiment about purity—and about miasma, the possibility of religious pollution. Sherman's march into Carolina awakened the terrors of impurity, further radicalizing the adversarial nature of South Carolina's Confederate religion. The very nature of Sherman's destructive march had much to do with the evocation of these fears. A number of states experienced Union occupation and suf-

Sherman's destructive invasion

fered the blights of war. None suffered the kind of ideological hatred, the destruction and pillage, of South Carolina. Sherman gave broad discretion to his Army of the West regarding the Palmetto State, the state he and his men referred to as the "the hell-hole of secession" and "the mother of traitors." The half-legendary terrors of Union invasion would do much to create ideological unity among white Carolinians across lines of tradition and denomination. Roman Catholics, a tiny portion of the upcountry population and very much isolated from the broad themes of evangelicalism, nonetheless united with their fellow southerners in their devotion to Confederate religion. Following the burning of the Ursuline Convent and the destruction of Saint Mary's College in Columbia, a rumor circulated among upcountry Catholics that Sherman's men had drunk whiskey from the sacred communion vessels and even performed a kind of black mass with the priestly vestments of Saint Peter's Church. One Columbia priest referred to Sherman and his men as "the very vandals of hell." Another upcountry rumor suggested that Sherman's men sought not only to break the southern will to fight but to degrade the southern woman, the symbol of the purity of the cause and the hearth-minders of Confederate piety. "Talk about your property Madam," one circulating tale had Sherman say to a distraught belle, "you ought to thank heaven that your life and virtue are safe."[35]

The reaction of South Carolinians to the invasion of the state used religious language to describe the hated invader. Emma Leconte recorded in her diary that Sherman's men were "fiends incarnate." Upcountry Christians worried over the "desecration of southern churches" by this demonic foe. Grace Elmore believed that these "very devils of hell" would take their hatreds out on the women of South Carolina and pondered whether or not she should take her own life rather than submit to the lusts of the invader. "God forgive me," she wrote, "if I had to choose between death or dishonor. I could not live—life is sweet but would have lost its savour. That which was taken could never be restored. God will, God must justify the deed."[36] The invading Yankee army meant both the loss of the purity of Carolina's sacred world and the possibility of a literal loss of purity, the rape and degradation of the southern lady. Like a Roman matron, Elmore vowed that she would seal her loyalty to the southern cause with her own death rather than submit to the hated invader. Elmore reflected in her private musings the public worries of a defeated Carolina. The loss of purity because of the failure to defend the sacred soil of Carolina would become an important theme in the celebration of the Lost Cause, with Reconstruction-era conservatives rallying former Confederates with a call to defend the state that had been "outraged" by the Union army, the Republican Party, and "disloyal" freedmen.

Sherman's march left Columbia in flames and brought Charleston to its knees. Fleeing into the upcountry, low-country families brought the news of utter defeat, and worse, the humbling of Carolina honor. "Humiliation spreads its ashes" wrote William Gilmore Simms after the burning of Columbia, leaving the novelist and proslavery ideologue to wonder about the ways of "that Providence which is so inscrutable to man." Some committed Confederate ladies of the upcountry felt that Providence might have less to do with it than the failings of their men. Elmore penned in her private diary the sum of all fears for the free white men of South Carolina; that the women of their households would question their masculinity. "Our men," she complained in January 1865, "have not done their whole duty en masse."[37]

The news of Appomattox and of the occupation of the upcountry found Carolina collapsing under the weight of its own tremendous failure. Chaos reigned as slaves left the plantations and took to the red clay roads of the upcountry. Union cavalry forays terrified the populace and disorganized the basic mechanics of upcountry life. In May 1865, Big Creek Baptist Church "dismissed Divine service" because of "the Yankees raiding the country." Meanwhile loss of life draped the upcountry in mourning. Thirty to thirty-five percent of South Carolina's young adult white male population had perished in the war. Maxcy Gregg's brigade lost more than four thousand men, with Gregg himself dying at the Battle of Fredericksburg. The fiery young secessionist, who had sought to shape the struggle into a war on northern economic centralization as much as against abolitionist fanaticism, told his aides that he "cheerfully gave his life for the independence of South Carolina."[38]

In the face of defeat, humiliation, and horrifying loss of life and property, Confederate religion reasserted itself. Confederate evangelicals believed that God had a transcendent purpose for the Confederacy, and the loss of the war did little to change that belief. Confederate religion became a vessel that preserved the dream of southern conservatism, a dream that would find expression in both political acts and aesthetic representations of the Lost Cause.

One of the earliest expressions of the Lost Cause in the upcountry occurred at Trinity Episcopal Church, in Columbia, South Carolina, in the early summer of 1865. After Appomattox, the rector of Trinity, Peter J. Shand, omitted from his services the customary "Prayer for the President" in the *Book of Common Prayer*. When word of this minor rebellion reached the head of the Union occupation forces in Columbia, the elderly minister received an order to include the prayer the following Sunday morning with a detachment of Union soldiers present. Shand did so, but the congregation, kneeling through the rest of the "Prayers of the People," as Episcopal ritual prescribed, rose defiantly to their feet as Shand began the enforced intercession. When he completed the prayer, Union soldiers looked on as the congregation continued to stand in stony silence, refusing to add a devout "amen." [39]

The experience of conversion itself provided, not only to Confederate veterans, but to the women of the ancien régime, a narrative within which to structure the experience of defeat. Florella Meynardie's 1879 novel *Amy Oakley; or The Reign of the Carpet-bagger* fashions the story of postbellum South Carolina as the creation of order out of chaos, a struggle with anarchy won by conversion to evangelical Christianity and loving remembrance of the Confederacy. Meynardie's narrative focuses on the tribulations of a daughter of the ruined rice aristocracy who attempts to make a new life for herself in the upcountry. Oakley's adventures in the upcountry, in which she must briefly disguise herself as a servant girl to escape greedy and lascivious carpetbaggers, end with a reestablishment of hierarchy—though a hierarchy based on evangelical values and the remembrance of the Confederacy. Revealing the continuing split between upcountry and low, the "republican simplicity" of the upcountry yeoman, rather than the low-country planter's aristocratic values, prove to survive the war. For example, one of the subplots of the narrative concerns the "pleasure-loving Marie," the daughter of a wealthy Columbia family whose postbellum move to the low country becomes her moral and spiritual downfall. Marie, though married to a patient cuckold, becomes a notorious flirt in fin-de-siècle Charleston, the "reigning belle," as Meynardie put it. She rejects the simplicity of plain-folk religion, leaving her "brilliant parties" only to mockingly attend revival meetings. Marie eventually finds peace in conversion to evangelical Christianity and rejection of the corruption of Charleston. She is able to have an experience of grace only when she attends a revival meeting with "a humble dressmaker." Marie, like Amy, finds planter values ultimately impotent in the face of change. Also like Amy, her conversion to evangelicalism does not constitute a rejection of the Old South, only of the low-country aristocrats' construction of that antebellum world. Marie's transformation saves her disastrous marriage, making her weak-willed husband into a loving patriarch. Leaving corrupt Charleston behind, Marie becomes the mistress

of a large upcountry cotton farm where republican simplicity and patriarchal values reign. Meynardie's novel stands in the long tradition of the
Carolina upcountry's distaste for Charleston's elitism and wicked habits
and also suggests that the breach in the mythic world of the Old South
could be restored only by conversion to Confederate religion.[40]

The idea of conversion itself, so central to evangelical Christianity, became central to the emerging Confederate religion that placed much emphasis on the returning veteran, who, following conversion, becomes the
embodiment of both evangelical and Confederate values. The soldiers represented objets d'art in the gallery of upcountry culture, heroes who had
"enlisted under the banner of the cross," combining Confederate identity
with a role in the upcountry congregational life. They embodied the upcountry ideal of faithfulness to God and the southern cause, even as the
Old South became a ruin to contemplate. The Reverend Joseph Peacock
serves as an example of just such a figure. A Confederate cavalryman who
had experienced conversion within the ranks, Peacock became a Baptist
minister in Aiken County following the war. He used his pulpit to preach
a Christianity that reveled in the aesthetic of the Lost Cause, representing
the struggle as part of his own conversion narrative and urging on his
congregation both the experience of evangelical salvation and the commemoration of the Confederacy.

The churches of the upcountry sought to validate these figures that
so clearly represented the Confederate cause. The Daughters of the Holy
Cross," a ladies organization at the recalcitrant Trinity Episcopal Church,
regularly presented to Confederate veterans who joined their communion
a ribbon made from sheaves of palmetto and featuring crossed Confederate battle flags. Veterans steeped in the sentiments and symbolism of
Confederate religion often became prominent leaders of educational and
religious institutions. G. W. Holland, who served as president of Newberry College from 1878 to 1895, had lost an arm in the war but found
religion when, the story went, a pocket New Testament stopped a bullet
that would have "surely" killed him.[41]

Ellison Capers represents the most influential of the veterans who "enlisted under the banner of the cross." Capers, a graduate of the Citadel,
had ties with the wealthy planter class of the low country but served
as rector of the prominent Christ's Church Episcopal in Greenville for
twenty years following the war. Capers had become a brigadier general at the age of twenty-eight, suffered a severe wounding at the battle of Chickamauga, and took part in the disastrous charge at Franklin,
Tennessee. Perhaps because of his time in the crucible of war, Capers's

thoughts turned to religion. He studied for the Episcopal ministry, and for the rest of his life—as the rector at Christ's Church and as Episcopal Bishop of South Carolina—preached Confederate Christianity. Capers continued to view the southern war effort as having a transcendent purpose and came to see the active commemoration of the Confederate experience as a sacred duty. Capers himself became a symbol of the Lost Cause in South Carolina second only to General Wade Hampton himself.[42]

The heroes of the Lost Cause who became local leaders in education and religion embodied the values of Confederate religion. Their narratives of conversion, often growing out of their experience in the southern ranks, became paradigms for the creation of a white Carolina united behind the experience of the Lost Cause. The tales they told of dead comrades, battles lost and won, and the transcendent meaning of the Confederacy became a set of aesthetic images to contemplate, teaching the values of prescriptive duty and, most important, virtue. The virtue of the Confederate holy warrior had little to do with simple moral behavior and respectable standards, though those elements certainly played a role. Confederate virtue meant duty, courage, and the high demands of honor. The determinative power of evangelicalism in the lives of these heroes made the South Carolina ministry more influential than ever before in shaping a sacred world, in part because many of these Confederate holy warriors became ministers. The world they created would see itself at war with modernity, seeking to preserve the folk mores of Carolina in the fading years of the nineteenth century. The construction of an aesthetic of the Lost Cause with Confederate religion as an organizing theme came to act as a standing critique of the world the Yankee made.[43]

The influence of Confederate religion in South Carolina suggests that the idea of civil religion does not provide the best theoretical explanation for the meaning of the Lost Cause. The celebrants of the Lost Cause used Confederate memory to embody a deeply conservative ethos that celebrated the past as a model for the present. Civil religion tends to assume a kind of eternal national present in which a dominant set of values unites a variety of religious, ethnic, and racial groups under a common banner. These values are often the pragmatic values of tolerance and an easy equality. In contrast, Confederate religion called upon defeated Carolina to sadly mourn a lost past by practicing the values of that past in the present. The ethos of the Lost Cause tended to emphasize the importance of duty, of the terrible struggle that attended a fight for liberty, and of the willingness to challenge the dominant ethos of the nation. Tolerance and equality played no role in Confederate religion. Confederate religion played a militant role in the Carolina upcountry, a continuing sense of Confederate nationalism.[44]

Celebrating the past to critique the present links the celebrants of the Lost Cause in the South Carolina upcountry with the romantic conservatives of Europe. The connection between the remembrance and active commemoration of the southern cause with Confederate religion strengthens this comparison, since European conservatism often conjoined with religion to create powerful aesthetic representations of past sacred worlds. In the context of the South, the power of an aesthetic of the Lost Cause connected to evangelical religion created an even more powerful configuration. This was true, first, because the "religion of the heart" as a discrete category already had a powerful hold on many in the upcountry at the time of Appomattox. The joining of such powerful religious and emotional impulses with the Confederate experience created an irresistible combination for Carolinians disoriented by the rapid change of war and emancipation. Second, the Confederate religion provided upcountry conservatives with a set of values they could, in fact, conserve. These values, the whole complex of which can perhaps be summed up as nonutilitarian civic virtue, provided both manners and morals for the organic society that conservatives sought to build out of the ruins of war. Figures such as Ellison Capers embodied these values, providing a narrative of self-sacrifice and courage, baptized by submission to a divine will and the divine order.

Why did South Carolina evangelicals take this path and why did southern conservatives, not all of whom had clear evangelical convictions, link themselves with this transcendent world of divine values? The question needs little explanation. The bête noire of conservatives in a variety of contexts has been the pragmatic nature of modernity, its failure to recognize that the true, the good, and the beautiful exist within the nontechnical, nonideological aspects of human life and social organization. Conservatism finds a natural ally in religion, itself a clearly nonfunctional phenomenon.[45]

Why did the religion of the upcountry have such close connections to southern conservatism? It seems problematic that a religion that put such heavy emphasis on the transcendent and on the experience of regeneration, of new life, would link itself so closely to a movement that looked to the past, to a failed experiment in political economy that had died a violent death on a thousand battlefields. What possible benefit did South Carolina evangelicals receive from entangling their sacred world with a political Lost Cause?

The theological problems that Confederate defeat raised for the churches of the South required a theological response. Barbara Bellows and Thomas L. Connelly have written that the South found itself "spiritually unprepared for Appomattox," and other scholars have explored the profound sense of spiritual despair that gripped evangelical hearts and souls when the holy cause collapsed.[46] However, it should not go unheeded how quickly South Carolina evangelicals moved from wondering over the immutable ways of God to finding in Confederate defeat an example of the workings of a divine order. A military defeat did not signal divine displeasure. The true faith, reminded a pastoral letter from the South Carolina Methodist Conference, had always suffered in this world. "To be innocent and to be oppressed," it proclaimed, "are the body and soul of Christianity."[47]

Furthermore, the centrality of the doctrine of human depravity in evangelical thought dovetailed nicely with the themes of the Lost Cause and the conservative tradition associated with Confederate memorialization. If the South had lost, if the righteous had suffered, if God's chosen had passed through what in biblical language was called "a fiery trial," then that merely confirmed the power of wickedness in the world, the intractable nature of human sin that evangelicals had always proclaimed. Southern conservatives, meanwhile, needed little convincing in order to believe in the perfidy of the human race. W. K. Easley became so incensed over what he saw as the evils of Reconstruction and the moral failures of the American "plebs" that in the years following the war he began to speak openly in the republican upcountry of the need for a European-style monarchy, perhaps with an alliance between throne and altar.[48] Evangelical religion provided a metaphysical explanation for the evils of modernity, providing southern conservatives with a grammar of transcendent dissatisfaction, sanctifying their hatred of the disordered and anarchic world they believed had been born at Appomattox.

Linked by the crucible of war and by the intermingled logic of their own ideologies, evangelical religion and southern conservatism looked upon the ruins of the Confederate idea. Together they created an aesthetic of the Lost Cause, drawing on the themes of the cause as a sacred effort, the role of southern women as vessels of purity in a world of evil, and the tragic nature of the southern experience. Unable to overcome the South Carolina upcountry's obsession with personal liberty in order to shape a prescriptive order, southern conservatives found in the Lost Cause a means to unite white Carolinians in a culture of defeat and renewal. The booming economic prospects of the 1850s seemed a distant memory, and emancipation threatened not only livelihood, but the very possibility of social order. Confederate religion, and its defiant attitude toward modernity, provided theological and cultural meaning to a young, vibrant society brought up short by cataclysmic defeat.

Of the southern ethos, novelist Walker Percy once wrote that "its most characteristic mood was a poetic pessimism which took a grim satisfaction in the dissolution of its values."[49] This poetic pessimism constituted the very heart of the aesthetic of the Lost Cause, a pessimism about the possibilities of society that issued in both sad praise for a conquered past and a critique of the materialistic and utilitarian present. Southern conservatism represented a contemplation of ruins and an insistent criticism of the new world that modernity sought to erect on those ruins.

CHAPTER THREE

No Tears of Penitence

Blue-Eyed Belles and the
Emergence of the Lost Cause

"When we look round the ruins of our country," William King Easley told the Pendleton Ladies Memorial Association in 1866, "we almost sink with despair." Appomattox, Easley intoned, had created an "hour of gloom" in the South, transforming the bridal blush of southern nationalism into "a time of mourning."[1]

Sorrowful as the former cavalry commander sounded, he and many other South Carolina Confederates would more often display an attitude of defiance than one of sorrow in the years following the war. The conservatives of South Carolina would come to view the war of secession as part of a running battle with the forces of the modern world; cold, godless, and materialistic forces that sought to undermine their liberty, take their property, and dismantle their social order. Practicing Confederate virtue, virtue undergirded by Confederate religion, remained the only hope of sustaining a prescriptive social order. The past became the standard for present action. "If we are true to our past," Easley told the women of Pendleton, "our country will one day emerge."[2] Fidelity to Confederate memory meant more than a romantic reflection on the deeds of Confederate heroes. It required action in the present, even militant action, to safeguard the citadel of South Carolina's soul from the ravages of the modern world.

White conservatives shaped the aesthetic of the Lost Cause, even as they struggled to maintain the hierarchical world of the Old South. The contemplation of the ruins of their social order—remembering the experience of combat, the loss of comrades and meeting together as veterans and Confederates—provided a mythic worldview that placed current struggles in a larger perspective. Conservatives leaders contrasted Confederate virtue with the very real corruption of Reconstruction-era government,

using the Old South as a prophetic standard with which to critique the
world the Yankee made.

The aesthetic of the Lost Cause united white conservatives in the years
immediately following Appomattox, developing in the midst of struggles
to limit the rights of the freedmen and recapture hegemony over South
Carolina's political and social order. Interpreters of the Lost Cause have
not focused on the emergence of the movement during these years or on its
aesthetic form. Heavy emphasis on the Lost Cause in the 1880s and 1890s
has led historians to ignore the role of the earliest organizations, groups
that often emphasized defiance and rejection of Yankee mores rather than
simple nostalgia and reconciliation with the North. Such defiance grows
out of the context of Reconstruction, a milieu that called into question
whether conservative whites could successfully stabilize their social order
after the destruction of their slaveholders republic.

The Lost Cause aesthetic exerted enormous power over white hearts
and minds in the years immediately following the war, an emotional force
much remarked upon in narratives of Lost Cause celebrations. The emo-
tion awakened by the aesthetic emerged from the way conservative whites
used a gendered language and symbolism to display Confederate virtue.
Women became repositories of a southern identity that defiantly survived
Appomattox. Their role in Lost Cause ceremonies and organizations not
only legitimated the Confederate struggle, but seemed to divinize the Confederacy in defeat.

The Lost Cause aesthetic, responding to the destabilizing influences of
war and emancipation, showed a special concern for the ideological uses
of women's bodies. Sources reveal not only public ceremonies in which
women are placed on public display but a further interest in describing
the beauty of those who founded Lost Cause organizations or marked the
graves of the Confederate dead. The power borne by women's involvement in the Lost Cause aesthetic grew from the insistence on the part of
conservative whites that the hierarchical relationships of the Old South
continue in the wake of defeat.

Laura Edwards describes resistance to "stay laws and homestead ex-
emptions" as receiving stiff opposition from those she labels "conservative whites."[3] Evidence from the South Carolina Upcountry suggests that
southern conservatism functioned in a different way, as whites, elite and
otherwise, appealed to the aesthetic of the Lost Cause to stabilize the
ownership of productive property, rightly viewing mastery over land as
a prerequisite for mastery in social relationships. Protests and challenges
offered to South Carolina's Radical Reconstruction government reveal

the same concerns over land and property, particularly in the taxpayers movement of the early 1870s. Concern over the preservation of antebellum hierarchy mixed with fear of the loss of mastery. The anxiety that the basis of the household itself—productive agricultural property—might disappear also influenced the early stages of the Lost Cause aesthetic. Conservatives whites had known that Confederate defeat meant the end of slave property and watched in even greater horror as the land the slaves had worked threatened to slip out of their grasp.

The power of the Lost Cause aesthetic energized conservative white men to challenge the Reconstruction regime. African Americans just as vociferously resisted the imposition of this world resurrected from the ruins. Black religious experience provided a way to assert independence from the visions of an organic society envisioned by white conservatives. The failures of the Reconstruction regime, a regime ostensibly reflecting *black resistance* black interests, reveal how black resistance could falter in the realpolitik of the era. Black resistance nevertheless plays a crucial role in the story of southern conservatism, forcing whites to define the meaning of white supremacy in a world where their aesthetic visions did not always conform to reality. Struggles over the meaning of white supremacy would sunder the unity of whites in the decades to come, playing a crucial role in the failure of southern conservatism and the transformation of the meaning of the Lost Cause.

Immediately following the war, the Lost Cause aesthetic provided a crucial impetus for political action. The conservatism nurtured through the rough-and-tumble, profit-hungry frontier period of South Carolina's history came to fruition as South Carolina white men sought to control and channel the forces unleashed by war and emancipation. Confederate memory, imbued with the power of evangelical religion, provided a repository of virtue, a moral aesthetic that called upon those mourning for the Lost Cause to continue the struggle. Easley and other emerging celebrants of Confederate memory may have pointed Carolinians to the ruins, but the contemplation of those ruins created defiance, not supine despair, and certainly not regret. "In all the mourning in our state over its Lost Cause," wrote Laurens County's John Leland, "there are found *no penitence* no tears of penitence."[4]

South Carolina's lack of penitence applied particularly to the matter of slavery. A meeting of the state legislature, headed by provisional governor Benjamin Perry, met at Columbia's First Baptist Church in September 1865, ostensibly to prepare the state to formally reenter the Union. Instead, those who gathered seemed to meet primarily to vent their

frustration at defeat. Rather than declaring the Ordinance of Secession
"null and void," as had been ordered by newly inaugurated Andrew Johnson, the legislature simply repealed it, implicitly recognizing secession's le-
gality and legitimacy. Emancipation received a grudging acknowledgment
that sounded nothing like acceptance. Slaves, the legislature granted, had
"been emancipated by the United States authorities." In December the
regular session would attempt to reshape the social reality of emancipation in the Black Codes. These codes created what Walter Edgar has called
"a judicial ghetto" for Afro-Carolinians, restricting their movement and
tying them to the land through the enforcement of labor contracts. The
codes even made use of the terms "servant" and "master," transposing
the vocabulary of slavery into the postbellum world. [5]

Yankee free-labor ideologues cheered the notion of contractual relationships breaking up the slave system, perhaps viewing this as proof
that the southern cause had truly been lost. However, the actual workings
of these contracts, and the assumption that the former planters brought
with them into these new economic relationships, challenged the sanguine attitude of many northern reformers. The new labor contracts attempted to tie black South Carolinians to the land, transfiguring slavery
into *villeinage*—essentially a form of noncontractual serfdom. South Carolina sought to subordinate black people in a neofeudal system that would
safeguard folkways and reflect attitudes regarding prescriptive hierarchy
and religious notions regarding the meaning and use of wealth and markets. The labor relationships of the postbellum period mark a break with
the capitalist order in their rejection of the notion of "absolute property" connected with slave ownership and their turn toward a relationship
between land and labor founded on reciprocal duties and obligations. [6]
White conservative Carolina attempted to transform the freedpeople from
their property into their peasantry. In the fall of 1865 Lutheran minister
and proslavery writer John Bachman expressed the hope that the Black
Codes would reflect the natural order, that "the Negro would be placed in
the situation for which God intended him—inferior to the white man." [7]

The attempt to structure upcountry society along hierarchical lines appears in the early labor contracts drawn up by planters. Many of the new
labor contracts seemed less like the opening wedge of free labor than the
paternalist compromise in written form. A contract used by Confederate
veteran John R. Jefferies sought to reinstitute antebellum racial hierarchies and to ensure his continued mastery over his "people." The allegedly
free people who worked for Jefferies in Union County had to agree to
"give no impudence or sauce nor leave my premises at any time without

consent." Compensation would not come in the form of cash, but rather in provisions of "corn, peas, syrup and potatoes." Contracts such as these troubled and exasperated Union authorities. John De Forest, a Federal officer in charge of the occupation of Greenville District, wrote that the labor contracts he read "contained all sorts of ludicrous provisions. . . . The idea seemed to be that if the laborer were not bound body and soul he would be of no use." De Forest encouraged the planters and farmers of Greenville to make use of the "weekly wage" as a means to ensure labor, but the Union officer lamented that such an innovation went "beyond the usual circle of southern ideas." Robert K. Scott, Reconstruction governor of South Carolina later attributed the failure of the state's agriculture to become quickly profitable in 1866 to "the ignorance of the free labor system." [8]

The labor contracts attempted to circumscribe African American agency as much as possible. Afro-Carolinians, meanwhile, sought to shape their freedom within this context, often in ways that corresponded to the worst fears of the postbellum South. The dismantling of slavery, events seemed to suggest, meant the complete unraveling of the social fabric. In August 1865 a local newspaper reported that "a gathering of the colored population" in Abbeville had been ordered to keep quiet so as not to disturb the peace of white residents. To their horror, the gathering grew even louder, and a local white man, known to be a defiant Confederate veteran, was threatened by the rowdy participants. [9] Freedpeople seem to have continued forms of resistance important during the antebellum era by stealing from whites, a practice given an extra impetus from the hard economic times. The *Anderson Intelligencer* complained of crime "on the increase with the freedmen in the way of depredations on the smokehouses of citizens." In 1866 Greenville's John D. Ashmore wrote to J. E. Hagood in Pickens that, "many depredations are being committed by freedmen . . . many of them have refused to sign contracts for labor and are very troublesome." The freed slaves' willingness to act "troublesome," to show their own agency in response to the attempt to reinstitute antebellum social relations, constituted the most basic challenge to the attempt to shape the upcountry into an organic culture. [10]

Southern conservatives saw such "troublesome" behavior as the very shape of evil, a rebellion against natural hierarchies. The search for order, so often stymied by prosperity in the antebellum period, seemed equally distant in times of economic hardship following Confederate defeat. Economic crisis challenged the old assumptions of liberty tied to property, the producer ideology of the free and independent farmer asserting mastery over family and land. The fear of losing property, and thus mastery, threatened to create a divide in the unity of white Carolina. The divide did not come in the 1860s. Tied together by commitment to the Lost Cause and united in the determination to restore the lost world of the Old South, white Carolinians attempted to shape an organic order and to beat back the threat of modernity. Fears over the loss of property and mastery found expression in the praise of the Lost Cause, the construction of the Confederate cause as a virtuous struggle that still continued.

"Money," wrote one Greenville dry goods merchant, "is scarce as hen's teeth."[11] The lack of currency in the Carolina upcountry may have troubled merchants more than the yeoman farmers, who worried over the loss of the land. The loss of productive property became an epidemic in the upcountry, largely owing to deprivation resulting from the war. The realties of emancipation and the seeming impossibility of recreating their antebellum worlds befuddled many returning veterans. One observer wrote that many who had shown "courage and steadfastness" on the battlefield had "failed utterly at adaptation." Such men would "sit around crossroads stores, expectorate tobacco juice, swap jokes and abuse Yankees and niggers." "Poor folks ha'nt no chance," one Confederate widow told a Greenville clergyman. "What's poor folks to do without land?"[12]

Whites publicly expressed anxiety over the meaning of the postbellum economic crisis. Many returning veterans, worried about their lack of land or the possibility of losing their productive property by a failure to pay their debts, hoped that the 1865 constitutional convention would address the issue. One writer to the Newberry County's *Weekly Herald* prophetically worried that "landless white people" might become "tenants with the negros," while "a few wealthy men, speculators and blockade runners" engorged the best land of the state. The brief controversy over the Stay Law, a wartime measure meant to safeguard the property and credit of soldiers while they fought for the Confederacy, conjoined fears of loss of property and mastery with an early use of the rhetoric of the Lost Cause. The South Carolina circuit court's declaration of the Stay Law as "inoperative" and "unconstitutional" caused a brief popular response. Confederate veterans Y. J. Pope and John P. Kinard, of Newberry County, challenged the court's ruling at a mass meeting in Newberry; similar mass meetings in Lexington and Edgefield Counties attacked what they called "the upheaval of property."[13] The farmers of Edgefield found such an upheaval readily apparent. By 1870, 43 percent of male heads of households owned no real estate in Edgefield County.[14]

One of the most interesting of the debtor protests occurred at Pickens

Courthouse in August 1866. The leaders of this meeting also played a prominent role in Confederate memorial activities and used the memory of the Confederacy to call for debtor relief and "a liberal homestead law." The state government, argued one of the meeting's resolutions, owed it to the memory of the Confederate dead to ensure that the men of the state not fall into "pauperism and misery." One resolution wondered at "the apathy and indifference of the distinguished men of the state" and expressed solidarity with the protests in Edgefield and Lexington Counties.[15]

In the 1860s, anxiety over the loss of the land in the South Carolina upcountry never became a true class movement, although Carolinians experimented with the languages of class. Those opposed to the end of the Stay Law, however, used a political "language of exclusion" rather than a "language of class."[16] In part, demands for debtor relief that swept the upcountry emerged out of the desire to prevent a class structure, an economic and social caste system, from dismantling the old hierarchical structures based on landownership, patron-client relationships, and planter paternalism. Rather than a progressive movement that sought to claim inherent rights deserving the watch-care of the state, Confederate veterans laid claim to inherited privilege, ancestral rights to land and productive property further solidified by their participation in the war for southern independence. One resolution passed at the Pickens protest noted that both creditors and debtors had supported the state's secession, and both must now suffer the results of Carolina's subjugation. Tacking away from a language of class and toward a grammar of marginalization, leaders of the debtor relief movement shaped a Lost Cause aesthetic that placed the practice of Confederate virtue at the center of its symbolic world. Though such movements are seldom seen as a reflection of the conservative South, the use of Confederate virtue as the center of gravity for their argument, combined with the concern that white men be enabled to ground their liberty in productive property, suggests a connection with the southern conservative ethos. The debtor relief movement sought no progressive reform, but only to safeguard the households and property relations of traditional white Carolina.

Historians of the postbellum South who have seen in the Lost Cause a class phenomenon that legitimized the emerging industrial order should take note of phenomenon such as the debtor movement. Centering the movement for debtor relief on the Confederate aesthetic suggests that the Lost Cause became plastic in the hands of warring camps in the postbellum period. Neo-Marxist theorist Stuart Hall has argued that ideological constructions can experience changes of meaning that open narratives to contest and conflict. Public symbols, Hall writes, become "ideological terrains of struggle" rather than simply labels affixed to class ideas.[17]

Confederate memorial associations helped to shape the narratives in which contest over the meaning of the Lost Cause would occur. The creation of the Lost Cause aesthetic acquired its ideological thrust in an arena of conflict. These local associations sought to ritually invoke the memory of dead comrades and lament the Old South, even as they shaped the memory of the war. The first Confederate veterans' organization in South Carolina, the Confederate Soldier's Association of Pickens County, contained many of the features that would dominate later memorial associations. Formed in the fall of 1866, the first meeting of the organization in September occurred under the auspices of Saint John's Lutheran Church of Walhalla, a predominantly German settlement in the extreme northwestern part of the state. The meeting at the Lutheran church heralded the central role that evangelical religion would continue to play in the Lost Cause, placing the celebration of the Confederacy under the auspices of Confederate religion.[18]

Gaines Foster and Edward Ayers have found an elitist tinge among the early Lost Cause organizations, but the group who met to form the Pickens County soldier's association bore little resemblance to the more status-conscious memorial associations formed in Richmond and Charleston.[19] A group of five appointed as a steering committee contained only one member of the professional class, the physician O. M. Doyle, who by 1870 had been driven by financial hardship to give up his practice and turn to farming. One member of this committee, S. P. Dendy, had been listed as a student in 1860 and lived with J. D. Franklin's prosperous farming family. Another founding member of the group, W. T. Cleveland, had lived in the home of the planter Bayles Hix, where he served as a classics tutor. In the 1860 census he had been listed as owning no property. J. M. Addams seems to have been a middling yeoman at the time of the war and may have supplemented his income with work as a tanner following Appomattox. He certainly had prospered little more by 1870. Both he and another leading light of the association, Robert A. Thompson, had been major participants in the Pickens County debtor protest in early August. Addams had in fact penned the resolutions connecting debtor relief to the memory of the Confederate dead. Thompson had been a signer of the Ordinance of Secession. The final member of the steering committee, J. W. Shelor served as a private during the war (most of the other founders were officers) and in 1866 had a taxable income of twelve dollars. Though not serving on the steering committee, another private, the German-born H. W. Pieper, helped write the constitution and by-laws of the organization. Pieper seems to have been the most economically successful of the group in the 1860s by continuing his dry-goods business·and running a local tavern.[20]

An examination of the backgrounds and economic positions of these leaders yields a number of insights. First, the men who met to form the soldier's association had important ties to the antebellum elite even though they themselves had not been part of the planter class. Only one member of the steering committee seems to have been a slaveholder before the war, but two had lived in the homes of wealthy patrons and likely admired their lifestyle and accepted the values of the slaveholding class. In some way these celebrants of Confederate memory could be described as "new men," but they were also men who entered the postbellum world firmly committed to the ideology of the Old South, an ideology forged into an even stronger mettle by their Confederate experience. In the years ahead, many of these men would become prominent members of the community but in ways that hardly marks them as members of a New South elite. Second, they had returned from the war to find themselves in a precarious economic position. Two had been landless in 1860; while the remaining three seem to have endured varying degrees of financial hardship in the years following the war. Like returning veterans all over the upcountry, the founders of the soldier's association anxiously pondered the link between liberty and property and worried that loss of one meant loss of both. Finally, the involvement of some of the prominent members of the association in calls for debtor relief challenges the assumption that the memory of the Lost Cause functioned as a simple gloss on New South materialism. C. Vann Woodward's assertion that the Lost Cause acted as a tool in the hands of Bourbon capitalists bears little resemblance to the meaning of Confederate memory for the veterans of Pickens County who used the rhetoric of the Lost Cause to safeguard the property of all white men.[21]

Significantly, this group called on the living embodiment of the antebellum ruling class, Wade Hampton III, to speak to the September meeting. Hampton, a scion of one of the wealthiest families in the South, had spoken out against secession in 1860 but quickly accepted the drift of the times when the war began. Though he had no formal military training, Hampton did have an enormous personal fortune, which he used to outfit a brigade of cavalry, infantry, and artillery appropriately called Hampton's Legion. Earning a reputation for gallant charges as a cavalry commander, he led the Army of Northern Virginia's horse soldiers after

Jeb Stuart's death in 1864. Unwilling to accept the reality of Appomattox, Hampton attempted to reach a fleeing Jefferson Davis in the spring of 1865 in order to escort the president without a nation into the southwest, hoping to continue the struggle.[22]

Though described by postwar observers as an "aristocrat to his fingertips," the Wade Hampton who came to Walhalla in 1866 had much in common with the founders of the soldier's association. Hampton returned from the war in near poverty, his family home in Columbia burned to the ground, and, like so many upcountry veterans, crushed by overwhelming debt. Hampton lived in genteel poverty for the rest of his life.[23]

The speech the bankrupted planter delivered managed to praise the old order, threaten the North, and urge moderation toward South Carolina's black population all at once. Hampton praised the Old South as a virtuous republic ruined by war, where the "artisan could ply his vocation" and "the farmer till his soil." Hampton evoked the imagery of warfare that played an ongoing role in the Lost Cause aesthetic, the evocation of "banners flying proudly, banners glistening brightly" and "desperate charges against the enemy." Recalling the hated invader, Hampton reminded his hearers that "the grasp of military power has not yet relaxed its hold," even as he urged continued defiance, particularly the continued defense of Confederate virtue. "Shall we who are freeborn men be so base as to declare that our country has met the fate it deserved?" Hampton asked.[24]

Hampton clearly connected manly independence with the Confederate cause. His speech to the recently returned vets, many who waited for the gavel to fall over farms and homeplaces, conjoined the aesthetic evocation of warfare with a continuing struggle of defiance. Hampton's praise for the old order, the virtuous republic of productive and property-owning white men at work in their fields, constructed the dreaming vision as a birthright that needed reclamation.

The freedmen had a role to play in the new order that would grow organically from the old, a clearly subordinate role in which emancipation did little to change the status of black Carolinians. "He has been faithful in slavery, he will be your friend in freedom," Hampton told the vets, inscribing indelibly the experience of slavery on the experience of Afro-Carolinians. In Hampton's praise for the Lost Cause, and in so many similar orations, the agency of Afro-Carolinians received no recognition. Hampton and other Carolina conservatives viewed African Americans as childlike and endangered by their severance from hierarchy and paternalistic concern, and they called for a protective shroud to fall around the African American experience in South Carolina. Unable to practice the virtues of the free white man who had shown his mettle in the war for southern independence, emancipated black Carolinians could only practice faithfulness and loyalty, the virtues of slaves. The refusal to allow, even rhetorically, the agency of African Americans became a central feature of South Carolina conservative culture, even as freed slaves and northern black people showed their clear and undeniable political subjectivity during Radical Reconstruction.[25]

Hampton would become the central figure in the celebration of South Carolina's Lost Cause. In the fall of 1866, Hampton spoke at a number of small soldier's associations and later became the head of the Carolina Confederate Survivors Association. In speech after speech, the former lieutenant general called for continued defiance and helped germinate a devotion to the Lost Cause that would come to fruition in his own 1876 campaign for governor. Speaking to the Anderson Soldier's Aid Association in the summer of 1866, Hampton told the veterans to "expect nothing from the government of the United States," which had branded them "outlaws, rebels and traitors." Though historians have argued for an apolitical interpretation of the Lost Cause movement, Union authorities thought differently. Following his Walhalla speech, a detachment of Union cavalry rode into town demanding information on the "traitorous and seditious" speeches that had lately been given in the mountain hamlet.[26]

Male organizations did not carry the banner of the Lost Cause alone. The role of women in the symbolic christening of Confederate regiments at the beginning of the war expanded into a central role in the celebration of the Lost Cause. The growth of the Ladies Memorial Association in South Carolina reveals the ways that women shaped the aesthetic of defeat while showing how class and gender conjoined in the celebration of the Lost Cause. South Carolina's Ladies Memorial Association had its beginnings in Charleston, organized by Mary Amarintha Snowden in May 1866. The organization grew directly out of wartime soldiers' relief organizations and preserved its basic organizational structure as it passed the torch to the United Daughters of the Confederacy in the 1890s. Throughout its history in South Carolina, the the association remained much smaller that the male memorial organizations and more elitist in its membership, even as it left Charleston and made its way into the upcountry. The founders of the association chapters, such as Lucy Holcombe Pickens of Edgefield, represented the women of the planter class. The "southern lady," it seemed, had a specific class location. Much as the yeoman farmer or the landless laborer might see in his rough-handed

wives and daughters the epitome of southern womanhood, the memorialization of the women of the Old South centered on the plantation mistress.
Praised for wearing homespun and suffering untold deprivations for the
southern cause, the women who formed these memorial associations just
as likely used their husband's political influence and wealth during the
war to maintain a lifestyle not very different from their days of antebellum glory. Nonetheless, at countless monument dedications, graveside
memorial services, and funerary orations, young belles, often chosen for
their beauty and family connection, stood beside the matriarchs of the old
order to praise the sacrifices of the Confederate dead.[27]

Several factors likely influenced the class orientation of women's
memorial associations. First, the ideal of the southern lady since antebellum times had been the sequestered belle free from the necessity of
labor. Slavery had made possible such a lifestyle for many in the planter
class, and even some prosperous yeoman families likely approached the
ideal, at least managing to keep women's labor hidden within the household. Emancipation and economic transformation forced many South
Carolina women, even in the families of small planters, to take up the
hoe. Women's labor came out into the open, challenging the ideal of the
patriarchal male who used his mastery over his slaves to assert a different
kind of mastery over the lifestyle of his women. Southerners preferred not
to recognize this basic change in social relations and so divinized women
able to approximate the antebellum ideal. The women of Carolina who,
sequestered by wealth, could still represent the ideal of the Old South
naturally became the keepers of its hearth fires.[28]

Second, southern women did not have the experience of combat or
fairly egalitarian camp life of the Confederate soldier to blunt class dis-
tinctions. The mass mobilization necessary for the Confederate war effort
opened the practice of Confederate virtue to men of all classes, from the
wealthy planter (who occasionally served as a private) down to the landless laborer. Massive loss of life within regimental units often propelled
even the poorest of farmers into positions of leadership in such a way that
postwar veteran organizations sometimes had a remarkably egalitarian
cast. Even members of the South Carolina working class, such as J. W.
Reid, could correspond with wealthy J. B. E. Sloan, of Greenville, regarding their common experience in the Fourth South Carolina Volunteers,
bound together by their common experience of battle.[29]

Finally, the role that feminine beauty played in the aesthetic of the
Lost Cause, and its connection to class structure, has often been passed
over. Physical beauty, though most often constructed as a "natural gift,"

actually functions as a social category structured by such diverse factors as dress, artistic paradigms, and even root metaphors of religious and ideological meaning. In postbellum South Carolina, beautiful bodies had a class location. John De Forest manifested these attitudes in his description of the "low down women" of Greenville and Pickens Counties who searched him out in hopes of receiving Federal rations. Their class location, he suggested in his memoirs, had been inscribed on their very bodies. De Forest described a mother and daughter as "ghastly," with the mother being "stooping and clumsy in her build," while the daughter, "nineteen years old . . . but looking twenty-seven," had the possibility of beauty, admitted De Forest, but failed to attain it because "of the miserable quality of her life and raiment." Two other young women of the "impoverished classes" who came to De Forest seeking help received a similar assessment: "tallow complexions, straight, light, dead hair, broad cheek bones and singularly narrow foreheads. One of them was made a little more repulsive than the other by a deformed hand."[30]

The women who took part in Confederate commemoration, on the other hand, seemed fit symbols for commemoration of the holy cause. Young women of prosperous families served as sponsors for Confederate veteran groups. Elected from the young, unmarried teenagers of the community, these women are invariably described as beautiful. Public spectacles such as monument dedications and political tableaux featured "the loveliest young women of the Town" acting as objets d'art in the aesthetic of the Lost Cause. Lucy Holcombe Pickens, founder of the Edgefield Ladies Memorial Association, became important in this respect because of her intimate connection with the Lost Cause, her marriage to Francis Pickens, the secession governor of South Carolina, and her renowned "Blue eyed beauty." Mary Chesnut described her as "young, lovely, and clever," and so widespread did the perception of physical attractiveness and Confederate loyalty become that the Confederate government had her likeness placed on the one hundred dollar bill.[31]

Beautiful white female bodies became crucial elements in the public presentation of the Lost Cause aesthetic. Mary Douglas has argued that cultural representations of the female body encode fears of impurity and assert systems of traditional patriarchy over against autonomy and capitalist individualism. The willingness to present eroticized, beautiful bodies, even in later political tableaux, when these bodies represent Liberty or South Carolina, suggests that sexual anxieties and patriarchal fears are being salved by this process, even as such powerful aesthetic perceptions incite political action. These female bodies on parade are not, as Julie

Kristeva might argue, metaphors of lack and nought, but rather powerful political symbols that assert the righteousness of the ancien régime against radicalism and social revolution. Class-based beautiful bodies thus played a central role in southern conservatism's challenge to modernity.[32]

Much of the Ladies Memorial Association's work during the early years of its existence centered on mourning the Confederate dead. Concern for the proper burial and memorialization of Confederate heroes spread from the early associations in Virginia into the Carolinas. The earliest initiative in the South Carolina upcountry involved simply gathering the names of each county's Confederate dead on a state roll of honor. Many of these rolls later achieved a kind of official codification as compilers meticulously attempted to include every fallen Confederate soldier, as if to fail in placing a single name would constitute an act of impiety. In the 1890s, for example, memorialists in York County set about the work of "perfecting the rolls" of the state's Confederate dead. A special concern for the keeping and marking of graves also moved the organization. Mrs. Robert McCaughin, of Newberry County, acted as an agent of the local association and sought to raise money "to turf and mark" Confederate graves. The ritual decoration of Confederate graves played an important role in the activities of individual associations. The celebration of Confederate Memorial Day spread into South Carolina in 1866, an attempt at inventing a tradition inspired by the reading of a German romantic novel describing European Catholicism's practice of decorating ancestral burial plots on special days.[33]

Mourning rituals became central to the Lost Cause aesthetic, bearing a similarity to the attachment to ancestral shrines so important in the romantic conservatism of Continental Europe. Martin Greiffenhagen has argued that such a romantic view of the ancestral past had all the power of a "revolutionary ideology" in its profound alienation from modernity. South Carolinians seem to have held to a similar conception of their Confederate dead, asserting that the virtue of dead Confederates stood as a bulwark against the forces of transformation and modernity. Gaines Foster, on the other hand, views the decoration of graves and public mourning as a way for the South "to acknowledge the death of its cause." The meetings of the Ladies Memorial Associations, Foster insists, included "little discussion of historical and political issues."[34]

An examination of one such meeting, a gathering in upcountry Pendleton, tells a different story. The 1866 gathering in which W. K. Easley spoke of the "ruins of our country" also included a call to action set within a ritual of commemoration. The act of memory meant more than a simple reflection on the settled facts of history. Easley called on the women of Pendleton to remember the virtue of the dead Confederates and suggested that such an act of memorialization would turn the resting places of the fallen into shrines of resistance, with much the same effect as the "graves of Thermopylae" had on the people of Greece. Easley praised South Carolina womanhood, using classical and medieval illustrations to show that Carolina women had inherited the task of preserving Christian civilization from the ravages of time and decay. Easley went on to compare the Confederate effort to other lost causes of history that the practice of virtue eventually made triumphant. "The bones of Pym and Hamden and Cromwell were thrown to the dogs," he reminded these keepers of graves, "and yet one day William of Orange stood in Whitehall and laid the basis of British freedoms." Easley clearly believed the cause to be anything but lost even as he urged the remembrance of those who had fallen in its defense: "Overpowered we are, but not vanquished! Prostrate we are, but not fallen!"[35]

Easley's elegant call to action represents only one example of the political orientation of some women's memorial associations. The attempt in Columbia to erect a monument representing the Confederate dead of the entire state openly challenged the hegemony of the Radical legislature. Seeking to reclaim the space around the statehouse for white conservative Carolina, a group, later known as the South Carolina Monument Association, formed in November 1869. Louisa S. McCord was its first president. McCord, the daughter of secessionist firebrand Langdon Cheves, was a published author of proslavery, antifeminist tracts in which she used her massive learning, sharp wit, and keen sense of irony to excoriate the assumptions of modernity regarding the nature of rights, the necessity of reform, and the inevitability of progress. A self-described conservative, McCord believed that she and other women of her class had the responsibility to practice the virtues of home and religion, preventing the world from becoming "a wrangling dog kennel." McCord, with the southern cause now lost, certainly would have seen the work of memorializing the dead as part of this effort to preserve the conservative ethos of the South against the tides of time.[36]

The South Carolina Monument Association attempted to have a statewide appeal and did have a somewhat more popular orientation than the memorial associations. An announcement of the monument association's formation, at a meeting during the state agricultural fair, urged women of all classes to participate; membership had been set at one dollar, an amount described as being "low as practicable." Despite this seeming

openness to all the Confederate widows of the state, the leadership remained the wives of the antebellum elite. Three of the general officers
had been the wives of Confederate generals. Representatives from the
elite Charleston Ladies Memorial Association also served on the board of
general officers. The majority of donations came from the wealthy ladies
of Richland County and Charleston, together raising donations of more
than three thousand dollars. Pickens County, on the other hand, con-
tributed only five dollars. Though clearly located in a differing milieu of
class and economic status than the memorial associations, the monument
association showed a similar ideological orientation as men's groups by
inviting Wade Hampton to serve as the inaugural speaker.[37]

Issuing an appeal for funds in 1869, the ladies of the association headed
by McCord declared that a monument to the Confederate dead would
"witness the justification by the decree of a God of Right" and create a
"sacred altar" where the women of the state could bring "pious oblations." The Reconstruction legislature, however, insisted that the ladies
take their "pious oblations" elsewhere. Only by 1872 did the association
have the funds to begin preparing a site for the monument's placement. In
that election year, the monument association, now headed by the daughter of Wade Hampton, chose not to make a request to place the monument
on "state House grounds," nor on "the main street of Columbia," owing
to the government of "carpetbaggers and Africans" who ruled the state.
The monument, a single Confederate soldier atop a marble shaft, was
placed at the Elmwood Cemetery, where numerous Confederate soldiers
had been buried. The placement of the memorial challenges Gaines Foster's assertion that the early women's memorial associations acted only as
"mourning societies" in their eagerness to place their funereal monuments
among the dead. The women of Columbia placed their statue of a defiant
Confederate soldier in the graveyard only because of political opposition
in the statehouse. They had, in fact, considered another location before
choosing the cemetery, only abandoning it when surveys discovered that
the sandy soil would not support the weight.[38]

After 1876, when, in the words of the South Carolina Monument Society history, the "men of the state" fought "to throw off the embrace of
the deadly serpent in whose coils they had so long been enfolded," supporters promptly moved the monument from Elmwood to the front of the
statehouse overlooking busy Main and Gervais streets. In an elegy on the
marble base, the women of the association praised those who "have glorified a fallen cause by the simple Manhood of their lives" and, "remaining

true to the instincts of their birth," had "died in the performance of their duty."[39]

The inability of white Carolinians to place a monument to the Confederate dead on the grounds of their statehouse reveals the great challenge of conservatism in the years following the war. The matter of labor contracts and black Carolinians' resistance to them forced white Carolina into a struggle to circumscribe an alarming political subjectivity on the part of the freedpeople. The first open acts of rebellion against the allegedly organic order of social relations occurred in the churches. As the evangelical fellowships of faith became centers of Confederate religion, black Carolinians made a speedy exit. In January 1866, the black membership of the First Baptist Church of Camden withdrew to form the Mount Moriah Baptist Church. New denominations grew out of the freedpeople's insistence on religious reconstruction. The African Methodist Episcopal Zion Church became one such new upcountry organization in the years following the war. Coming to Chester County, South Carolina, in 1867, the fellowship of faith had spread by 1890 into much of the northeastern tier of the state, with congregations in Lancaster, York, Spartanburg, Newberry, and Fairfield Counties.[40]

The response of white evangelicals varied from attempts to retain control of their black flocks to an attitude of "good riddance." One Baptist church in Greenville County sought to continue control of the emancipated by making their new congregation an extension of the mother church. In June 1866, the congregation of Milford Baptist granted "a letter of dismission to Sister Lydia, a freedwoman, for the purpose of constituting a church at Jubilee Meeting House." Milford Church also attempted to continue the practice of discipline against its remaining black members, such as freedman Jack Scott, who "was excluded from the church for stealing a watch." Most commonly, white evangelicals saw the departure of their former slaves as evidence of degeneration in the race, a blow struck by the emancipated against Christian civilization. Failing to exert spiritual control over black worship, Carolina evangelicals relegated it to realms of darkness and religious pollution. In the eyes of Confederate religion, the emotional worship of the freedpeople constituted "devil dances."[41]

The Reconstruction Acts of 1867 provided freedpeople with the political leverage to lay claim to their freedom and represented the greatest challenge to the organic social order that southern conservatives hoped to shape. The coming of Radical Reconstruction meant more to conservatives than the fear of "bottom rail on top," the terror of black republican domination. Certainly this played an essential role, but Carolina conservatives found even more disturbing the determination of the new legislature to fundamentally reshape South Carolina society along the lines of nineteenth-century liberalism. The new legislature, and the constitutional convention, made clear its purpose. One participant later said that the 1868 constitution had hoped to follow "the progressive advance of the age," and conservatives would have agreed, finding the new constitution nothing less than revolutionary.[42]

Resistance to the state constitutional convention and its work would likely have been roused had the delegates composed a conservative document. Even the demographics of the convention represented a revolution for South Carolina. Out of 124 delegates, 76 were African American. Out of this group, 57 had been enslaved a mere three years before they met to reshape the political culture of Carolina. Native whites made up a tiny minority of the delegations.

Unfortunately for the freedmen, their leaders at this crucial historical moment left much to be desired. Bourbon Democrats would work hard to create a legend of the convention and the Radical legislatures that followed as a circus of illiteracy, corruption, and criminality. Political inexperience, illiteracy in a small number of cases, and naïve idealism out of keeping with Reconstruction realities constitute the only "crimes" of the majority of the delegates. However, many of the Radicals seemed determined to prove their critics correct. A former slave from Union County spent several nights in prison during the convention for the theft of some of his fellow delegates' personal belongings. Afro-Carolinians were unluckiest of all in the white "scalawags"—white southerners who collaborated with Reconstruction governments—who represented their interests: Joe Crews, of Laurens County, had been a slave trader before the war, and Franklin J. Moses combined a reputation as a thief, liar, opportunist, and notorious seducer. In time, the state government would earn the appellation "carnival of debauchery and corruption." One New York Republican who served in a minor clerical position wrote that to breathe the very air in the state capital "made one feel like going out and picking a pocket."[43]

The state constitutional convention, white scalawags and eager black reformers, met in the summer of 1868 and initiated a number of reforms that sought to strike at the heart of the conservative ideal. The most important of their speedy reforms certainly centered on opening both the ballot box and the jury box to black South Carolinians, thus radically

changing the configuration of South Carolina politics. Of as much concern to conservatives was the introduction of South Carolina's first divorce law and other marriage reforms that undercut the power of the
southern patriarch to rule his household. An insurgent women's suffrage
movement among black women in Carolina supported these measures,
beginning a strong tradition in the postbellum period of political militancy among Afro-Carolinian women. The Radical constitution writers
even struck at some of the ritual behaviors of the Carolina ruling class by
outlawing dueling. In the enthusiasm of the moment, some of the more
idealistic delegates called for laws making the use of the words "nigger"
and "Yankee" illegal in the state; another, who seemed to have a utopian
turn, suggested an amendment that would "outlaw crime and poverty."
Francis Butler Simkins dryly comments that the convention tabled the
latter suggestion "due to problems of enforcement."[44]

White men of Carolina also trembled at the clear move toward the land
confiscation of white property heralded by the work of the South Carolina Land Commission. The land commission went further than any
other southern state agency in the attempt to grant the much-longed-for
forty acres and a mule promised by Radical Republican congressmen,
but like so many of the reforms of the Radicals, the plan bogged down
in corruption and mismanagement. The land commission clearly served
as an instrument of vengeance in the hands of the Radicals, awakening
the strongest opposition from large landowners and frightening the small
farmer, who already feared the loss of property, liberty, and manhood.
The animus of small farmers and the white working class turned against
the Republicans and the northern domination they represented rather
than against the aristocrats who had ignored their concerns in 1865–
66. Losing their freehold for nonpayment of taxes awakened their greatest fears—impoverishment, dependency, and, ultimately, effeminacy. In
1873, 270,000 acres fell under the gavel for nonpayment of taxes. The
amount of property lost nearly doubled the following year. One carpet-
bag Republican openly referred to driving white Carolina "to the wall
through taxation."[45]

The Lost Cause aesthetic faced a deadly enemy in the goals of the
land commission. How could the world of the Old South, glorified in
the Lost Cause aesthetic, be maintained by landless paupers? Concern
over losing the foundation of the household made taxation the rallying
point for white conservatism during the early years of Reconstruction.
John S. Preston, husband to the head of the South Carolina Monument
Association after McCord's retirement, described the "Black Republican

Government" as a "revolutionary mob" who had "the power to tax without limit." In an open letter responding to the 1868 constitution, white conservatives, led by Wade Hampton and former Confederate general Samuel McGowan, complained that taxation combined with the disenfranchisement of veterans meant taxation without representation, a policy repugnant to "Anglo-Saxon Liberty." These conservative leaders drew a connection between the land commission's "wild and ruinous" schemes of confiscation and the relatively high taxes of the Reconstruction regime. The property of the white veteran, they declaimed, would fall victim to "spoliation" by "northern adventurers, southern renegades and ignorant negros." Hatred of the relatively high taxes of the postbellum period extended from large landowners to the poor yeoman, whose economic fragility made him especially anxious over the doings in the statehouse. Rumors of extravagant expense by the black legislature brought his frustration and anger to the danger point. In Anderson County, an editorialist worried that high taxation, combined with the overwhelming debt of many farmers, would result in South Carolina's farms passing into the hands of "northern capitalists," while white South Carolina men would become "serfs and tenants to Tad Stevens and his radical friends."[46]

One ironic upcountry incident reveals the continued anxiety over the loss of property evinced by Confederate veterans and their willingness to lay claim to the right of property because of their practice of Confederate virtue. In May 1869 several Confederate veterans from upper Greenville County wrote a letter to C. P. Leslie, the Republican head of the land commission, requesting "distribution of the lands of the state" to "a democratic, moneyless, landless set of men" who had faithfully served the Confederate cause. Clearly misapprehending the political situation in the state, these Confederate representatives of the "democratic, moneyless, landless" set received an open letter from Leslie in the *Greenville Southern Enterprise*. Leslie expressed his sympathy for their plight, all the while reminding them that their white democratic leaders had been the most vocal opponents of the land commission's work. Leslie also chided them for assuming that their service on behalf of the Confederacy meant that the state government owed them anything. The state would recognize them as "citizens" rather than as valiant warriors.[47]

In this debate over land, Confederate veterans who argued for recognition as practitioners of courage and virtue met the firewall of modernity. These landless Confederates demanded the traditional practice of reciprocal obligations in a patriarchal and paternalistic society, the grant of land in return for the practice of virtue. The Radical Republican land

conservatives were against up modernity 77

commission, on the other hand, used a language of rights and citizenship, of partisanship and political interest. The state did seek to aid its needy "citizens," Leslie asserted, but had to struggle with competing interests to accomplish its task. The omnicompetent state thus had to use the power of taxation to bend recalcitrant interests to its will. Such an answer constituted no answer at all for the white veteran who saw in this expansion of state power the very shape of his fears: taxation and debt leading to dependency. These fears resulted in a determination to maintain independence even if that meant, in the words of a Fairfield County man, "a refusal in a solid phalanx to pay no further taxes."[48]

Democratic leaders shared concerns over confiscatory taxes. The 1871 and 1874 taxpayers conventions highlighted a number of these themes, asserting the need for tax relief and white unity while also favoring a hierarchical social order. The makeup of these gatherings looked as conservative as the 1868 constitutional convention had looked revolutionary. W. D. Porter, the president of the taxpayers 1871 convention, told the opening session that he saw "so many familiar faces, so many of the good men and true, to whom South Carolina, in her better days, was accustomed to confide her honor and interests." Familiar faces indeed. Eleven of the thirty participants had been Confederate generals. One delegate had served in Jefferson Davis's cabinet. Most of the remaining members had served in state legislative capacities during South Carolina's Confederate experience. Viewing itself as an "advisory body," the 1871 convention went beyond its self-imposed mandate to investigate taxes and bond issues and criticized the nature of South Carolina's Reconstruction government. Not only excessive taxation but the "useless" number of officials that made up local Reconstruction bureaucracy concerned the convention. These two conventions became vehicles to unite the Democratic Party in an ideology that paradoxically combined calls for reform with appeals to Carolina conservatism. Democratic leaders proposed an end to excessive taxes while refusing the remedy of debt repudiation as damaging to the honor of the state.[49]

The Lost Cause as a center of gravity for resistance played a crucial role in both the 1871 and 1874 conventions. The very makeup of the conventions signaled that this movement represented a continued Confederate war effort by different means. In his speech to the 1874 convention, former Confederate brigadier general Martin W. Gary, of Edgefield, made specific reference to the issue of the war, an issue he insisted had not yet been settled. "The cardinal difference between the two parties in this country," he asserted "has been the construction of the Constitution." Moreover, Confederate defeat "has not determined which is correct." Gary asserted his own belief in state's rights, a principle he believed excessive taxation and domination by a "black republican" government had overturned. Gary and other conservatives also used the taxpayer's convention to address the issue of universal suffrage, Gary asserting that such an idea acted simple as "the tool of the demagogue."[50]

Historians have argued that the taxpayer's convention offered little to the "democratic, moneyless, landless" set of white men in whose name it met. Even its attacks on the Radical legislature failed to sound a clear note of reform regarding spending cuts and state-funded debt. The taxpayers convention did, however, result in a popular movement, despite the antidemocratic rhetoric and demographic of the convention. By 1874 most South Carolina counties had "taxpayer unions that monitored taxation levels and state and county expenditures, and happily persecuted offending revenue agents." This taxpayers movement, headed largely by Confederate veterans who saw their participation as part of the ongoing struggle against Yankee perfidy, linked with the Democratic paramilitary organizations known as rifle clubs, the Ku Klux Klan, and even the agricultural reform societies of the Grange to create a political culture of dissent, growing out of the memory of the shared struggle of the Lost Cause. Following 1874 Robert K. Scott did make some concessions to the Democratic leadership, resulting from fears of a looming taxpayer revolt and the precipitous drop in value of the Radical government's bonds in London and New York, a plunge caused largely by the taxpayers convention's having shined a light on the corrupt manner in which Radical leaders handled the state-funded debt.[51]

The taxpayers movement represents one organizational element of the conservative response to Radical Reconstruction. Stephen Kantrowitz has noted a connection of membership, method, and goals between the taxpayers movement, agricultural clubs that attempted to control black labor, and such emerging paramilitary organizations as rifle clubs and the Ku Klux Klan. Kantrowitz assumes that the connection of these groups centers on their common commitment to white supremacy. Subsequent disagreements on the meaning of white supremacy among Carolina white men suggest that in the late 1860s and early 1870s, they found unity in a more complex ideological system that included, but did not limit itself to, the goal of white mastery over black Carolina. The ideology of the Lost Cause created a greater sense of corporate identity than did white supremacy as white men used the memory of the Confederacy to shape a conservative order in the upcountry. However, the assertion by black men and women of their own rights, and the creation of their own spheres of agency in black churches, raised questions about the meaning of white supremacy, questions that would later help to sunder the southern conservative ethos and its expressive aesthetic. One faction, led by Hampton would call for continued paternalism and the invitation to social organicism as the meaning of white supremacy; other whites, led first by Gary and then by Ben Tillman, saw white supremacy as finding its clearest expression in extreme violence against black bodies.[52]

The strength of Confederate religion provided a broad-based consensus within which to construct this ideology, and the celebration of the Lost Cause and its aesthetic appeal provided a public forum for the explication of a southern conservative ethos. Maidens walked among the ruins, their bodies representing the desire of conservatives to construct an image of purity amid the imperfections of time and history.

The creation of an aesthetic, a set of timeless images that represented the beauty of social harmony, faced seemingly insuperable odds in the 1870s. Not only did a restive black majority resist the social organicism that would have made a mockery if the Fourteenth Amendment, but southern conservatives also found themselves conquered and occupied by the northern legions. Nevertheless, southern conservatism, long bound by the contradictions of the antebellum world, ironically became a powerful force in the forging of the postbellum southern mind as its "poetic pessimism," to use Walker Percy's phrase, raised a new ideological world, a world based on the contemplation of the southern ruins.

CHAPTER FOUR

All the Natural Bonds of Society

The Lineaments and Language of Southern Conservatism

South Carolina, according to Presbyterian divine David E. Frierson, warred with Leviathan in 1868. In the year that Republican Radicals created a new constitution for South Carolina, the Anderson County minister used the mythical beast of the Old Testament to describe what he called "the spirit of atheism" that walked abroad in the land. Leviathan, the primeval monster who struggled against the God of the Hebrews, had now been incarnated as "the spirit of innovation that nullifies statute and precedent." Making clear reference to attempts by the 1868 constitutional convention to root out the conservative mores of Carolina, Frierson declared that all human attempts to restructure society sought "to nullify law by multiplying laws," thus turning society "into a military camp." The entangling systems of human law seeking to create utopia interfered, according to Frierson, with the organic growth of law shaped by Providence through prescriptive tradition and historical experience. The spirit of Leviathan embodied in the Federal government and the Radical South Carolina legislature sought to "ignore precedent and the experience of mankind and make law . . . with the spirit of the nineteenth century."[1]

Frierson's critique of the Radical efforts represents the epitome of conservative upcountry ideology. The "democratic, moneyless, and landless" set of men, though never as articulate as Frierson and other men of mind, held to similar conceptions of the postbellum world. The exigencies of war and emancipation meant that they could no longer rely on networks of reciprocal obligation, assured in their positions as representatives of virtuous Carolina manhood. Instead they had to deal with a Radical government seemingly bent on destroying the basis of their social order, seeking to treat them merely as citizens afloat on a sea of partisan interests. In the late 1860s and into the decades of the 1870s and 1880s, South Carolinians who pondered the meaning of their Lost Cause found in it a critique of this new world and a defense of the old. The lineaments of the tradition they created, though appealling in many ways to all classes of Carolina whites, contained enormous tensions that would later help to sunder southern conservatism. However, in the years between 1868 and 1886, the aesthetic of the Lost Cause shaped a culture of dissent in South Carolina, a rejection of "the spirit of the nineteenth century" that had animated the 1868 constitutional convention.

Southern intellectual life emerged in the last two decades of the twentieth century as a productive field of study, breaking from the common view that the antebellum South suffered from an "intellectual blockade." The traditional attitude toward the southern mind has been best summed up by Wilbur J. Cash, who wrote that "in general, the intellectual and aesthetic life of the Old South was a superficial and jejune thing." However, new efforts at taking seriously "the mind of the South" have yielded important insights into the proslavery argument, southern constitutional theory, and the South's critique of bourgeois materialism. Studies have also explored the emergence of the Southern modernists in the twentieth century and the agrarian conservatism of Vanderbilt "fugitives." However, the great gap in our understanding of southern intellectual history has been roughly the period between 1865 and 1920, a period that C. Vann Woodward has described as a time of "cultural famine," when learning and literature fell victim to "bonds of mind and spirit."[2]

Woodward's characterization ignores the sophistication of southern conservatism's critique of American society during Reconstruction and the Gilded Age. This critique had its intellectual touchstone and public platform in the celebration of the Lost Cause. Charles Reagan Wilson has argued for the importance of this prophetic challenge to American mores in understanding the Lost Cause movement, exploring several of the "Lost Cause prophets," especially the Virginian Robert Lewis Dabney. Wilson notes the importance of ministers in this critique and shows how they excoriated the mammonism of the New South by praising the aristocratic and agrarian values of the Old. Woodward, on the other hand, ignored the importance of this critique, suggesting that materialistic, go-ahead southerners of the New South paid scant attention to these Confederate jeremiads and so relegated them "to the dustbin of the 80s."[3]

Woodward's dismissal of the Lost Cause critique seems surprising, since he believes that the populist challenge to American capitalism, which the emerging national order relegated to the dustbin of the 90s, as it were, can be regarded as the fulcrum of the late nineteenth century. Wilson, on the other hand, has paid too much attention to the ministerial critique of

American society and to ministers' attacks on the New South. Though, as Frierson's example shows, ministers played a crucial role, other former Confederates became equally important in the South's culture of Lost Cause dissent. Moreover, the prophets of the Lost Cause challenged much more than the entrepreneurialism of the New South. The romantic conservatives of the Lost Cause quarreled with the entire course of western civilization.

The position of these postbellum conservative intellectuals differed radically from their antebellum forebears. Antebellum Southern intellectuals, according to Drew Faust, huddled together in a "sacred circle" owing to their experience of "personal loneliness, social alienation and intellectual futility."[4] Such was not the case for the conservative intellectuals of South Carolina's Lost Cause movement. The very public memorialization of the Confederacy, combined with these spokesmen's record of wartime courage and gallantry, provided them a platform to proclaim their views on the social order. Organizations such as the Confederate Soldier's Associations, the ladies memorial movements, and other efforts offered numerous barbecues, picnics, and other social events at which South Carolina's men of mind could publicly ponder the meaning of history, the results of Confederate defeat, the relevance of traditional social rankings, the moral justifications for slavery, and the crisis of the western world. The importance of evangelical religion often provided these figures, not always especially devout themselves, an idiom with which to appeal to the often-enormous crowds of farmers and townsfolk who attended monument dedications and other public spectacles. The Lost Cause became the gravamen of South Carolina conservatism, providing a vocabulary of dissent and a forum within which to express that dissent to all ranks of Carolina society.

William King Easley became a representative figure in upcountry conservatism in the years following the war. Easley's thought not only embodied much of southern conservative ideology, his intellectual bent urged him to think through the complexities of this tradition and to press it toward its logical conclusion. Following his service during the war as a cavalry commander, Easley continued to express many of the themes that concerned him in his days as a secessionist agitator. The experience of war and of defeat solidified some of these themes in his thought, particularly the meaning of history and the historical process. The experience of Reconstruction convinced him of the dangers of mass democracy and pushed him toward an extreme conservative position that despaired of the intractable dangers of left-wing republicanism. The experience of

Confederate defeat became an important feature in his thought, becoming for Easley an example of the tectonic convulsions that had shaken the foundations of western civilization since the time of the French Revolution, convulsions that, in his words, had sundered "all the natural bonds of society."[5]

The southern conservatism that connected itself to the lost Confederate cause insisted on the defense of slavery, largely because white South Carolinians, through the Black Codes and their efforts against Radical Reconstruction, sought to recreate the antebellum world of hierarchical social relations. In February 1871 Easley gave an address honoring George Washington and Robert E. Lee, showing how southerners continued to connect their attempted secession with the American Revolution. Easley's speech lamented the Lost Cause, calling the end of the war "the overthrow of the constitution." He reminded his audience that both rebel warlords, had been "slaveholders and sons of slaveholders," asking if slavery could truly have been a pernicious system if it "could produce such men as Washington and Lee." In fact, Easley contended, slavery had been responsible for the nobility of character found in the Old South. Slavery had, according to Easley, acted as a preservative for southern mores in "this commercial age," giving the southern war of independence "the high tone of the crusades." Easley's view of slavery, in retrospect at least, was similar to that of many modern historians; a protective shield around the South that isolated it from the depredations of modern capitalism.[6]

Easley's defense of slavery represented a rear-guard action by 1871. His real interest in defending slavery hinged on his hatred of the idea of equality and his consequent belief in the necessity of organic hierarchies rooted in history and Providence, rather than an ex post facto defense of the antebellum institution. In the speech on Washington and Lee, Easley suggested that hierarchy in nature revealed a basic inequality in the world; he asserted that African slavery in South Carolina had merely reflected this inequality. Basic inequality, he insisted in another public oration, "is as old as nature and wide as the world." Southern conservatives again and again showed this tendency to root hierarchy in the facts of creation that no human fiat could change. Martin Gary, for example, told the 1874 taxpayers convention that unequal social relations remained fixed by divine decree and that "it is vain that man attempt to solve the laws of creation."[7]

Not only had slaveholding reflected the designs of nature and Providence, it had supposedly prevented the southerner from learning the dark passions of profit-seeking and commerce. The late nineteenth century, influenced by the laissez-faire ideology of Victorian liberalism, gave free reign to the entrepreneurial impulse. Southern conservatism linked modernity with social relations based on contractual relationships that provided entrepreneurial opportunity for the strong while crushing the weak on a wheel of social Darwinism. The image of "the Yankee" played a central role in this vision of modernity, a role similar to that of the antebellum conservative's view of northern perfidy. The northerner, corrupted by "this commercial age," became the symbol of all southern conservatism fought to prevent. The South, Easley asserted, had "developed a higher type of manhood than the north." Emerging from the intricate pattern of paternalistic social relations, the southern man had opportunities for moral heroism unknown to the northerner who "goes on in an eager, ceaseless struggle, jostling elbowing and trampling down his competitors in the race for wealth." Easley feared the influx of visitors from the North seeking wealth, anxiously worrying that the southern people would "become imbued with the leading ideas of the Yankee mind," a mind in which "everything good and noble, all that exalts and dignifies human character is made subordinate to Thrift." The image of the Yankee as the agent of entrepreneurial capitalism thus served as a cautionary tale as the tentacles of finance capitalism slithered over the upcountry. A popular ballad, "The New Yankee Doodle," sung at South Carolina Confederate reunions and even at family gatherings, managed to mock northern manhood, suggest that the secession crisis resulted from little more than a northern attempt to impose their cultural mores, and portray the Yankee as the villainous agent of profit-seeking;

> Yankee Doodle had a mind
> To whip the southern traitors
> Because they did not choose to dine
> On Codfish and potaters
>
> Yankee Doodle oh for Shame!
> Your always intermeddling
> Let guns alone their dangerous things
> You'd better stick to peddling

Such balladry expressed not only hatred of the conquering foe but also anxieties over the New South world of town and mill. A social world of hierarchical harmonies seemed an Eden in comparison to the banalities of commercial capitalism.[8]

The pessimism often displayed by South Carolina conservatives prevented them from escaping into the illusory world of romance, as some
interpreters of the Lost Cause have argued that they did. Carolina conservatives did not simply defend slavery as if emancipation had never occurred. Willing to abandon the slave system, conservative thinkers refused
to relinquish the ideology that undergirded the proslavery argument. In
an 1875 sermon, Pastor Frierson expressed the opinion that God may not
have ordained slavery as a sacred institution, since "relations of master
and slave in the Bible are treated not as a matter of doctrine but as a
matter of history. . . . The sacred scriptures on questions of social condition are profoundly silent." God did however "regulate the orders and
institutions of society." Frierson thus allowed for the possibility that God
would allow slavery to die, but his concession did not include the notion
that equality should shape human relationships. According to Frierson,
differing ranks developed organically in society because of "diversities
of capacity," and any attempt to create equality represented a challenge
to "the order of nature." The institution of slavery had been ephemeral,
Frierson could admit in 1875, but the need to reflect a divine and natural
order in the hierarchy of the social order remained.[9]

Easley, Frierson, and other South Carolina conservatives believed that
the experience of Reconstruction underlined the dangers of ignoring natural hierarchies. Easley himself took an active role in white democratic
efforts to challenge Reconstruction and became certain that Reconstruction evinced all the characteristics of a violent revolution, the very opposite of the conservative revolution he believed both the American Revolution and the war for southern independence represented. "The abuse of
democratic principles," he told one Reconstruction audience, "is more to
be feared than despotism." Easley based this declaration on the notion,
borrowed from classical political theorists such as Aristotle and Cato the
Elder, that a people could more easily resist a single despot than "universal licentiousness." Easley used Rome as an example of how "public
virtue" could become tarnished in "universal debauchery."[10]

Easley's postbellum thought shows significant continuity with his antebellum concerns. Civic humanism remained the load-bearing pillar of
his political thought, an emphasis sharpened by his praise for an entire
generation of South Carolina men who had given their lives for the sake
of safeguarding a virtuous southern republic. However, the experience
of Confederate defeat had forced South Carolina conservatives to reflect
more deeply on the meaning of history and the function of the historical process. Reaching back to Renaissance humanism and its classical

sources, learned Carolina conservatives explained Confederate defeat and
Radical Reconstruction within the context of a cyclical view of history
that allowed for the degeneration of liberty and virtue over time and yet
offered hope and a call to resistance.[11]

Ellison Summerfield Keitt best embodies this view of historical ex-
perience. Keitt, a Confederate cavalryman and the brother of fire-eater
Lawrence M. Keitt, had become a leading figure in South Carolina's Lost
Cause movement, in part, because he perceived himself as the caretaker of
his brother's memory (Lawrence Keitt had died in 1864 at Cold Harbor).
Both a dedicated aristocratic supporter of Hampton and an agrarian critic
of finance capitalism who became a leading figure in the South Carolina
Farmer's Alliance, Keitt challenged the view that Bourbons and agrarian
Radicals confronted one another as inimical opponents in the late nineteenth century South. His southern conservative critique of the Gilded Age
combined elements of white supremacy and a view of history informed
by classical and Renaissance sources.[12]

Keitt pondered the meaning of South Carolina's experience in Reconstruction and believed he found in it an explanation for the decay of cultures through time. Nations and peoples, he told a Democratic campaign
club in New York City, move "from refinement to corruption; then back
to barbarism, tyranny, despotism and oppression." Keitt believed that the
1868 constitutional convention gave evidence of such a skeptical view of
the historical process. The "refined" culture of the Old South had been
barbarized by "one hundred black negros, fresh from the shovel, the hoe
and the waiting saloon." An avid reader of Aristotle, often asked by contemporaries to orate on and explicate the ideas of "the master of those
who know," Keitt held to the classical view of history as a cyclical process. Republics also moved in cycles, a process that led to decay unless
resisted by virtue. Easley shared this notion, likely drawn from some of
the same sources. "The democratic element," Easley told the provisional
South Carolina legislature in 1866, destroys "every conservative element"
in society and then builds upon the tottering foundations." Such a whirl-
wind force can produce good governments, but after establishing new
political structures, it becomes "a malevolent scourge."[13]

The dangers of mass democracy concerned most South Carolina conservatives not because they longed for a monarchy, but rather because
democracy would shatter the possibility of a conservative republic. Conservative ideology saw a causative link between universal suffrage and
tyranny, twin poles conjoined by the congenital weakness of human nature. An Anderson County essayist in October 1866 admitted that South

Carolina fought the tides of inevitable change in this "age of democracy" that had seen "the enlargement of popular influence." The state must stand athwart the tides of change, the essayist warned, because "there has never been an establishment of popular democracy from which one may not trace the ultimate result of autocracy." The French Revolution served the essayist as a cautionary tale. The "wretched sans-culottes, reeking with the blood of the noble and the good," had shown the dark face of the new democratic juggernaut. The writer had little hope for the future of constitutional liberty, since, "with the overthrow of the patrician society and civilization of the South, the last obstacle to radical democracy was destroyed." If the South could no longer act as a bulwark against the Leviathan of centralized power, then some "some modern Marius, flattering the populace, shall assume the role of dictator."[14]

Postbellum conservatives found themselves in an age that increasingly accepted the notion of unlimited suffrage, often in tandem with the notion that the rule of the majority could solidify the power of the managerial elite, either political or economic. The centralized state, for thinkers influenced by Victorian liberalism, became a receptacle for abstract rights. The 1868 constitution seemed to crystallize these ideas for many Carolina conservatives. In the year of the convention, Spartanburg's J. Banks Lyle, a South Carolina College graduate who had served as a captain in the Fifth South Carolina Volunteers, told the Limestone Springs Democratic Club that the degeneration of public virtue had helped give rise to the "hypocritical rulers" who now controlled the Palmetto State. Lyle argued that this had been, in part, the outcome of "the unbridled power of the ignorant masses" and "absolute democracy." Drawing on Burkean notions of British constitutionalism, Lyle asserted his belief in "chartered rights—fixed and established by local government." Only by rejecting the tyranny of the majority and respecting liberty embedded in tradition could the state enjoy "peace and order."[15]

Southern conservatism, never sanguine about schemes of moral and social improvement during the antebellum period, became even more wary of such optimism after the war. Southern slaveholders had not rejected economic and social progress, but instead believed that conservative institutions such as the patriarchal family, slavery, agriculture, and the influence of evangelical churches slowed the pace of change and prevented reform from becoming revolution. The shocks of war and emancipation created an even more dour view of the historical process. In his private musings, Easley pondered the course of ancient civilizations by drawing examples from biblical and classical sources. His study, he believed, challenged the notion that one age truly represented a progressive development over another. The growing power of money over personal, paternal relations, of contract over obligation, convinced southern conservatives that the Western world had fallen into its dotage. An editorial in the June 9, 1869, *Newberry Herald* worried over "the growing influence of money," the way in which the "commercial age" in which southern conservatives lived had helped to coarsen rather than improve the American social order; "The decay of chivalry . . . and the decline of republican simplicity are certainly not signs of progress to a higher moral level." Southern conservatives, their view of history grounded in a lost cause, could never accept Victorian liberalism's dreams of economic, social, moral and political progress. Instead, experience and inclination drew them to a much older view of history in which degeneration followed cultural achievement ending in barbarism with, perhaps, some hope of slow improvement on the other side of ruin. Such a hope belonged to generations yet to come, because the work of Providence moved slowly by human standards. J. Banks Lyle agreed that human societies must progress, but argued that advance must be "gradual and uniform," a fragile process of organic growth easily "disturbed by being advanced a generation at a single step."[16]

The southern conservative view of history, culture, and politics grew directly out of its view of human nature. The evangelical doctrine of utter human depravity and sin that corrupts the best intentions made them wary of all schemes of improvement. Human beings had a transcendent nature that subordinated them to an unchanging moral order, but they also had a tendency to subvert that moral order. "God governs this world," wrote W. K. Easley in his private journal, "by laws which are fixed and immutable." These laws included a certain symmetry in human nature: human beings have a spirit, Easley asserted, "that promotes individual activity," while on the other hand, they have a will that God has granted to "restrain man from his folly." The problem for civilization comes when, as often happens, these twin laws of human nature fail to work in tandem. The result of these forces spinning off in opposite directions was, according to Easley, "blows and convulsions," in short, revolution. Easley's view of human nature, though much more complex than that of most of his fellow upcountrymen, was shared by the evangelical faithful in their struggle to reign in the desires of the depraved human heart.[17]

The southern conservative view of history also owed much to the German romantic conservatism learned through Carlyle. German romanticism tended to accept a notion of history dominated by the idea of crisis, moments of almost apocalyptic transformation, that lay waste to prior institutions and raise up new worlds on the ruins.[18] George Fredrick Holmes, while living in South Carolina under the patronage of the secession convention president David Flavel Jamieson, wrote an article on Fredrick von Schlegel in which he referred to the study of history as the explication of "the mysteries of the downfall of nations, and the successive cycles which have arisen upon the ruins of their precursors." The shocks of history could never ultimately lay waste human civilization, since even seemingly disconnected, chaotic strings of human events had meaning "within the controlling hand of God, without which the whole scheme becomes unintelligible." Human sin could create enormous mischief within this system, however, and the entire Western world, to the minds of southern conservatives, suffered from just such a crisis. The French Revolution, bête noire of all conservatives since Burke's opening volley against the sansculotte regime, provided a favorite explanation for the crisis of the West. Jamieson held this view, one that he had learned from his intellectual hero, Michelet. During Reconstruction, Easley gave a speech in which he called the French Revolution "unequalled in the annals of human depravity," a spiritual and moral as well as a political crisis in which "all the natural bonds of society were broken asunder." Easley explicitly linked the French revolutionary spirit with northern abolitionism and presented the South as having resisted the virulent strain of revolutionary fervor to the last. Former Confederates could look to their resistance with the same pride that the Greek looks to Thermopylae.[19]

The frequent use of classical imagery and political theory by men of mind like Easley played an important role in the construction of southern conservatism. Again and again, learned South Carolinians drew on their repository of knowledge regarding the classical world to shape their argument and thought. The influence of republicanism stemming from the Renaissance and the transatlantic world has become much discussed in the southern context. However, many Carolina conservatives took their republican theory straight, without the filter of the American Revolutionary experience. Aristotle and Roman republicanism played an especially important role in their thought, and in fact learned postbellum South Carolinians can be said to have lived in the rhetorical and symbolic worlds of ancient Greece and Rome. In 1869 Wade Hampton, speaking at a state agricultural fair, referenced the barbarian invasions of the third century to describe the horrors of Reconstruction. He called upon listening Confederate veterans to look to the courage of legions who had cried "Rome

Forever!" amid the ruins of their empire. Even so, should Confederate veterans "plant our colors on the graves of our ancestors and invoking reverently the protection of our God shout with more than Roman patriotism 'The South Now! The South Forever!'"? Ancient Greece and Rome even provided justification for southern racial mores. Radical governor Robert K. Scott brought the full fury of these classically trained conservatives on his head in 1869, when he told a convention of freedpeople that the Roman emperor Septimius Severus had been "a colored freedman." An editorial in the conservative *Columbia Phoenix* responded bitterly to this "demagoguery" insisting that the emperor "had been born in a city of Africa, but was of a noble Roman family." The writer suggested to Scott that "he might improve his classics as well as his politics." [20]

The appropriation of classical themes shows the conservative tendency to view the past as a prescriptive tradition that should guide the present growth of society. Greece and Rome seemed especially appealing to the educated Carolina conservative because they represented ordered, agrarian, hierarchical societies that practiced a conservative republicanism. In the case of Rome, the decline of the Empire represented a perfect trope to describe the cultural and historical crisis of war and emancipation. Roman emphasis on the necessity of public, civic virtue dovetailed with the Confederate celebration's emphasis on southern virtue. Hampton, in his 1869 address at the fair, used the experience of Rome to warn the veteran yeoman of the dangers of "luxury" that would corrupt virtue and turn even the white electorate into little more than a "mobocracy." Confederate virtue coalesced with the notion of Roman *pietas* to serve as a southern conservative ideal that could safeguard the fragile social relations of the South. Contemporaries described the Confederate veteran, Bourbon Democrat, and Lost Cause orator Leroy W. Youmans as "a splendid old Roman," an apt description for one whose scrapbooks included his own Latin transcriptions of the odes of Horace, combined with pictures, signatures, and other memorabilia of the fallen Confederacy. [21]

Invocations of classical sources became important in shaping the aesthetic of Confederate memory, in lending it a certain style that set it apart from the perceived barbarities of late nineteenth-century life. Concern over the style of their opponents reveals southern conservatism's deep attachment to ritual behaviors, to public expressions of their belief in rank and degree. Hierarchy, "the natural bonds of society," in Easley's phrase, faced terrible danger when the rituals of deference were ignored or scorned. An editorial in the *Columbia Phoenix* in November 1869 worried that the "Yankee schoolmarms" who came south to train "the

against schoolmarms

light infantry of radicalism" had taught the freedmen to forsake the use of "Massa" and "Miss." Conservatives worried even more over the tendency of the freedmen to perform their new emancipated state by jostling white men and women on street corners, by refusing to stand up and remove their hats in the presence of whites, and by ignoring other rituals of servility. In part, the use of a language of classical elegance recreated a static world where such rebellions against order did not occur, an arena of mythical action in which Confederate heroes eternally charged the Yankee lines inspired by the wisdom of Cato and the courage of Brutus. The importance of this style helped make beauty of expression and feeling awakened by expression of crucial importance and helped created an aesthetic of Confederate commemoration. One editorial comment on Hampton's agricultural fair oration admitted that "no new or novel view" had been articulated but that Hampton's address had evinced "an elegance of language and an elevation of tone" that had reminded veterans of the unity of white male southerners, forged on the battlefield. Public men like Hampton, Easley, and Keitt fashioned a language of classical elegance in which free white men spoke to free white men, a grammar of hierarchy, deference, duty, obligation, and virtue that became the language of southern conservatism.[22]

Such evocations of a mythical past had the power of aesthetic experience. A powerful aesthetic, according to Delacroix, contains two important components. On the one hand, aesthetic representations of the self and the world "contain a possible dream"; its form must not simply invoke the unlimited. Aesthetic representations suggest certain possibilities, hopes that have some chance of coming to pass, dreams that are realizable. On the other hand, the subject who contemplates aesthetic representation engages in what Delacroix calls a "game of ghosts." This game of ghosts imagines worlds that could be or have been but often are not, grounding aesthetic enjoyment in the experience of yearning. Aesthetics, according to Delacroix, have an explosive effect on human beings because they contain these profound tensions—a possible world that incarnates our most deeply felt yearnings that exist as a ghostly reality, often in some constructed "golden age," past or future.[23]

The Lost Cause aesthetic became a game of ghosts in which yeoman farmers, anxious over the new liberty, property, and changing social relations, could express and experience profound yearning for the world they had lost, that their captains reminded them they had fought heartily to save. This aesthetic leap into a constructed past prevented the powerful tensions within southern conservative ideology, the devotion to liberty

grounded in productive property straining against the belief in hierarchy
and prescriptive tradition, from creating an open breach. The language of
the aristocratic elite, recalling past glories and grounding the Confederate
experience in a prescriptive organic tradition, prevented the development
of languages of class. Such an open breach in the southern conservative ethos would have to await the much rougher language of Captain
Tillman.[24]

The aesthetic of Confederate defeat memorialized by southern men of
mind stood in stark contrast to the America in which they lived. The Civil
War not only emancipated slaves but also placed America on a course
of centralized economic power and entrepreneurial pragmatism that has
been called "the incorporation of America." This trend began during
the war itself, as Republicans, unimpeded by the southern democrats,
forged links between the Federal government and emerging corporate
America in the form of railroad subsidies and a new, centralized banking system friendly to industry. Tax policy during the war and after favored business organization with a high degree of internal integration,
thus promoting the corporate model. Economist Jeffrey Hummel notes
that Carnegie, Morgan, and Rockefeller all began their piratical careers
with help from the Federal government during the war years. Meanwhile, a number of United States Supreme Court rulings in the 1870s,
particularly the well-known *Slaughterhouse* cases, strengthened the partnership of government and finance capitalism. William Graham Sumner,
the influential Yale economist influenced heavily by the work of Herbert
Spencer, wrote in the 1880s that the "savings bank depositor is the hero
of the age."[25]

Celebrants of the Lost Cause in South Carolina held to a different set
of values. Youmans praised the Confederate soldier because the soldier's
courage and gallantry challenged the "utilitarian age." Hampton urged
Confederate veterans to remember their native attachment to agriculture
instead of turning to professions in the pursuit of the main chance. Easley
warned southerners not to adopt the "utilitarian" ideas of the north and
not to assume that "utility is . . . the sole standard of moral conduct."
Aggressively unpragmatic, the conservatives of South Carolina used their
own Confederate experience as an example of lavish expense of blood and
treasure on behalf of a cause that served no purpose other than the embodiment of the moral good. Defeat did not mean moral turpitude. "That
we failed," Ellison Keitt told the South Carolina legislature in 1867, "is no
argument that our cause is unjust." Reconstruction, he continued, repre-

sented "the ruins of vandalism," but firm attachment to the conservative principles of southern life "survives the shock of revolution and time."[26]

Southern conservatism's lineaments and language existed as a cultural ideology embodied in a variety of forms. Few conservative South Carolinians put their critique of modernity into writing. Their attacks on the new order of incorporated America, a new America they believed mongrelized by mass democracy and guided by a cold pragmatism, appear in private musing, letters, and, above all, in public orations that commemorated the Confederate dead. These public ceremonies not only provided an open forum for the explication of southern conservatism, but the ritual of these ceremonies themselves evoked the nostalgic defense of the Confederate *public* prescriptive order.[27] *rituals*

The dedication of Columbia's soldier's monument serves as an example of how southern conservatism became embedded in ritual occasion. White South Carolinians after 1876 sought to have their Confederate monument, originally placed at Elmwood Cemetery, moved to a more prominent, and a more political, location. The fashion in which this relocation occurred challenges the notion, put forward by Edward Ayers and Gaines Foster, that Confederate memory participated in the entrepreneurial ethos of the Gilded Age by transforming the Lost Cause into a commodity, legitimizing the new economic order. In the late 1870s, South Carolina, to the contrary, acted very much like a traditional *gemeinschaft,* commemorating its fallen warriors rather than a society dominated by private economic interests. South Carolina's Confederate monument became a public trust, with money raised all over the state for its construction. The thrifty Bourbon government allocated $650 to fund the moving of the statue. The engineer responsible for its relocation, himself a Confederate veteran, donated his time. The marble base had been a gift from the owner of a quarry on the Congaree River. The Italian sculptor seems to have been the only one who took profits from the commemoration, profits raised from contributions at ice cream socials, barbecues, and other social events. Even South Carolina's railroad companies, which lived under the watchful eye of a Bourbon railroad commission that set freight and passenger rates, gave special passes to veterans on their way to the celebration.[28]

The ritual honoring the defeated Confederacy began at 6:30 A.M. on the morning of May 13, 1879, as Columbia awoke to the sound of booming cannons. More cannons would rattle the city throughout the day as the survivors of Confederate regiments arrived from around the state.

Charleston's Washington Artillery fired guns, using cartridge boxes made in 1860 by the women of South Carolina to celebrate the signing of the Ordinance of Secession. Columbia's veterans of the Richland Volunteers waited at the depot of the Wilmington, Columbia, and Augusta line, greeting incoming troops from Sumter and Camden.[29]

The organizers of the event made every effort to shape an aesthetic of the Lost Cause. The event not only recalled the memory of the war, but sought to invoke the very experience of combat. The ladies of the monument association had requested that the visiting volunteers bring with them, for a grand march down Main Street to the statehouse, the regimental colors that had been carried into battle. The Jenkins Rifles of York County carried the last battle flag removed from Columbia before Sherman's entrance. Flags bearing the names of various conflicts and slogans that celebrated Carolina liberty played a prominent role in the activities throughout the day. A number of ritual presentations of regimental colors underlined their importance. Ellison Capers, for example, presented his daughter with the flag of the Twenty-fourth South Carolina Volunteers that had been hidden in her cradle during the closing days of the war to prevent it from falling into the hands of Sherman's troops. One regimental flag notable in its absence was that of the famed Hampton Legion. The colors of this regiment had been used in 1864 as the death shroud of Hampton's son, Preston, and so moldered with him in the graveyard of Trinity Church.[30]

A march of the Confederate survivors down Main Street played an important role in the day's events. The parade transformed the thoroughfare, in the words of one observer, "into a long glittering line of steel." The presence of women along the line of march, in the words of one commentator, "completed the beauty and harmonies of the picture." Carriages that contained "the ladies of the monument association" brought up the rear. Prominent on the platform at the soldier's monument, along with Governor W. D. Simpson and Bishop Ellison Capers, stood "four young ladies whose fathers gave their lives for the Lost Cause." These young ladies had not been chosen from the thousands of yeoman families filled with orphans of the Confederate cause, but from South Carolina's elite—all of them bearing names like Dargan, Cheves, and McCord.[31]

More than fifteen thousand people crowded into the capitol square and surrounding streets to take part in the ritual dedication. The aesthetic of Confederate defeat had a profound effect on these crowds. A number of emotional outbursts occurred along the route of the regimental march, one observer noting that even a number of men turned away to hide tears.

Celebratory cheering greeted the marching veterans who echoed back the cheers and rebel yells.

Ellison Capers, by 1879 the high priest of Confederate religion in South Carolina, prayed a dedicatory prayer. Capers's intercession revealed the centrality of virtue at the heart of the Lost Cause and suggested that remembrance of southern valor should shape the behavior of the present. Capers prayer called for the legislators who would daily pass the monument to look upon the soldier and recall his "sacrifice and courage." "May they and all Carolina's children," Capers intoned, "be true to the valor and virtue that death could not corrupt."[32]

The public oration sought to remember the Confederate experience and to place it within a history of struggle on behalf of ordered liberty. John S. Preston, a Virginia native, Harvard graduate, and son-in-law of Wade Hampton, delivered the elegant oration. Preston had been a Confederate general and an adamant opponent of Reconstruction, briefly fleeing the South for Europe after the war.[33]

Preston drew on both biblical and classical language to describe the pilgrimage of South Carolina since Appomattox. Carolinians had wandered in a wilderness like ancient Israel. The Red Sea had parted for Carolina upon the election of Wade Hampton, and now Carolinians could raise a stone column to the gallant dead just as the Greeks raised a column to the immortal three hundred at Thermopylae. The placement of the monument in the *agora,* Preston cried, recalled the cry of Brutus at the assassination of Caesar—"Rome again is free!"[34]

The theme of the struggle for liberty against tyranny became the central symbol of Preston's address. Liberty did not, however, mean unbridled individualism but rather, as Capers prayer had suggested, the ability to practice Confederate virtue within the context of ancestral tradition. Eternal truths inhered in this tradition and had a public, material embodiment in the Confederate soldier's monument. The lone soldier on the shaft of marble represented "the emblem and substance of Truth."[35]

The truths embodied in Confederate memory had a deep instinctual appeal, according to Preston. The orator borrowed from romantic conservatism's tendency to root identity, ideology, and moral virtue in blood and soil. The former general, midway through his address, called on the four young women, "maidens whose fathers died in the field," to come forward and unveil the monument in its new location. "Your veneration is but tradition," he said, as he called forward the young women who had been children at war's end. "Memory may be lost in oblivion but nature knows no apostasy. In obedience to her dictates," he told these vestal virgins of the Lost Cause, "kneel in the pride and purity of filial piety and dedicate this monument to the Truth for which your fathers died. Their justified spirits are approving your act." [36]

The four young ladies did not, in fact, literally kneel, but they did come forward to draw the ropes and unveil the monument. Increasing the aura of religious ritual that surrounded the event, observers claimed, was that as the veil fell away to reveal the soldier, the clouds "parted as cheer after cheer" exploded from the overwrought crowd.

The combination of religious symbolism and the public display of white elite female bodies proved a powerful symbolic configuration. The explosive reaction of the crowd to this symbolism underscores the power of this imagery. The monument, after all, had already been unveiled at its Elmwood Cemetery location. Most participants in the event had already looked on the rather pedestrian sculpture. This ritual performance of southern conservatism, placing the monument at the very center of law and governance and surrounding it with the profundities of Confederate religion, released a sense of mystical devotion to the Confederacy. The women who played such a prominent role in the ceremony performed the task so often assigned to female symbolism in religious faith; they evoked purity and suffering, made poignant by their youth, beauty, and class position. If Preston and Capers sought to initiate the thousands of South Carolinians into a Confederate religion of virtue bounded by or-dered liberty, no stronger set of symbolic acts could have been imagined on that May afternoon.

The women may have played the role of *mater dolorosa*, but the po-litical undertones of the event remain clear. The move to the statehouse constituted an act of purification and defiance, a symbolic cleansing of the Augean stables of Reconstruction and a demand that South Carolina's Confederate identity receive recognition. The task of memorialization, Preston insisted as his oration continued, contained not only a sense of mourning but also the possibility of continued struggle against "our con-querors." Looking out on a sea of former Confederate regiments, many of which on this day wore the red shirt that had symbolized their involve-ment in the state's 1876 struggle for redemption, Preston noted that the North already had a monument to its struggle, "consolidated power from the Atlantic to the Pacific." The dedication of this monument, however, showed that the power of the consolidated nation-state had ground to a halt in South Carolina, and faithful remembrance of the Confederate struggle could keep it at bay. Women would continue to play a special role in this continued defiance. Preston believed that the women of South

Carolina, whose efforts had made the soldier's monument possible, occupied a central position in the cult of the Confederate dead: "Not even at the cross and tomb of the Son of God did the women kneel with surer trust in the sublime truth for which He died than these women do here kneel today by the monument their hands have raised in testimony to truth for which the Confederate soldier died."[37] The practice of Confederate religion by South Carolina's faithful women would continue to structure the defense of the South's holy cause.

This game of ghosts could not continue forever. The veterans listened to their former captains but would become increasingly restive in the decade to come. Evocations of the past and the language of longing could not hold the forces of economic and social change at bay. Southern conservatives spoke the elegant language of the past in a rough-and-tumble democratic present, when the political situation necessitated a mass movement. In the struggle with radicalism, southern conservatives reveal the paradoxes at the heart of their ideology. Though seeking to live in a static society enveloped by old usage and custom, they had unleashed popular forces that would ultimately undermine the organic culture they sought to create. The struggle to end Reconstruction had itself unbound these often-violent forces. The heritage would not be a society enveloped by order and sustained by custom, but rather would be a disintegrating social order, strapped by vicious racial pathologies and stricken by the consequences of war and emancipation.

Southern conservatism's desire for an organic social order broke on the rocks of the realties of Reconstruction, even as had the hopes of Radical Republicans with their much more utopian designs. The Carolina yeomen who listened to the evocations of Rome and the praise of the old order did much more than listen to the promises of the past. In an increasingly chaotic social and economic situation, they sought to salvage their lost world by the use of main force. Though they did not understand it until much later, South Carolina conservatives had summoned a beast out of the depths.

CHAPTER FIVE

Killed by a Damned Rebel

The Lost Cause Militant

Calvin Crozier, a Confederate soldier returning to his home in Texas, stopped in Newberry, South Carolina, on September 7, 1865. Crozier had been slowly making his way home by train and by foot, his return having been delayed by sickness and a stay in a northern prison camp. At the train depot in the low-country town of Orangeburg, a fellow Confederate soldier asked Crozier to escort two young belles on a trip to visit their relations, and Crozier, as romantic as any other Confederate cavalryman, readily agreed. The jaunt turned deadly in the small upcountry town of Newberry, when a group of allegedly intoxicated African American soldiers, the Thirty-third U.S Colored Troops, boarded the train and began, in the language of one version of the story, to make "gross insults" to the young women under Crozier's care. Infuriated, Crozier pulled his bowie knife and slashed one soldier, who cried out, "I'm killed by a damned rebel." The soldier's compatriots quickly hustled Crozier off to their regiment's bivouac, where they took a speedy revenge. Crozier was ordered to dig his own grave, an order he refused, and so received a severe beating. Citizens of Newberry attempted to make contact with Crozier, but the Union troops refused. At daylight the next morning, the Thirty-third formed into a firing squad, and successive volleys dropped Crozier to the ground. The soldiers placed Crozier's bullet-riddled body into a shallow grave, though Newberry whites later retrieved the body and buried the remains with full Confederate honors.[1]

The Crozier incident would live on in the memory of the Lost Cause, in part because it evoked all the fears of white men in the postbellum world. Charged with the protection of defenseless belles, Crozier had allegedly fought manfully with the African Americans who had subjected the women to "gross insults." Successfully fending off the attack, he nevertheless found himself at the mercy of Federal power, ultimately losing his own life because of his defiance. Crozier's story exemplified the struggle white men believed themselves to have been engaged during the postbellum years, a war to defend their mastery, to preserve the racial and gendered mores of the Old South against the intrusions of Federal power.

The memory of the Crozier incident represents the darkest impulses within the aesthetic of the Lost Cause, how the memory of battlefield struggle could legitimize the use of violence against African Americans and other representatives of northern hegemony. Conservative whites sought to use this violence to reassert their own control over South Carolina's political, social, and cultural life. It also points out that the freedpeople did not simply accept the imposition of a conservative order. South Carolina blacks, many of them under arms in either the Republican Party militias or as uniformed Federal troops, refused to simply accede to the wishes of white conservatives and struck back. The members of the Thirty-third U.S., for example, refused to accept Calvin Crozier's assertion of manhood, refused the world that southern whites hoped to maintain after Appomattox. Whites would in turn respond with overwhelming force, the power of the aesthetic of the Lost Cause pushing them far from the conservative ideal of an organic society.

The original impetus for upcountry violence came from the desire to end the chaos of postbellum South Carolina. The Lost Cause became militant in the upcountry after 1868, a militancy that pleased conservatives who hoped to reassert their hegemony. The aesthetic of the Lost Cause expanded to embrace this violence, creating folk legends and heroes for whites to contemplate, figures whose primary characteristics included defiance to Federal authority, a connection to Confederate memory, and an eagerness to assert mastery over dependents. Conservatives often failed to construct the kind of aesthetic they desired as the upcountry descended into a maelstrom of violence, upsetting the conservative dream of an ordered society.

Violence in the upcountry thus showed tension within the aesthetic of the Lost Cause and raised questions about the larger project of southern conservatism. How could an ideology that inspired violence pretend to admire social harmony? Conservatives may have believed that the formation of groups such as the Klan and their support for "outlaw" banditti represented a proportional reaction to Federal tyranny. They watched in horror as these same groups and individuals struck at the roots of the southern social order by ignoring paternalism and dismantling traditional hierarchies. The white elite did successfully reassert hierarchical control over the white masses in the rifle clubs of the 1870s, showing the continuing strength of the elite and the power of the Lost Cause to unite white men behind the cause of Carolina. Even this return to hegemony would, however, be short-lived.

Laura F. Edwards has written that gender, along with race and class, "shaped the political terrain" of the Reconstruction South.[2] The explosion of violence that upcountry South Carolina witnessed is best understood as the outcome of anxieties unleashed by those powerful forces. White conservatives sought to protect their liberty, a word that encoded their control over households. The elite, hoping to shape an aesthetic to call to their aid the white masses, watched in horror as the desire to protect the household turned into the destruction of household, the dismantling of social harmony. The political intimidation conservatives hoped would be provided by the Ku Klux Klan quickly turned into racial and sexual terrorism. Violence that began as political violence quickly descended into subpolitical behaviors, actions that did not, as Laura Edwards has argued, act as means to restore hierarchy, but actually laid waste to them. Ironically, only the intervention of the Federal government, the great terror of southern conservatives, brought a halt to this violence when they could not. Summoning the aesthetic of the Lost Cause to their aid once again, southern conservatives successfully revivified the Confederate cause for one last great charge into the cannon mouth of modernity.

The Crozier incident serves as only one example of the extraordinary amount of violence in the postbellum upcountry, violence that almost always exhibited racial and political overtones. Controversy has raged over the cause of this excessive violence, particularly with regard to the rise of the South Carolina Ku Klux Klan. Joel Williamson has argued that the upcountry regions where the Republican Party's largely African American militia was most proactive had the greatest degree of white-on-black violence, suggesting that the Klan represented a response of whites to Radical Republican domination. Williamson shows that counties with a special taste for extreme violence played unwilling host to a large black militia well supplied with Winchester and Springfield rifles, eager to do battle.[3]

Richard Zuczek has taken Williamson to task over this view, pointing out that white violence began even before a Republican-controlled militia existed. Zuczek correctly notes that the South Carolina Klan operated as early as 1868, although, in his words, "no militia of any kind existed until the spring of 1870." He rightly views white violence, especially the Ku Klux movement, as emerging from on-going resistance to northern rule that began at Appomattox. Zuczek's description of white conservatives struggle against Reconstruction as a "people's war," similar to guerrilla

insurgencies around the world, represents a fruitful approach to understanding the era.[4]

Zuczek's argument, however, ignores the degree of militancy among
Afro-Carolinians in the period immediately following Appomattox.
Though not organized into a formal militia immediately following the
war, blacks throughout the state asserted their newfound freedom, sometimes through purely symbolic acts. Right after the war, black occupation
troops throughout the state often involved themselves in such incidents
in ways that left white Carolinians howling in frustration and fear. In
Anderson County, for example, black United States troops protected a
group of slaves, accused of having murdered their master, from a white
lynch mob. One such group walked into an upcountry church and infuriated the white congregation by "attempting to sit with white women."
Rumors of the rape of white women by black troops circulated in whis-
pers throughout the upcountry, though this ultimate horror of the southern white mind received little public attention, often mentioned in veiled
language. Churches frequently became centers of symbolic struggles. An
Anderson County historian relates that Prince Rivers, a soldier in the
same Thirty-third that had been part of the Crozier incident, walked into
the First Baptist Church of Anderson, angering whites when he "took a
seat in the middle of the church." One local white grumbled that "carpetbaggers, scalawags and negros were in the ascendant and the congregation did nothing to resent the indignity." Meanwhile, frightening stories
spread among whites that a black revolution, on the bloody model of
St. Dominguez, would come on the Fourth of July, 1865. When that
date passed with only some noisy, public celebrations of freedom, whites
looked in fear to January 1, 1866, and then to July 4, 1866. The fear
that former slaves would rise up and slaughter their former masters kept
anxieties on the knife-edge. The defiant behavior of individual freedmen
and the very presence of armed, African American soldiers did little to
quell this anxiety.[5]

The Union Leagues (Republican Party political cells similar to the
Democratic clubs), the first organization of Radical Republicans in the
South, showed an armed militancy that accompanied their increasing political sophistication. One recent historian of this movement, in describing
the Leagues' varied work, has called this movement "one of the largest
black social movements in American history." In 1867 the Union League
of Pickens declared martial law after shooting a local white Democrat.
Pickens whites cowered in their homes over the next several days as the
armed Union League members paraded about the streets, questioning and

imprisoning whites known as outspoken ex-Confederates. In other parts
of the upcountry, white violence against blacks created a bloody peace.
In Anderson, one local woman remembered that, although the black soldiers of the Thirty-third had been stationed there, "so many of those
niggers disappeared and could never be accounted for . . . the garrison
was removed and white men substituted."[6]

Attempting to untangle the complex genealogy of upcountry violence,
interpreters have ignored the possibility of its roots in the celebration of
the Lost Cause and the perception among whites that they defended an
organic ideal of society. Former service in the Confederate cause runs
as the common thread among white participants in these killings, riots,
melees, and other forms of violent resistance. The willingness of Afro-
Carolinians to resist the imposition of conservative order stirred anger,
awakened fears, and pushed the white elite into an open advocacy of violence. Through a variety of means, interlinked with more public forms
of protest, such as the taxpayers movement and the commemoration of
the Confederate dead, Carolina conservatives asserted their defiance in
the face of Reconstruction. Indeed a people's insurgency, the violent activities of white conservatives had as its underpinning the mystical faith
of Confederate memory and the desire to shape a society founded on the
ideals of Confederate virtue and religion. The Lost Cause became militant.

The earliest efforts to use force to defend southern conservative ideals show a significant lack of coordination. Immediately after the war,
economic hardship and the desire to reassert the antebellum racial caste
system led to the formation of "agricultural clubs," vigilance committees
that saw their primary mission as the control of black labor and the enforcement of the Black Codes so as to limit the gains of emancipation.
These armed groups seemed particularly concerned that the contract system, which had the full support of the Freedmen's Bureau, not interfere
with the planter's control over his antebellum slaves. In 1866, a Union
officer in Greenville County complained of mounted companies of whites
who went about "whipping and driving back freedmen found employed
away from their former owners." Similar actions occurred in Newberry
and in Laurens County, where men described as "mounted desparados"
defiantly challenged Union infantry and "sought to prevent the freedmen
from hiring out to any but their former owners."[7]

The militancy of the agricultural clubs did not represent a highly organized effort by white conservatives, though it clearly evinced many of their
concerns. Seeking to restore the traditional order of South Carolina society, these men, likely former Confederate cavalrymen, sought to tie black

Carolinians both to the land and to their former masters. The elasticity
of the contract system greatly troubled conservatives, and they hoped to
use it to create a system of *villeinage* rather than to allow contractual em-
ployment to become the opening wedge of free labor. The ties between
these vigilante bands and later efforts at resisting Reconstruction are hard
to find, since by their nature such groups maintained utmost secrecy and
kept few records. However, evidence suggests that the agricultural clubs
had a leadership well represented in the taxpayers movement and the rifle clubs. The clubs apparently worked in tandem with the Democratic
Party, combining violence and economic coercion to restore the "natural" relationships between the freedmen and the property-owning class.
In 1866 Martin Gary, later leader in the taxpayers movement, apparently
took part in the killing of a Federal soldier in Edgefield to ensure white
control over black labor in the region.[8] Local Democratic Party leaders
certainly helped raise funds to purchase arms from the North, arms used
by the agricultural clubs, the Klan, and, later, the Democratic rifle clubs.
The Liberty Hill Democratic Club of Edgefield worked to tie black people
to the land by decreeing that its members "hire no traveling farm hands
that have made no contracts for the year but are working from place to
place."[9]

The Liberty Hill Democrats are one example of a "political cell" that
planned and carried out insurgency against the new regime. Founded
in 1868, and clearly a response to Radical Reconstruction and the new
constitution, its members met for the purpose of discussing "the salvation of our country." The Liberty Hill Democrats perceived this effort as grounded in Confederate religion, evangelical faith exfoliating in
the celebration of the Lost Cause. The first meeting, as would all subsequent meetings, opened with prayer and included an address by the
vice-president calling for "patience under trial," citing the example of
the children of Israel, "who were the chosen people of God and who
nevertheless wandered for forty years in the wilderness." South Carolinians represented a new chosen people, who would suffer under Radical
rule but ultimately receive divine deliverance and justification. Led by
Confederate veterans Colonel J. F. Talbert and J. B. Crutchfield, the club
members even debated whether or not they should describe themselves as
"national" Democrats. Though deciding to use the adjective for descrip-
tive purposes, many members remained uncomfortable that such a notion
as "national" politics might not be "true to constitutional liberty." The
principles of consolidation and centralization that they fought seemed the
underlying assumption of "national" identity.[10]

The militant Lost Cause often expressed itself through much more subversive channels. The decentralized nature of the white conservative effort
sometimes took the form of vigilantism practiced by Confederate veterans and guided by white property-owners. In May 1865, William Walker
Russell, formally a scout for Wade Hampton, led an armed band of Pickens County men against a detachment of Federal troops who had allegedly
stolen a number of mules and horses. Russell's former Confederates retrieved the livestock, killed one of the Federal soldiers, and conspicuously
"buried him in a Negro graveyard." In the same county, local folklore
claimed that the famed postwar evangelist Sam Jones allegedly took part
in an attack on Federal soldiers. A local historian explained that Jones's
"home was just across the river on the Georgia side" and that he "dearly
loved adventure."[11]

Armed gunmen and their cohorts, like the bloodthirsty Texas Brown,
of Laurens County, and Mance Jolly and the Jolly gang, of Anderson,
passed into folklore as Confederate Robin Hoods who continued the
southern struggle through their illegal activities. Using the Lost Cause
to justify their activities, such groups and individuals embody Eric Hobsbawm's theoretical paradigm of "social banditry." "Social bandits," as
opposed to practicing a simple, unambiguous criminality, are viewed by
their people "as heroes, as champions, avengers, fighters for justice, perhaps even leaders of liberation." Hobsbawm views such figures as engaging in "the defense or restoration of the traditional order of things."
Social banditry constitutes a violent response of traditional society to the
forces of "modernization," a phenomenon that Lacy K. Ford has used to
describe the Klan in a study of York County. Outlawry in the postbellum
upcountry certainly fits this paradigm, as desperate men embodied for
many white South Carolinians the defense of the southern conservative
ethos grounded in the celebration of the Lost Cause.[12]

Manson Sherrill "Mance" Jolly is as an example. Jolly, a former Confederate soldier, made himself a nuisance to Union occupation forces
throughout the end of 1865 and into 1866. John De Forest wrote that
Manse Jolly and his "bushwackers" hailed from Spartanburg County,
and before the war he had been "a farmer by occupation" who had "lost
a brother in the war and had avenged his death by taking the hand in
the murder of some straggling Union soldiers after the proclamation of
peace." De Forest especially lamented the tendency of Anderson County
farmers to give Jolly and his "desperate men" shelter "out of admiration
of their defiance to the Yankees."[13]

The activities of Jolly and other ex-Confederates led Lieutenant Colonel Haughton, commander of the Union garrison in Columbia, to issue a proclamation in the upcountry requesting the assistance of "peaceful and law-abiding citizens" to aid in the capture of "armed bands of marauders." The Union commander received little help from the respectable citizenry. An article in the *Anderson Intelligencer,* whose editors tended to preach an open cooperation with the forces of occupation, decried the common practice of "incursion upon public and private stores" that had too often been "encouraged by good and true citizens." By 1866, even the *Intelligencer* had placed itself on the side of the social bandits. One article described Union troops invading the home of "Ms. Jolly whose son stands in unenviable light with the military" and reported that the Yankee troops had not only stolen jewelry but had handled Jolly's sister "in a rough manner." Jolly would eventually flee to Texas in 1866 after the bounty on his head reached seven thousand dollars in gold. Recognizing his talents, the Texas cattle town where Jolly sought refuge made him its sheriff in 1867.[14]

Violent resistance to Yankee rule often had even clearer connections to the Lost Cause aesthetic, revealing Confederate commemoration as anything but apolitical. J. C. Keys, of Anderson County, hosted a reunion for the Palmetto Sharpshooters and later promoted the creation of the Anderson District Soldier's Aid Association, an organization similar to the soldier's association of Pickens. Keys, a prominent citizen, also apparently played a role in the murder of three Federal soldiers at Brown's Ferry on the Savannah River. Some of the social bandits seemed to seek to restore rituals of deference between white Carolinians and their former slaves. The brutal Texas Brown, of Laurens County, not only robbed freedpeople but also forced them to "take off their hats and get on their knees" in a ritual of subordination.[15]

Significantly, much social banditry in the upcountry centered not only on race and Republican politics but on South Carolinians' discomfort with aspects of modernity that their conquerors sought to impose. The case of moonshine and the Reconstruction-era internal revenue laws serve as one example. Except for a brief period during the War of 1812, no internal taxes had been levied on home brew since the Revolutionary era. South Carolinians, enraged by the confiscatory taxes on property, took equal umbrage at the tax on homemade liquors. The upcountry counties of Pickens, Anderson, Greenville, Spartanburg, and the newly created Oconee, took special offense at this seeming attack on a traditional practice of the piedmont farmer. Often living on a subsistence level in isolated mountain hamlets, Carolina yeoman in these counties found it easier to ship their corn to market in liquid form and thus turn a ready profit on sales day. In a bitter irony, the need for cash in hand had become a special concern since the beginning of Reconstruction as other forms of taxes mounted. Thus, internal revenue laws came as a special burden and further evidence of Federal perfidy.[16]

Stirred to defiance, piedmont farmers continued to make their corn liquor, known variously as "busthead" or "popskull." Many of these yeomen had not cared for their congregation's attempts to regulate their distilling and so paid even less attention to attempts by the Yankee conqueror. Such resistance led Reconstruction officials and United States Marshals to attempt to enforce the Federal tax in ways that enraged upcountry conservatives. Marshals and their scalawag informants could enter homes at will, as they did in a number of cases, in search of the elements of "mountain dew" production. J. W. Porter, of Pickens County, had his home raided by Federal troops, behavior which Porter loudly protested as "a high-handed outrage." Porter's resistance earned him a severe pistol whipping.[17] William King Easley took it upon himself to defend many of the arrested bootleggers, viewing Federal attempts to squelch the practice as further evidence of Yankee meddling, and resistance as another form of the Confederate war effort. The Lost Cause often functioned as the basis of his appeal to juries. In defending a bootlegger named Stack, Easley reminded the jurors that the accused had served in the Confederate army as a partisan of "the Cause Lost." He praised Stack's record as a defender of the South, calling to the jurors' minds the glories of Confederate virtue. Easley balanced this praise by attacking the Leviathan state's imposition of internal liquor taxes, seeing it as an effort to corrupt the virtue of a free people. The "incomprehensible provisions regarding taxes of distillation" had undermined southern virtue. Such laws, said Easley, "breed a race of informers who feed upon chicanery and fatten on treachery."[18] Many upcountry juries agreed. Hubbard Garmony, a Greenville farmer and likely moonshiner, shot and killed a revenuer who had trespassed his property and received an acquittal from a Greenville jury on the basis of "self-defense."[19]

The southern conservative elite sometimes expressed distaste with the methods and actions of these rowdy moonshiners and bandits. Wade Hampton, for example, rather blandly expressed concern in the 1870s that "the people must obey the laws."[20] The tendency among many conservative leaders to accept outlaws as allies, however, suggests that they

but more often, the outlaws
conservatives as allies

viewed the bootleggers and blockaders as allies against a common enemy, modernization imposed from above by the Federal government. General Easley, who so despised the tumult of democracy, ironically seemed comfortable with defending social banditry as an expression of Lost Cause defiance to the United States. Nonetheless, the common ground of the Lost Cause functioned as a uniting factor as these figures became folk heroes of Confederate virtue. This phenomenon appears most clearly in the case of the most famous upcountry bootlegger of them all, Lewis Redmond, of Pickens.

Redmond had roots in western North Carolina but came to Pickens in 1876 after shooting and killing a North Carolina scalawag informer named Alfred Duckworth. Redmond lived in the isolated mountain district of Pickens County, with a brood of women and a cohort of followers, in what one account describes as "a natural fortress in the mountains."[21]

Redmond had clear attachments to the Lost Cause. Though too young to enlist formally in the southern war effort, Redmond had run away to join his brother in the Confederate army. Redmond, much like Manse Jolly, maintained a lifelong hatred of the Yankees, a result of his brother's death in the war. Deeply loyal to the southern cause into the 1870s, Redmond used his influence in the mountainous sections of the upcountry on behalf of Hampton's Redemption campaign of 1876 that ended Reconstruction in South Carolina, even supplying wagons to take the old and infirm to the polling places. His legend included the unlikely notion that he used his earnings in the whiskey trade to help poor upstate farmers pay exorbitant Reconstruction taxes.[22]

Folk legends centered on Redmond's resistance to Federal rule show the people of the upcountry constructing a hero-deliverer out of the bootlegger, a partisan Confederate who refused to surrender. His efforts on behalf of Hampton, which had a basis in historical fact, show that Redmond became a social bandit, seeking to restore traditional society. South Carolina's attitude toward Redmond and his banditti shows him as something more than a hoodlum. All the respectable voices in the state spoke in defense of the outlaw following his 1878 capture, including the genteel Wade Hampton. Confederate veteran D. Wyatt Aiken, the aristocratic leader who had participated in the agricultural clubs, the rifle clubs, and the Granger movement, spoke out in Congress on behalf of Redmond and against the Federal revenue laws, particularly against the part of the statute that allowed the clearly unconstitutional search of private homes without a warrant. Even the deeply evangelical Grace Brown Elmore took part in the effort to have Redmond freed, showing that Confederate religion could even stomach moonshining and banditry if such actions had the patina of defiance to the Yankee conqueror.[23]

The Redmond case reveals the deep antipathy, and the deep anxieties, South Carolinians had toward the new world being shaped by Confederate defeat and Reconstruction. Such discomfort clearly continued even after Redemption. In the late 1860s, however, white conservatives had only one goal—to end rule by "black republicans" and resist the making of their society along the lines of "the progressive nineteenth century." Rather romantic individuals like Redmond and Jolly pale in importance to organized efforts by white conservatives to subvert Yankee rule, resist the tides of change, and reassert a hierarchical order over black Carolinians. Ironically, and ultimately to their hurt, white conservatives attempted to use the tactics of popular politics and the mechanisms of mass movement to attain their goal of a balanced, hierarchical, organic society. Believing in a limited style of politics, they awakened the unlimited passions and prejudices of white Carolinians to accomplish their goal. The most well known and controversial of these movements, the Ku Klux conspiracy, began in the year of the new Radical constitution, 1868.

The hooded order had begun in Pulaski, Tennessee, organized by Confederate veterans and headed by "the wizard of the saddle," Nathan Bedford Forrest. Though not formed until 1868, the South Carolina Klan had clear connections with the Tennessee order, and South Carolina's York County Klan became perhaps the most organized and pervasive of such movements in the South.[24] However, the secretive, underground nature of the Klan prevented centralization of control, and each state functioned independently or, in Klan terminology, as a "realm."[25] Even within the state, leadership devolved on local veterans who headed individual Klans. The organization became so loose-knit that individual Klans in Union County occasionally battled one another, with their membership divided between groups engaged in a feud over a community dispute extraneous to Reconstruction politics.[26]

Controversy over the meaning of the Klan has centered on its purpose. J. C. A. Stagg has argued that the Klan represented an effort at "labor control," though much of his evidence relates to the agricultural clubs that appeared shortly after Appomattox rather than to the Klan. Charles Flynn uses a version of the social-banditry thesis to describe the Klan, noting that they often punished white adulterers and usurers as well as blacks and scalawags. Trelease argues what has been called the "liberal definition" of Klan goals, "a terrorist organization aiming at the preservation of white supremacy."[27]

Richard Zuczek combines the most convincing elements of these views, suggesting that the work of the Klan should be seen as largely a political effort, arising specifically to challenge Republican rule. This does not contradict the view that white conservatives sought to control black labor or community mores. The Klan, however, had a more specific purpose: by using terrorist methods, to end Republican domination of the state. Such methods, dependent on a strong base of participation among whites of all social classes in rural South Carolina, created a movement, in the phrase of another era, of "massive resistance" that became an escalating spiral of violence of which elite leaders soon lost control.[28]

Klan violence swept the upcountry in the summer of 1868. Significantly, the strongest Klan organizations appeared in the upstate counties that shared three characteristics: a clear white majority, a large number of white republicans, and a well-organized, well-armed Union League membership. Historians have largely ignored the strength of white Republicans in these counties, since their interpretation of Klan violence has been much influenced by the liberal school that sees the early Klan as largely an organization devoted to racial purity. Though clearly seeing themselves as defenders of white supremacy, the leadership of the Klan viewed blacks through the paternalist eyes of the Old South, believing their "faithful negros" had been led astray by scalawags and carpetbaggers. The intention, at least of the southern conservatives who led the movement, centered on the methods of the antebellum slave patrol to enforce order on black Carolinians and to intimidate and, if necessary, murder, black and white carpetbaggers and Republican politicians. K. L. Gunn, a member of the York County Klan, told a congressional investigation committee that he understood the organization's purpose as "the killing of white Radicals and the whipping and intimidation of the negros."[29] The violence that would be brought against the freedpeople would not be deadly violence, but rather violence meant to control and subjugate.

Not all local Klan units, or klaverns, shared the paternalistic view of African Americans, and these small groups, at times individuals, seemed dedicated to the murder of blacks on the basis of a belief in racial purity. White conservative leaders did attempt to limit the violence of the Klan, and the call by Wade Hampton in late 1868 for moderation lessened the spreading Klan terror.

In 1870 terrorist intimidation would be renewed, as white Democrats attempted a fusion with Republican leaders disgusted with the corruption of their party. The result, a reform-minded third-party effort, had the support of leaders such as W. K. Easley and his friend and former brigade commander, J. B. Kershaw. Richard B. Carpenter, a reform Republican, ran at the head of the ticket, with Confederate brigadier Matthew Calbraith Butler as lieutenant governor. Openly courting black votes, white democrats attempted coercion where salesmanship failed. Despite these efforts, Radical Republican Robert K. Scott took the gubernatorial seat, and the regular Republicans made other important gains as well.[30]

Frustration boiled in the klaverns at Scott's reelection, frustration that turned to rage as the new governor, working in tandem with the Grant administration, created a militia drawn from the membership of the Union Leagues. A period of unrest, described by Richard Zuczek as "the most violent period in South Carolina since Sherman burned a path across the state," commenced in 1871, leading Grant to declare martial law in nine upcountry counties.[31] The Klan came out for blood.

The attacks of the South Carolina Ku Klux Klan repeated tactics in use throughout the South. Dressed in robes—at times white, at other times red or black—the Ku Kluxers dressed in what Charles Flynn has called "stylized anachronism" in an effort to evoke the tradition of charivari, the "rough music" that served as a means of social control and moral regulation in old Europe. Klan members invariably came upon the homesteads of politically active freedmen and white scalawags in the middle of the night. One York County white Radical received a night visitation by the Klan heralded by the sound of clattering hooves and voices crying, "Here we come, we are Ku Klux, straight from Hell!" as they crashed into his cabin. Members of the Union Leagues most often received these visits, showing the political intent and focus of Klan violence. Other times, the Klan simply used the threat of violence to frighten and intimidate. In 1873 Confederate veteran and Ku Kluxer J. N. King participated in one such episode. Sending a coffin to the Greenville Republican county treasurer J. M. Allen, who reportedly had stolen more than twenty thousand dollars during his administration, the Klan persuaded Allen to flee the state and return to New York City.[32] Public notices traded on the supernatural aura of the Klan. For example, Republicans in one upcountry town found the following posted at the courthouse "KKK . . . The Serpent and the Scorpion are Ready . . . Burst your cerements asunder and meet at the Den of the Glow worm." The cryptic language ended with a warning clear in its intent—"THE GUILTY SHALL BE PUNISHED!"[33]

Some interpreters have seen the gothic elements of Klan activities as a tactical attempt to draw on the freedmen's fears of "han'ts" (spirits of the dead, not unlike zombies) and similar paranormal phenomenon. Evidence suggests that at least some freedman evinced much more sophistication than this. Focus on the supernatural likely results from the Klan's close connection to the Lost Cause; they posed as the spirits of vengeful Confederate soldiers as an act of pious remembrance and to draw on the powerful memories connected to Confederate defeat. Rather than the probably unsuccessful effort to appeal to the superstitions of the freedmen, the Klan's appropriation of ghostly themes shows their own obsession with the aesthetic of the Lost Cause.[34] Most Klan members had served in the southern war effort and made the Confederacy central to their violent activities. Initiation ceremonies into the Klan, according to testimony in the South Carolina Ku Klux trials, featured an examination of the neophyte's war record. Efforts to frighten freedmen drew on Confederate memory, as individual Klansmen, speaking in sepulcher tones, announced to freedmen that they had come from hell where they had been since their deaths at Shiloh or Antietam.[35] Federal and Republican authorities certainly saw clear connections between the Klan and the Confederate experience. Scalawags in Oconee County referred to the night riders as "the Rebel KKK." Governor Scott referred to the klaverns as "organized and disciplined ex-Confederate soldiers."[36]

The bizarre behavior of the Klan represented the mystagogy of Confederate religion, a ritualistic invocation of the dead that in some ways embodies all the elements of the Lost Cause aesthetic. Calling upon the memory of the Confederate struggle, evocative of the experience of battle and appropriating these memories in their struggle against modernity, the Klan linked itself firmly to Confederate religion. South Carolina's evangelical churches often functioned as headquarters for Klan raids, and some ministers participated in and protected the klaverns. Initiation ceremonies in York County called on the neophyte to swear an oath "upon the Holy Evangelists of Almighty God." One recruit who had "protested that he did not care for organizations except for religious ones" had been assured that "this is about the same thing."[37] The Klan, making use of the aesthetic of the Lost Cause, became a primary expression of Confederate religion.

Southern conservatism, because of its American context, has found itself in the ironic position of making populist appeals on behalf of an essentially elitist ideology. The Ku Klux conspiracy provides a perfect example of the southern conservative inability to ride the tiger of mass participation. The cycle of violence, initiated by their evocations of the Lost Cause aesthetic, became uncontrollable and attracted a bevy of sadists and murderers to their hooded ranks. Southern conservatives conjoined reports of some of the more outrageous activities of individual Klans with their own fears of turbulent democracy. In the words of Union County attorney Robert Wallace Shand, the activities of the Klan had "induced the lowish white element of our white people" to "diabolical outrages."[38]

Shand rightly saw diabolism in activities of many Carolina Klansmen. Violence increasingly became less overtly political and expressed savage psychosexual desires and anxieties. Individual Klans moved from beating and whipping political opponents toward sadistic acts of patriarchal violence, at times even directed at white women. One white upcountry prostitute, allegedly sleeping with a number of freedmen, received a severe beating and then was forced to lie in the middle of her yard while the Klansmen poured hot tar onto her vagina, burning her horribly. Freedman Amzi Rainy looked on in horror while Klansmen beat his wife and raped one of his daughters.[39]

Some of the white conservative leaders, who had administered an oath to the Klan members to make white women "the especial objects of our regard and protection," looked on somewhat helplessly at the horrors they had allowed to walk Frankensteinlike in the Carolina upcountry. Conservative leaders made attempts to quell the turmoil, in part because they knew that such extreme violence dared the Federal authorities to intervene. Newspapers such as the *Carolina Spartan* and the *Yorkville Enquirer* circulated petitions calling for peace and quiet. The Grand Cyclops of the upcountry Klan, J. Banks Lyle, of Gaffney, called together his upcountry klaverns and ordered them to "restrain their excesses." If they did not, he threatened, he would "wash his hands of the whole business." The aristocratic Lyle's pleas had little effect. The rowdy klaverns simply reminded Lyle that "your oath binds you to us and if you break it we will kill you."[40] Lyle would ultimately flee to Texas, though it is unclear whether he sought to escape prosecution in the Ku Klux trails or from his fellow Klansmen.[41] York County Klan chief, former Confederate James Avery, also sought, with little effect, to end the worst excesses of the Klan in that county.[42]

Conservative leaders, and in later years their defenders, would claim that they had disbanded the Klan. The cases of Avery and Lyle suggest that these leaders had become ineffectual. Ultimately, the tardy willingness of the Grant administration to use military force brought an end to the terror. Elements of the United States military, which had been busily "pacifying" the Plains tribes and breaking northern labor strikes, received the assignment to quell restive southern whites. White conservative leaders had little to do with the first Klan disbanding. Some conservatives, such as Shand, believed that the "low elements" in the Klan turning state's evidence against their leaders brought an end to the terror, simultaneously expressing their belief in the perfidy of the "swinish multitude" and ignoring the Federal government's positive role in bringing an end to the horror. Though Carolina conservatives never admitted it, the Klan's effort failed because of the Federal army's willingness to crush the Ku Klux by making close to six hundred arrests from late 1871 into the spring of 1872. More than four hundred of those arrests occurred in the Klan hotbeds of Spartanburg and York Counties.[43]

The reluctance to continue the Klan's rampage of psychotic violence does not suggest that South Carolina's white leadership had undergone a change of heart. The savage turn taken by the South Carolina Ku Klux Klan did little to weaken conservative desire for militancy, even if at times they seemed shocked by the level and type of violence employed. Waiting out the 1872 presidential race, as their old enemy U. S. Grant rolled to reelection after a brief challenge from Horace Greeley and the Liberal Republican movement, Carolina conservatives began organizing rifle clubs in hopes of mobilizing for the struggle against Radical Republicanism. The organization of such troops had begun as early as 1869, with Charleston's Carolina Rifle Club, whose members stockpiled sixteen-shooter Winchesters that they insisted were only for sporting. The same club uniformed themselves in gray hunting shirts, an homage to the partisans of Francis Marion, "The Swamp Fox," South Carolina's famed Revolutionary War hero.[44]

Similar clubs began to appear in the upcountry only after Federal efforts scattered the klaverns. Conservatives perhaps felt that a more public expression of armed militancy, serving under strict military discipline, might prevent the rifle clubs from engaging in the excesses of the Klan.

The organization of the rifle clubs reflected the complex web of white conservative organizations in the upcountry, revealing a continuing culture of dissent. The Palmetto Sabre Club and the Sweetwater Sabre Club both drew their membership and organizational structure from the agricultural clubs that had sought to tie a black peasantry to the fields. Headed by former Confederate generals, their command structures resembled that of Confederate regiments formed into brigades. One upcountry club, the Richland Rifle Club of Columbia, drew its membership directly from Company A of the Second South Carolina Volunteers, who had fought at every major battle on the Civil War's eastern front. This rifle club even drew on older precursors in its membership and organizational structure since the Second South Carolina Volunteers had been formed from an antebellum militia known as the Governor's Guards, first organized in

1843.[45] Reflecting a common culture of resistance that resonated across
a range of issues and social groups, several rifle clubs in Greenville County
drew their membership from mountain bands of distillers.[46]

Technically illegal under the 1871 Enforcement Act, or, as it became
known, the Ku Klux Act, the rifle clubs represented themselves as social
organizations. They did, in fact, have a social aspect that the klaverns
never did, taking part in public parades as well as in banquets, balls,
sporting events, and barbecues. Such activities inevitably involved a celebration of the Lost Cause, since so many veterans participated in the rifle
clubs. James Connor, a Confederate brigadier general, served as the ad-
ministrative head of the clubs. Other prominent generals in the movement
included Matthew C. Butler, Martin Gary, Johnson Hagood, James B.
Kershaw, and, of course, Wade Hampton himself.

The social activities of the rifle clubs did little to stymie their pen-
chant for violence. The Army's effort in breaking the Ku Klux conspiracy
marked the swan song of Federal involvement in South Carolina's Reconstruction. After 1874, the combination of an armed Republican militia
and white determination to end Radical Reconstruction created an explosive cocktail in the upcountry. Conservatives became particularly restive
as the Franklin J. Moses gubernatorial administration replaced that of
Ohio Union officer Robert Scott. Moses, from 1872 to 1874, headed one
of the most corrupt state governments in American history. Corrupt bond
issues overwhelmed the state with debt, and Republican officials profited
from a scandalous misappropriation of funds. High taxes on landowners
paid for $125,000 worth of sherry, brandy, and whiskey, all purchased by
the gallon and used to entertain the legislators and their cronies. Conservatives especially raged that their taxes paid for the publication of Radical
journals such as the *Columbia Daily Herald*.[47]

The kind of violence that exploded in the upcountry in 1874 was different from earlier white efforts at intimidation and terror. Instead of relying
on subterfuge and night-riding, the rifle clubs openly battled Republican-
controlled forces, particularly in Aiken, Edgefield, and Laurens Counties. Democratic leaders like Martin W. Gary insisted that such activity,
which came to be known as the "straight-out," or, more appropriately,
the "shotgun," policy, offered the only hope for white Carolinians who
had tried fusion, night-riding, and political intimidation.[48]

An aesthetic can evoke horror and terror as quickly as it summons the
more tender sensibilities. Dreaming an older world led South Carolina
whites to use extreme violence in an effort to reconcile their desires and
fears with the realities of society and politics. The South Carolina rifle

clubs reveal the militancy of the Lost Cause, the political uses of Confederate memory. Viewing the aesthetic of the Lost Cause as a mourning ritual or a simple exercise in nostalgia fails to take into account its political power in the Reconstruction upcountry. In truth, the rifle clubs functioned as the Confederate army *recidivus* and openly battled the largely African American Republican militia for control of the state. The aesthetic of the Lost Cause may have evoked the ghosts of the Confederacy, but these were vengeful spirits who violently revealed their influence among the living.

CHAPTER SIX

Hampton or Hell!

The '76 Campaign

1876 Gubernatorial Campaign

Wade Hampton rode again on October 7, 1876. Flanked by the paramilitary arm of the South Carolina Democratic Party—which was made up of local rifle clubs—Hampton entered the midlands town of Sumter, South Carolina, an important stop in his gubernatorial campaign tour. In the center of town, a speakers stand had been erected, and on it a black-robed figure, bound in chains, stood solemnly before a crowd of farmers and townspeople. As the hopeful candidate assumed his position on the platform, the shadowy figure flung off its chains and cast aside its robe of mourning, revealing a beautiful young woman, white of skin, dressed in gauzy white, and wearing a tiara emblazoned with the words "South Carolina." The journalist Alfred Brockenbrough Williams witnessed the crowd erupt at this performance, with many of the men openly weeping. Late into the night, Williams reported, frenzied horsemen rode through the town crying out, "Hampton or Hell!" The candidacy of Wade Hampton in the 1876 governor's race seemed to these white South Carolinians to be the chance to restore South Carolina to home rule.[1]

The defeat of Reconstruction in South Carolina resulted both from the creation of a conservative culture and from conservatives' willingness to use violence, intimidation, and less extreme methods of coercion to unify the state behind the Conservative Democratic ticket. The creation of a white consensus in the state, of course, could not have brought the end of Reconstruction on its own. Ultimately the unwillingness of the Federal government to enforce the Fourteenth and Fifteenth amendments in South Carolina and throughout the South meant the end of Reconstruction. The triumph of 1876 became, however, much more than this to white South Carolina. It became, for white South Carolinians, a redemption in a political, cultural, and theological sense.

The historiography of southern Redemption has tended to focus on the ways in which conservative whites used fraud and violence to overturn *historiography on southern redemption* (handwritten annotation)

Reconstruction regimes. Whether the story is told as a heroic narrative of redemption or as a dream of democracy deferred, the emphasis has centered on votes—whether bought, coerced, or fraudulently counted.[2] No new evidence challenges the role of intimidation and violence in this and other Redemption contests. Former Confederate brigadier general and leading "straight-out" Democrat, Martin Witherspoon Gary, certainly believed that for the Hampton campaign to succeed without compromise or cooperation with Republicans "every Democrat must feel honor bound to control the vote of at least one negro."[3]

Even Gary, however, believed that the Hampton campaign must "get up all the enthusiasm we can among the masses."[4] South Carolina conservatives, like Gary, recognized that these white masses were the key to Democrats' regaining power in postbellum society. They understood, moreover, that power functioned best in a context of cultural consensus. If conservatives could control the tenets of that consensus in such a way that the white masses acquiesced to domination by the Democratic elite, then conservative rule would certainly be assured. To this end, in the 1876 campaign conservatives successfully created and celebrated a public spectacle that drew upon the racial and gendered obsessions of white Carolina culture. The ritual and rhetoric that accompanied the so-called Hampton Days of September and October 1876 depicted the conflict between Democrat Wade Hampton and Republican incumbent Daniel H. Chamberlain as a religious struggle between good and evil (between "Hampton" and "Hell") and preyed upon white anxieties about ideas of race and gender. As public representations of cultural ideology, the Hampton Days celebrations bring us into a tightly woven network of memory and myth.

Conservatives had looked on with horror as their state slowly came under the control of the Federal government and the Republican Party. Even as the Lost Cause movement took shape in the years after the war, South Carolina seemed on the verge of gigantic transformations. When the Republican-dominated Congress passed the Reconstruction Acts of 1867, a special "conservative state convention" warned of the "ignorant mob" that would come to power should black suffrage become a reality. Federal military power and the large number of newly enfranchised African American voters made real political resistance to Reconstruction ineffectual. Uncertainty over how to respond perhaps explains the paradoxical strategy of combining Ku Klux terror and cooperation with Republicans.[5]

This strategy, however, proved futile from the point of view of some

of South Carolina's white leaders. The 1872 governor's race ended with
the election of Franklin J. Moses Jr., a scalawag who had participated in
some of the worst corruption of the outgoing Robert K. Scott administration. Conservatives looked apprehensively on the fact that Moses
had been elected by the midlands and black-majority low country. Martin Gary and his compatriot from Edgefield, former Confederate general
Matthew C. Butler, began to look on the past attempts at cooperation
with Republicans as collaboration with an unyielding enemy and promoted instead the militarization of conservative resistance. Agricultural
and Democratic clubs, formed immediately after the war to coerce black
labor, transformed themselves into rifle clubs as early as 1874. The rifle
clubs, unlike their predecessors, were organized under military discipline
and a strict command structure. Although these organizations would play
a central role in the Hampton campaign in 1876, Democratic leaders
in the meantime found themselves at odds over the proper deployment
of the paramilitary groups. Gary and the Radical straight-outs of Edgefield County hoped to use the armed bands, composed mostly of battle-
hardened Confederate veterans, to reopen a shooting war between South
Carolina and its enemies. In contrast, Wade Hampton, with much of the
rest of the Democratic leadership in tow, sought to use the clubs only to
make a display of military might and so fulfill his policy of "force without
violence."[6]

Dissension in the 1876 campaign would become a crucial moment in
the history of South Carolina conservatism, even though disagreement
did not become, at that time, an open breach. White conservatives shared
a unity of purpose even if they differed on tactics. First, Radical Reconstruction must come to an end with home rule taking its place. Second,
conservatives, who had largely given up on the Confederate nation, believed that their state could become an ordered agrarian republic with a
significant measure of independence from the Federal government. Rejecting the notion of a Confederate nation-state, the memory of the Confederacy provided a model of virtue that would shape social and political
configurations through aesthetic and memory.

Historians have tended to collapse the straight-out position into the
shotgun policy, but these different descriptors represent different, though
not contradictory, aspects of South Carolina conservatism's desire for
state redemption. By 1875–76, most Carolina Democrats could be described as straight-out, in that they accepted Gary's position that the
Democrats must run on their own ticket and with their own organization, eschewing fusion and third-party efforts. The much more radical

[handwritten margin notes: ...ampl, ...emerging, ...among, Settler, whites, constructive + radicals]

"shotgun policy," or "Edgefield policy," caused more controversy and would have grave consequences for the conservative movement in South Carolina. The advocates of the shotgun policy believed that wanton political fraud and violent intimidation offered the only means of restoring home rule and self-government. Perhaps most important, they disliked the tendency of Hampton and his followers to speak favorably of the freedmen and to suggest the possibility that the emancipated slaves had a place, albeit a subordinate one, in South Carolina's social and political order.

Ultimately, this disagreement signaled changing attitudes toward the meaning of racial difference. The Ku Klux movement, and other acts of violence, radicalized many conservatives in their racial attitudes. Support for Gary and his proposal came from his own Edgefield County, as well as from the Klan hotbeds of Laurens and Spartanburg.[7] Throughout the state, the rifle clubs' running battles with the Republican militia, almost entirely African American, had sharpened the sense of a racial, rather than political, divide. Gary had, in fact, insisted at the 1874 taxpayers convention that the issue between conservative Carolina and its enemies "was one of race, not of politics."[8]

Both Hampton and the more radical straight-outs, then, saw the clubs as integral to their effort to restore Democrats to power. Often these clubs acted as a militia at the command of conservative leaders while cloaking themselves as social organizations. The constitution of the Richland Rifle Club, for example, simply referred to the group's central objective as "social intercourse," along with "target shooting and such other amusements as they [the members] may determine." These "other amusements" would ultimately include acting as the military arm of Hampton's 1876 campaign. Each club typically had fifty to sixty members, with altogether about thirty thousand white men under arms. A later congressional investigation found that the rifle clubs were led by men who had "long borne military titles obtained not by service in the militia, but on the fields of Manassas, Malvern Hill and Gettysburg."[9] *[handwritten: Chamberlain]*

The 1874 gubernatorial election of Daniel H. Chamberlain, a Yale graduate, abolitionist, and commander of black Union troops in the Civil War, did little to allay the anxieties of white conservatives. As the 1876 election approached, a number of conservatives made plans for a straight-out campaign in which they would use any means necessary to overthrow a government that they considered fundamentally illegitimate. Hampton M. Jarrell, whose description of events sometimes suffers from his tendency toward apologia, has nevertheless correctly written that this campaign should be seen as a "counter-revolution" rather than as an election.[10]

The choice of Wade Hampton as the Democratic standard-bearer seemed a natural one, perhaps in part because Hampton, unlike many former Confederate leaders, had no clear connection to the Ku Klux terror of the early 1870s. White conservatives, usually Confederate veterans, saw clearly that South Carolina would rally behind this embodiment of the Lost Cause in a bid to overthrow the Reconstruction government. To ensure this result, leaders planned public celebrations of Hampton's candidacy. For two months the general toured the state, beginning in the solidly Democratic white counties of the upcountry and ending in Charleston, completing what Richard Zuczek has described as Sherman's March in reverse.[11]

The upcountry town of Anderson was the first stop in Hampton's campaign tour, on September 2, 1876. Thousands of firmly Democratic supporters turned out to see the mounted rifle clubs, sixteen hundred members strong, and to listen to a cornet band compete with a cannon that, to one listener's ears, made the roaring sound of "salute and triumph." When Hampton began to speak to the crowd, he immediately had to "stand a long while and look and listen," as Anderson greeted him with "the yells of men frantically screaming their heads off and the shrieked love and frenzy of women." Hampton's cavalcade proceeded from Anderson to the mountain towns of Walhalla and Pickens, then to Greenville. Engineering the largest spectacle thus far in the campaign, mounted rifle club members and the R. E. Lee Fire Company greeted Hampton in Greenville with a torchlight procession and a parade of "citizens afoot and in wagons," many dressed in the red shirts that had come to symbolize devotion to Hampton and support for white conservatism. The *Greenville Southern Enterprise and Mountaineer* noted that "cheer upon cheer" greeted Hampton both at the torchlight procession and at the rally the following day on the grounds of Furman University.[12]

The Hampton Days celebrations exemplify how southern conservatives found themselves in the paradoxical situation of maintaining and institutionalizing an elitist ideology while having to appeal to popular political support.[13] Nevertheless, their use of ritual and spectacle to unite public opinion hardly constituted a new methodology of power in the political history of the West. Late in the fourteenth century, the cities of northern Europe celebrated the arrival of sovereigns with rituals both intricate and colorful. The visual elaboration of the theme of sovereignty, which often included the strategic use of motifs from the Catholic Church's Advent

[handwritten margin note: traditions of political rite]

liturgy, furnished a structure of meaning with which most early modern bystanders would be familiar. Gordon Kipling, one of the foremost interpreters of these celebrations, has argued that royalty often used such political rituals during inaugural ceremonies to reinforce the notion that the sovereign inherited both an immanent and a transcendent legitimacy. At the same time, these rituals had a folk aspect, since they constituted "a deeply felt assertion of communal solidarity."[14]

Traditions of political ritual in colonial and antebellum America provide further encouragement to examine public spectacles in the context of the Reconstruction South. One study has made the point that the investigation of public ritual in early America moves political history away from its standard role of interpreting "the words and actions of the ruling elite." Historians have also made use of ritual as a category for analyzing southern mentalités. Charles Reagan Wilson drew heavily on the anthropological work of Clifford Geertz and Anthony F. C. Wallace in his groundbreaking study of the Lost Cause. Bertram Wyatt-Brown and Kenneth S. Greenberg have similarly examined rituals of dueling, honor, and manhood in the Old South.[15]

Although historians who have focused on ritual have successfully shown how symbolic human actions reflect the values of the ever-elusive "folk," they have yet to recognize fully that public spectacles also shape and embody political ideology from above. The Hampton campaign reveals that southern conservatives used the Lost Cause movement to promote their own ideology and to shape public behavior. They sought to define and encode the boundaries of racial identity, to reaffirm antebellum attitudes regarding gender, and to express a revivified Confederate nationalism. Neither a self-conscious religion nor simply a gloss on New South economic concerns, the Lost Cause functioned in 1876 as an aesthetic of yearning, an attempt to represent the world that southern conservatives had watched go down in flames at Appomattox. The power of these images blossomed into a new Confederate nationalism that would haunt South Carolina into the twentieth century.[16]

Democratic leaders, almost all of whom were former Confederate generals, manipulated the aesthetic of the Lost Cause to herald a revival of the Confederate South, united to face its enemies. A Greenville newspaper reporter, for example, wrote that the Democratic club hoped that the town's planned torchlight procession, along with the other elements of pageantry, would "have the best effect upon the people of Greenville."[17] The hoped-for effect certainly seems to have been achieved. Hampton's journey through the upcountry towns appears in the sources as a succession of ovations. After leaving Greenville, Hampton moved on to nearby Spartanburg, where the thunder of cannons and fireworks and the light of torches and "burning balloons" greeted him that night. "South Carolina white men," a journalist noted, "were going into this fight with more determination and desperation of purpose than they went into the Confederate war." The mounted processions seemed to embrace all classes of South Carolina whites, as evidenced by some of Hampton's less "knightly" supporters, who resembled southern Don Quixotes, perched on mules and wearing some unkempt version of a red shirt and "shabby, ragged and patched breeches." [18]

The uniform of the Hampton supporter, the red shirt, became the most important visual symbol of the campaign. Oddly, its origin and meaning seem to have been uncertain, even for the participants. Opponents of Hampton claimed that its blood-red color represented the willingness of the straight-outs to use violence against Afro-Carolinians. However, had this been the case, Hampton himself would likely have publicly rejected such a symbol for undermining his vision of white supremacist paternalism. A more likely story relates how Martin Gary modeled the red shirt on Giuseppe Garibaldi's 1860 Red Shirts. Gary, a Harvard graduate, had a library well stocked with European history and would have appreciated this nationalistic symbolism. Regardless of its uncertain paternity, the red shirt quickly became the most public symbol of devotion to Hampton's reanimated Lost Cause. William Watts Ball, a young child in 1876, remembered the impossibility of finding a store in Laurens County that had not sold out of red flannel. Undeterred, the young Hampton supporter had his red shirt made out of red calico. [19]

In the eyes of conservative South Carolina whites, Hampton embodied both the ideology of the Lost Cause and the memory of the Lost Eden, the Old South. The emotional reaction of the crowds as he took the speakers platform mirrors the responses of South Carolinians at other public celebrations of the Confederacy. Contemporaries saw him as both "an aristocrat to his fingertips" and a blunt soldier in the War for Southern Independence, who would "chat on the war with the humblest private of the Confederacy or on the merits and characters of dogs and horses." One observer described the former cavalryman in language redolent of the medieval chivalric tradition, evangelical fervor, and the cloying magnolia scent of the southern elite: "Hampton, simple, unaffected gentleman, dauntless warrior of South Carolina, loving and reverencing his God, his cause and his commonwealth to the last recess of his clean soul." From a different ideological line of vision, a hostile *Atlantic Monthly* article claimed that Hampton had "strikingly crystallized all the arrogant old plantation qualities of the South."[20]

The image of Hampton as Lost Cause warrior received immeasurable support from the fact that not a few Confederate veterans served as his partisans. The response to Hampton's campaign suggests that a resurgence of Confederate sentiment occurred in 1876, an open and public awakening to feelings long fermenting in small, local memorial associations. As early as 1866 a Confederate Soldiers' Association had formed in the South Carolina mountain town of Pickens, with Wade Hampton as its first featured speaker.[21] After a decade of reliving the war in private celebrations, "old Confederate cavalrymen" embraced the announcement of Hampton's candidacy, "shout[ing] along the roads and in the streets of court house towns that with somebody like Wade Hampton to lead they could and would storm Hell." A member of the Richland County Democratic Club later recalled that a precampaign rally of mounted Red Shirts, as Hampton's supporters had come to be known, in Columbia had reminded him of the glory days of the Confederate cavalry or, as the Hampton supporter called it, "the day of Lee's Critter Companies."[22] Reporting on the September 13 parade and mass meeting in Laurens, the *Greenville Southern Enterprise and Mountaineer* described the common opinion that the marches, thunderous cannonades, and hospitality of the townspeople recalled "the times of 1861, when the boys were starting off to the army."[23] Governor Chamberlain himself claimed, "Never since the passage of the Ordinance of Secession has there been such scenes in the state." These invocations of the Confederacy suggest a society filled with profound yearnings. The rifle clubs, placed on public display, offered a way for South Carolinians to contemplate and reenact the past. The Hampton campaign thus became another example of Delacroix's "game of ghosts."[24]

The Hampton Days hoped to enlist ghosts of the Old South other than the former Confederate veterans. Hampton's understanding of white supremacy, one that employed paternalistic and hierarchical notions of the social order, meant that former slaves would have a role to play in the campaign symbolism. Black Red Shirts made a prominent appearance in many of the parades and were often placed conspicuously on the speakers platform. One observer noted that Democratic campaign managers appeared "solicitous about them and gave them front seats on the stands." Hampton's understanding of paternalism and social harmony fueled this appeal to African American cooperation. The Democratic Party leadership hoped, moreover, that such public expression of black support announced to the Federal government that the spectacle of armed ex-Confederates did not constitute another illegal Ku Klux movement.[25]

The 1876–77 congressional investigations into South Carolina electoral fraud uncovered several examples of former slaves who did in fact join companies of Red Shirts and march in the Hampton Days celebrations. Merriman Washington, of Richland County, led a Red Shirt club of sixteen black South Carolinians to the polls, half of whom, he later testified, were chased off by "a heap of the republicans." Aaron Mitchell, a black resident of Abbeville County, became a poll manager for the Democrats and testified that he had "voted as many [black Democrats] as between one and two hundred at Abbeville Court-House." The black supporters of Hampton had diverse reasons for casting their lots with the very embodiment of the master class. Some continued to benefit from white paternalism, like Jonas Weeks, of Richland County, who had been a slave belonging to Wade Hampton's father. Other African American Red Shirts had more complex motives, like Asbury Green, of Abbeville County, who was wearied of sharecropping and simply hoped that a change of administration would improve his prospects. "I want a change in the government," he remembered thinking. "I never have got no good out of the republican party. I never have got ten cents out of the party."[26]

Wade Hampton had long called on South Carolinians to view their southern world as both biracial and white supremacist. Speaking in 1866 to one of the earliest organizations of Confederate veterans, Hampton encouraged his former comrades to remember their duty to the freedman: "As a slave, he was faithful to us; as a freedman, let us treat him as a friend." Refusing to recognize that Afro-Carolinians could exhibit agency of their own, Hampton viewed them as either loyal friends or Republican pawns. He maintained a tight web of paternalism and control over the former slaves of the Hampton family and believed that other southern whites should do the same. Within this context black voting became acceptable. White supremacist paternalism, Hampton believed, could control these votes just as it could control other aspects of blacks' lives. He told a biracial audience in Abbeville, "We want your votes, we don't want you to be deprived of them." Martin W. Gary rejected this strategy, telling a supporter that he would rather "sing psalms to a dead mule" than speak to black audiences as Hampton did. Nevertheless, Gary, who viewed the campaign of 1876 as a war between races rather than political ideologies, for the most part remained quiescent in his criticism of Hampton for the sake of the straight-out campaign. He would not, however, hold his tongue under Hampton's gubernatorial administration: as

Stephen Kantrowitz has shown, Gary's philosophy of white supremacy came to fruition in South Carolina's Tillman movement of the 1880s and 1890s.[27]

Southern Christianity, symbolically tied to Confederate memory, played a prominent role in the conservative campaign, as it did in shaping the larger Lost Cause mythology. The postbellum white South created what can only be called a "Confederate religion," as Christian leaders transposed the virtue of Johnny Reb with the teachings of Christ and celebrated the memory of the fallen nation with the language of Zion. In the 1876 campaign southern religious practice structured the ritual of the Hampton celebrations. Just as sovereigns in the premodern West shaped their royal pageantry around the liturgical world of the Catholic Church, so did white South Carolinians mold their political performances around the ethos of evangelical religion. Prayer and the singing of hymns created a revivalistic atmosphere in the mass meetings that occurred along Hampton's route. The county Democratic clubs began their gatherings with prayer and, in the case of the Richland County Democratic Club, resolved to sing "joyful hosannas" upon Hampton's election.[28] Moreover, the central dogmatic and subjective experience of southern evangelicalism—personal conversion—easily conjoined with the category of the political. In a particularly evocative phrase, Democrats termed the decision (often made under duress) by white Republicans to throw their support to Hampton as "crossing Jordan." Rifle-club members similarly claimed that those who joined the Hampton campaign had "[come] over to the Lord's side."[29]

[margin note: see themselves as on God's side]

Profoundly shaping the Hampton-Chamberlain struggle as a Christian crusade, the religious imagery employed by campaigners was matched by the rhetoric of South Carolina church leaders, who had already prepared the ground for a conservative challenge to the Republicans. For example, Ellison Capers, the Episcopal priest who had served as a brigadier general in the Confederate army, became one of the most active and outspoken Hampton supporters. Converted to faith in both Christianity and the Confederacy by the experience of war, Capers became a kind of high priest of the Lost Cause in South Carolina, described as one of those who "pledged themselves to its [the state's] redemption under a white man's government." Only a ministerial assignment to Selma, Alabama, in 1875 kept Capers from more personal involvement in the campaign itself. A letter to the state's Baptist newspaper, the *Working Christian,* called on "The Christian Patriots of South Carolina" to refrain from violence and yet to do all in their power to support "our great ambition." The state's

Democratic Central Committee appointed a "day of prayer and fasting" for Hampton's supporters. Testifying to the widespread religious support, one seemingly amazed observer noted that "even Episcopal and Catholic" churches observed the rite. The encouragement given by church leaders clearly urged white South Carolinians to think of themselves as Confederate Christians.[30]

Hampton thus clearly fits into Charles Reagan Wilson's paradigm of "Crusading Christian Confederates." Hampton has been described as "a churchman of influence," though he made few statements about and evinced little personal interest in theological matters. Nevertheless, conservative Carolinians, whose religious devotion had intensified in the crucible of Confederate defeat, structured the celebrations of his candidacy so that the campaign seemed blessed with divine legitimacy. The general, who already embodied the virtues and values that white southerners believed constituted the noble crusader for southern independence, was now enveloped in a patina of religious expression. The way in which the Hampton campaign combined the religious and the political suggests that the multiple themes scholars have noted in the celebration of Confederate memory often merged. Hampton's 1876 campaign mingled the concerns of those, like politicians, who "interpreted the Lost Cause as a defense of states' rights, and . . . waved the gray shirt to enable former Confederates to win election," with the priorities of those, like ministers, who utilized the Lost Cause as "a set of symbols of virtue and an overarching myth which embodied threatened values." The Democratic Party leadership sought to summon the aesthetic vision of a lost world, a world of brave Confederate soldiers and faithful slaves surrounded by an aura of Confederate religion.[31]

In addition to the expressed longing for a lost past, the campaign's symbolic tableaux, such as the young woman's casting off her black robes and chains upon Hampton's arrival, became a theater of racial and gendered anxiety. It chronicled white South Carolinians' humiliation at their perceived loss of traditional freedoms and their fears that domination by Yankee radicals and their black "pawns" might continue. These fears had deep antebellum roots. A number of historians have made the argument that white male southerners, especially those who lived during or who could remember the slave system, became particularly jealous of their liberties, since they had seen with their own eyes the terrors of bondage and servitude. Heavily invested in the construction of their political identities as freeborn and independent, they fiercely asserted that no slippage into bondage would occur.[32] After the Old South society failed at war, southern conservatives, wanting to protect their own liberty within an ordered polity, worried over the often amorphous shape of postbellum racial and gendered identities. Tableaux, performed in connection with the political struggle of Redemption, became a way to exorcise these anxieties by establishing clear racial and gendered boundaries. Joel Williamson has written that the notion of "place"—designated social spaces within hierarchical systems—was a central concept in the vocabulary of southern conservatism. The Hampton campaign tableaux sought to establish "place" for emancipated African Americans and deployed the bodies of white women to exhibit, and legitimize, conservative ideology in the postbellum South.[33]

Reconstruction-era South Carolinian white men had much to ponder as they contemplated their identities as freeborn and independent citizens. Total subjugation already seemed to be a reality to many white South Carolinians. John Leland, of Laurens, who had been imprisoned in 1872 for "Ku-Klux" activity, wrote two years later that he felt "irresistibly impelled to publish to the world that the grand old State, declared to be free, sovereign and independent, an hundred years ago, is now deposed, gagged, and trampled in the dust." Similarly, the Greenville *Enterprise and Mountaineer* anxiously reported in the midst of the 1876 campaign that the Federal government planned "an armed invasion of the State."[34]

These fears of domination by a regnant radicalism using black "pawns" also appeared prominently in the Redeemers' rhetorical trope of "corruption" in the state government. One South Carolinian, though no supporter of Hampton, referred with disgust to the state's Reconstruction government as "a grand carnival of crime and debauchery." Similarly, Robert Barnwell Rhett, writing in 1875, grumbled that the political subjugation of South Carolina constituted at its heart a moral problem, having been occasioned by "the decline of virtue, and the depravity of the people." Benjamin F. Perry, in one of the opening speeches of the Hampton campaign, declaimed against "the corruption of the State and federal Government," its "extravagance," and its "enormous taxation." Tyrannical power, with tendencies essentially venal and corrupt, threatened the state, these critics protested. Using the language of outraged republicanism, South Carolina conservatives thus constructed for themselves an enemy deeply immoral and opposed to virtue; with the images of "carnival" and "depravity," it was also an enemy tainted by religious impurity.[35]

The anxiety over the corruption of the Reconstruction government and the threat it posed to white Carolina liberty escalated after Governor

Chamberlain's October 7 decision to ban the Democratic rifle clubs. These fears were further exacerbated by the fact that the Democrats did not have a monopoly on paramilitary organizations. A black militia, under Chamberlain's command, served as the militant arm of the Republican Party. Conservatives worried about this "lawless mob," making accusations that "the Republican party has precipitated riot and murder upon the State." The possibility of so-called riot and murder had steadily increased with armed clashes occurring between blacks and whites, particularly in Hamburg in early July and in Cainhoy in mid-October. Perhaps most ominous of all to white South Carolinians, in Aiken County two African American men allegedly attacked and attempted to rob "a respectable white woman, in her own home with . . . her husband at work in the fields. . . ." Conservatives thus thought they saw their deepest anxieties coming to pass even as they sought to reassert their political hegemony. The image of "a lawless mob" debauching the state's wealth and honor in the legislature coalesced with the image of two emancipated slaves assaulting a white woman in the home, while her husband performed the work in the fields.[36]

Carolina conservatives surely felt that they had stepped through Alice's looking glass to a world where white men found themselves disarmed, former slaves joined militia units with the blessing of the state government, and sacred white womanhood suffered insult within the enclosed household. These confused patriarchs responded with a gendered rhetoric of resistance that had long been a part of the rhetorical panoply of South Carolina conservatives. Stephanie McCurry has argued that low-country planters appealed to yeoman farmers during the nullification and secession crises with a language that equated the invasion of the state with the invasion of the household. South Carolina secessionists rendered this "invasion" in terms of sexual violence, suggesting that the "violation" of the household's women and the undermining of the patriarchal prerogative would be the outcome of federal "rapacity." Both a South Carolina gendered as feminine and the actual wives, sisters, and mothers who inhabited the domestic sphere faced "violation," if yeomen did not resist an intrusive central government. The only options available became "manly resistance" or effeminate submission.[37]

A similar gendered language appears in the Lost Cause aesthetic of the Hampton campaign. J. P. Thomas of Charlotte's Carolina Military Institute, at a Democratic meeting in Edgefield on August 10, 1876, called upon the "sturdy yeoman" to take a stand for "Old Mother, South Carolina." John Leland, who dedicated his memoirs "to the Women of South

Carolina," also used gendered terms to describe the allegedly illegitimate Reconstruction government: "Her [South Carolina's] seat and name has been usurped by a brazen-faced strumpet. . . ." Leland, so fearful that the government of his beloved state had turned to foreign gods, ascribed the intensity and the excitement of Hampton's march to "the women of the State," to whom he sang numerous paeans.[38]

Gendered images such as these drew both on the antebellum ideal of the "Southern Lady" and the increased importance this concept had acquired in the mythology of the Lost Cause. The peculiar concerns of the antebellum world had already fashioned the white southern lady, in W. J. Cash's unforgettable words, into "the South's Palladium, . . . the shield-bearing Athena gleaming whitely in the clouds." The crushing defeat of the Civil War created an even more elaborate mythology of womanhood. With white men fearing that the Old South had gone down in flames because of their moral failure, white women became the repository of southern virtue. Furthermore, Gaines M. Foster has suggested that women protected their male relatives from insecurity about their masculinity and its prerogatives by welcoming home their Confederate husbands, sons, and brothers with enthusiasm and by declining to use the interstices of war to challenge the patriarchy of the Old South. After the war, the idea of pure Confederate womanhood thus became an essential element of the Lost Cause mythology, stabilizing the hierarchy of the family and of southern society by buttressing the sagging defenses of white southern manhood.[39]

Perhaps it assumes too much to think that anxieties over the meaning of masculinity and sexuality found relief simply because the women of southern households had welcomed their men home. Proof that such uneasiness remained a feature of the white male southern mind into the 1870s appears in Leland's depiction of the state government as "a brazen-faced strumpet." Conservative fears about the decline of republican virtue and the dangers of a Radical government that conservative rhetoric rendered as a "loose woman" intermingled with concerns about the potency of white manhood. Calling on Carolina men to once again stand up for their "Mother, South Carolina," the 1876 campaign offered them another opportunity to live up to their charge to defend home and hearth. The fact that Chamberlain could disband their rifle clubs while arming a black militia viscerally reminded them of the humiliation of 1865. Would the white southern lady remain faithful during this new crisis? Could white southern men defend their domestic and political space, ensuring the loyalty of their women and destroying the "brazen-faced strumpet" in the Columbia statehouse who threatened their liberties?

The Hampton Days answered these questions with a resounding rebel yell of affirmation. Hampton's cavalcade passed from acclamation to acclamation in its triumphal tour of the upcountry. The celebration in the small town of Ninety-Six, for example, featured a mounted procession of Confederate veterans reportedly two miles long. At stop after stop, the Hampton Days became a stylized round of torchlight parades, fireworks, cannonade, and speeches by Hampton and lesser Confederate lights that called for resistance and unity among white conservatives. Although women had always played a prominent part in the organization of these campaign events, the proscription of the rifle clubs in October seems to have thrust them into an even more crucial role. Alfred Brockenbrough Williams called the tableau performed at Sumter on October 7 the "unspoken answer" to the disbanding of the clubs. He wrote of the sheer emotive power of seeing a chain-wrapped figure, wearing clothes of mourning, transformed into "a radiant young woman in pure white[,] . . . tall and stately, head up-lifted and eyes shining like stars. . . ." Her liberation galvanized the audience into a congregation of overwrought men and women, whooping rebel yells and willing to do anything to insure the defeat of radicalism.[40]

A similarly gendered spectacle made the Hampton Day at Winnsboro even more elaborate than Sumter's offering. As Hampton made his way to the speakers platform amid yet more rebel yells and a greeting from Confederate hero Matthew C. Butler, a young girl with a cap and staff, designated *Liberty,* raised another young belle, a prostrate *South Carolina,* to her feet. Nearby stood a feminine *Justice* bearing a sword, while a choir sang "patriotic songs." The tableau reached its climax as a local minister offered prayer. The participation of ministers in these tableaux, along with the evangelical hymn-singing and religious rhetoric, made the image of white womanhood an even more powerful symbol. By juxtaposing Confederate symbolism with white womanhood, and combining both these powerful ideas in the iconography of the South's revivalistic faith, celebrants of Confederate memory transformed onlookers into a true people's army for the coming revolution.[41]

White South Carolina women's public expressions of loyalty to Hampton and his cause strengthened post-Appomattox southern manhood. The rich symbolism they enacted linked Carolina conservatism to divine values. Their bodies became public texts in which the conservative ethos challenged and defeated Reconstruction radicalism. Nina Silber has written that gender, "[b]ecause of its association with 'natural' and immutable functions, . . . has offered a potent metaphor for legitimizing political relationships, for making power arrangements seem basic and fundamental." The Hampton campaign not only used the legitimizing language of gender but also fused it with the sacred values of the evangelical South. Concerns over the loss of rights and the invasion of property blended with the mythic dimensions of the images of womanhood used in the campaign, transforming the women of the Hampton tableaux into the verisimilitude of purity and divine endorsement for the Democratic effort. Beautiful white southern bodies, central to the aesthetic of the Lost Cause, shaped the inchoate longings of yeoman Red Shirts into a conservative ethos that celebrated evangelical truth and depicted the Hampton campaign as a battle for ancient Carolina liberties.[42]

Perhaps the most elaborate tableau occurred at Aiken on October 20. Tensions ran at fever pitch in this region throughout 1876. The Hamburg Massacre had occurred in Aiken County in July of that year. Just three days before Hampton's arrival, President Ulysses S. Grant issued a proclamation supporting Chamberlain's earlier disbanding of the Democratic rifle clubs. When Hampton arrived in Aiken, South Carolina's Palmetto flag greeted him, flying above a stand adorned "with garlands of evergreens." Aiken celebrated southern womanhood by building a platform for the white women of the town and decorating it with mottoes such as "Truth," "Virtue," and "Honor." Hampton, saluted with a legend that read "Hampton—We Love, Welcome, and Honor Him," spoke of his "sorrow that the people of Aiken had been subjected to so much undeserved persecution." Chamberlain, almost as if he desired to play his assigned role in this unfolding drama, decided to arrest a number of suspected "Ku Klux" on the day of Hampton's arrival.[43]

Conservatives used the Hampton campaign's gendered symbolism to dramatize basic power relationships and stave off anxieties about masculinity. Race also played a crucial, if surprising, role both in the iconography of the campaign and in its rhetorical constructions. The anxieties of South Carolina conservatives seem to have been primarily connected to the threat of "radicalism"; images of emancipated blacks as sexual threats to white southern women rarely played a role in the campaign. Hampton's policy toward South Carolina blacks seems to have been to "fuse" with black Republican leaders by offering them some of the spoils of patronage. Such intended cooperation, therefore, played a part in the campaign imagery. The garlanded speakers platform at Aiken, for example, featured what Williams described as "a large cartoon" that "represented the Palmetto [tree] prostrate and white and Negro men working together to lift it and the caption 'While's There's Life, There's Hope.'"

This poster suggests a very different symbolic world from the one that would emerge in the 1890s. In 1876 black men were still seen as faithful retainers with a role to play in the southern social order. Only later, in the late 1880s and 1890s, would they become "black beasts"—inherently dangerous political, sexual, and economic threats—in the white southern mind. The Lost Cause aesthetic in 1876 allowed that white women's bodies had been symbolically, but not literally, victimized by the politics of radicalism. The complete dismantling of the southern social order in the coupling of black and white bodies lay beyond the margins of this generation's cultural imagination, a lurking terror hidden from view.[44]

The racial demonization of African American women, however, did occur. The use of young, white, female bodies to legitimize and explicate an ideology implicitly assumed the marginalization of other bodies. The language of the Hampton campaign placed African American women outside the conservative dream for South Carolina. In part their exclusion resulted from the strong political consciousness that they exhibited before and during the Hampton campaign. Disfranchised and economically vulnerable, African American women believed the Republican Party's suggestion that a Hampton victory would mean a return to slavery. Thus, black women willingly shamed black men who had "crossed Jordan" to the Democratic cause. African American Red Shirt Edward Henderson described how some of his comrades found that their wives "wouldn't sleep in the same bed with them" if they voted with the Democrats; Jonas Weeks, the aforementioned Richland County black Democrat, testified to a congressional committee that a crowd of angry black women had "called me all kinds of names and they would pull off my breeches and call me a devil." Preston Taylor, a black Democrat who had the temerity to cry "Hurrah for Hampton!" as he left the polls, later reported that "the women jumped on me and tore off all my clothes...."[45]

The political consciousness of black women clearly horrified white conservatives as much as it rattled black Democrats since the women's political actions challenged the sacred boundaries of the social order both as women and as black people. Thus, African American women became symbolic counterpoints to the purity of white southern womanhood, that integral symbol of the southern conservative ethos. The rhetoric of the campaign contrasted the "southern lady" sharply with black female supporters of the Republicans. Fashioned by the Democrats as unruly, disorderly, and violent, black women became a symbol of Radical Republicanism in its most appalling aspects. One of the chief charges leveled against "scalawag" Franklin Moses, for example, concerned his alleged dancing "with mulatto prostitutes." Williams wrote that Moses, by "flaunting his vices," helped move white Carolinians from the "habit of submission" to "burning anger and craving for combat." Conservatives believed that black women used their bodies as instruments of political subversion, corrupting Carolina liberties.[46]

Images of disorderly black women abounded in Alfred B. Williams's accounts of the Hampton campaign. Describing a Republican meeting of black South Carolinians on Edisto Island, Williams noted the "very ugly mood" of black women, who seemed "especially maddened and foaming with rage." In another article Williams suggested that the faithfulness of black men to their former masters faced a twin threat from the Union Leagues and the "taunts and abuse of incensed women." Black women greeted the final Hampton Day in Charleston with jeers and catcalls that Williams described as "frantic."[47]

The idea of black women embodying political and sexual disorder epitomized for conservatives the forces of social chaos that threatened the ordered world of white Carolinians. South Carolina matron Florella Meynardie's 1879 novel, *Amy Oakley; or The Reign of the Carpet-Bagger*, contains a fictional representation of a Hampton Day celebration in Charleston in which black women, described as "female demons," shout "bitter, insulting invectives" at the Red Shirts. Significantly, the language of religious impurity also fills Meynardie's descriptions. She uses terms such as "polluted wretch[es]" to describe the black and mulatto women who made up the derisive crowd. Moreover, these unruly women are depicted as destroyers of their own households, with much of their venom directed at their own husbands. In one of Meynardie's scenes, a black woman threatens to rip the red shirt off of her "old man, dat varmit Ike," if he were to don it and join the Democrats.[48] Thus for Meynardie, and it seems for many South Carolina conservatives, politically aware black women came to represent the obliteration of distinction, boundary, balance, and limitation—all quite important terms in the political and social grammar of conservatism. When these women rejected the patriarchal prerogative of their husbands by criticizing their political choices and refused to support Hampton as the new white "master," the women's behavior seeped into the political realm. Unlike the young white southern women who acted out the drama of Carolina's struggle for liberty while personifying the virtues of the defeated South, African American women's uncontrolled bodies flaunted their subversion and challenged the harmony of household and republic. In the cathedral of the Lost Cause, jeering, taunting, politically aware black women became, in the eyes of Carolina conservatives, the gargoyles leering out from the shadows.

Hampton's victory would be a narrow one. Both Radical Republicans and Conservative Democrats perpetrated fraud and used violent coercion to manipulate the vote. The byzantine machinations that led to Hampton's accession to the governorship need not be recited here. Certainly pervasive fraud and extreme brutality made Hampton's victory possible; testimony before Congress later revealed that intimidation had occurred in every South Carolina county, with Aiken and Edgefield, the bailiwick of Martin W. Gary, supplying the most egregious examples. Nevertheless, the commitment of the former Confederates to the resurrected Lost Cause represented by the Hampton campaign provided the crucial unifying element for a white populace that had shown little unity since Appomattox. By April 1877, with the Federal government unwilling to intervene, Hampton would inaugurate what William J. Cooper Jr. has called "the Conservative regime."[49]

The celebration of Hampton's election reemphasized the themes of divine vindication that had been so important in the campaign. An article in the Baptist *Working Christian* announced, "God has crowned the closing year with another blessing. Wade Hampton is our governor. We cannot doubt that every good and perfect gift (and this among them) cometh down from the Father of Lights." "What hath God wrought!" a jubilant John Leland wrote at the end of the campaign: God had delivered South Carolina from her "more than Egyptian bondage."[50]

Most important, Hampton's victory justified the persistence of Confederate memory. "In all the grief and mourning of our stricken State over her 'Lost Cause,'" Leland wrote, "there are found no tears of penitence." South Carolina had not renounced her stand for Confederate nationhood. A sense of Confederate identity continued to play an important role in the southern conservative ethos by informing its defiance of interference by the national government. Confederate memory seemed more sacred than ever, as conservative South Carolinians saw in the Hampton campaign and victory a resurgence and exoneration of the southern cause. Post-Reconstruction South Carolina was, Leland asserted, "re-baptized with the blood of some of her bravest and best." The honor of the state, in question during Radical rule, was restored, as "she once more proudly holds forth her time-honored escutcheon."[51]

Recent interpreters of the Lost Cause have seen it as a nonsectional memorial to sacrifice and death and a celebration of white Americanism that could "easily enter the mainstream of national memory." This view fits easily with an earlier analysis that saw Confederate mythology as a colossal effort to restore southern self-esteem, an effort that never challenged the idea of sectional reunion. Edward L. Ayers has even postulated that the proliferation of Confederate veterans' organizations signaled the South's involvement in a broad, national culture of nostalgia rather than an assertion of its militant difference.[52]

The Hampton Days celebrations challenge these conclusions. An examination of these public spectacles suggests that the interpretation of the Lost Cause has suffered from scholars' shifting the focal point of Confederate memorial culture to the 1880s and 1890s. The perspective of those years, during which towns raised monuments in their squares, and women's memorial societies laid flowers on the graves of dead Confederates, gives credence to the notion that the Lost Cause, for many white southerners, functioned as little more than a nostalgic look at the past and a prop for flagging self-esteem. An analysis of the Hampton campaign, and perhaps other Redemption political contests, demonstrates instead that the Lost Cause provided an idiom for continued resistance to the Federal government and a ritual embodiment of the southern conservative ethos. Hampton's campaign shows that South Carolinians publicly celebrated the Lost Cause as a direct challenge to the Federal and Republican-dominated state governments. The bodies of white southern women were placed on display, exhibiting in sometimes elaborate tableaux the hopes and yearnings of South Carolina conservatives, even as the language of the campaign expressed the terror of uncontrolled black female bodies.

The powerful reaction that the aesthetic of the Lost Cause provoked among South Carolina whites did little to salve some of their most pressing concerns. Land loss and the slide into tenantry continued unabated and worsened in the 1880s. Despite the defiant tones of the Hampton campaign, Carolina yeoman could not even protect their own homesteads from creditors, much less defend "our Mother, South Carolina." Bourbon leaders in South Carolina, traditional historical views to the contrary, attempted to protect the freeholds of their constituents. They could not, however, reverse the economic fate of the farmer in the gilded age. Their failure would sunder the conservative worldview and make way for the Tillman aegis.

CHAPTER SEVEN

The Maintenance of Honor and Manhood

Southern Conservatives and the Agrarian Revolt

S. E. May had seen the struggle for southern independence, Wade Hampton's Red Shirt campaign, and the farmers' protests of the 1880s. The last decade of the nineteenth century promised even more catastrophic change. In 1895, a letter from May to a fellow Confederate veteran described how the Palmetto State had been experiencing "a great upheaval of the people." May was convinced that the rabble-rousing Ben Tillman, of Edgefield, who had become governor in 1890 and would dominate the state into the twentieth century, had not been the man to lead that upheaval. Hampton should have led the charge, May asserted, but "made the mistake of his life by allowing himself to be entangled in a faction." This was a reference to Hampton's brief flirtation with the Haskellite movement that had attempted to challenge Tillman by putting together a shaky alliance of Bourbons and black South Carolinians. May had left South Carolina, uneasy with the excesses of Tillman, disappointed in the behavior of Hampton, and disgusted with the turn taken by Confederate memorial associations; no longer were they brave warriors attempting to remember their dead. May referred to the leaders of the South Carolina United Confederate Veterans as "the most incorrigible skulkers from real duty in the Army of Northern Virginia." In May's eyes, the guiding light of Confederate virtue had grown dim, and the state's political culture had suffered accordingly.[1]

S. E. May embodies the ideological stance of numerous Confederate veterans and Red Shirts who saw no paradox in their involvement in the farmers movement and their Confederate identity. In the 1890s, many of the South Carolina Alliancemen continued to hold to the conservative ideal of an organic society shaped by the aesthetic of the Lost Cause.

Many of this generation saw themselves engaged in a lifelong struggle to preserve this social order against the forces of political and economic centralization, forces that threatened to end their way of life. They expressed this struggle by joining the Confederate army, the Klan, the Grange, the rifle clubs, and the Southern Farmer's Alliance. The unrest at century's end would unhinge the commitment of these Carolina white men to the notion of an organic society. Former Confederate leaders, like Hampton, would indeed find themselves "entangled in a faction," as the state divided along lines of economic interest and cultural change that transformed the meanings of the old symbols. The Farmer's Alliance represents the last great charge of traditional southern conservatism in South Carolina, a charge as ill-starred as Pickett's and of much more consequence for the state's racial, social, and economic history.

Interpreting the South Carolina farmers movement as growing from roots entangled with southern conservatism requires a break with much of the current historiography of the postbellum South. Historians have sometimes divided the agrarian radicalism of the 1880s from the celebration of the Lost Cause, often creating a melodrama in which protoradical farmers challenged conservatives over issues of economic justice. In this telling of the tale, Conservative Democrats successfully overreached the flanks of the farmers with a two-pronged assault of Confederate memory and white supremacy. C. Vann Woodward's magisterial *Origins of the New South, 1877–1913*, as well as other works by this late dean of southern historians, has been largely responsible for structuring this dichotomy between Bourbons and agrarians, seeing a clear dividing line between "the populist South" and the "planter-Confederate South."[2]

Historians such as Steven Hahn, Robert McMath, and Lawrence Goodwyn have buttressed this view with their intensive studies of southern populism. Interpreters of postbellum agrarianism have tended to view it as "a manifestation of American radicalism," a sort of rural variety of labor unionism. Lawrence Goodwyn believes that a progressive "movement culture" in the Farmer's Alliance helped fashion a cooperative ethos that then found expression in the People's Party of the 1890s, a third party whose platform included a radical critique of the American economic order. Steven Hahn argues that southern populism drew on rural traditions of helpfulness combined with sharp class antagonism.[3]

The desire to find in populism an example of genuine American radicalism has been motivated in part by the understandable desire to revise an earlier historiography that portrayed the farmers of the South and West as reactionaries. Richard Hofstader, and many students of western and midwestern populism, framed this argument, seeing in populism a "paranoid-style" of American politics. Populism, according to this older interpretation, became a social and political hothouse, where all the exotic growths of America racism, paranoia, and xenophobia bloomed under the care of rural creeps and cranks. Woodward particularly attempted to correct this view, noting that it grew from an older generation of historians' distaste and distrust for "mass man," a fear of the fascistic tendencies of the great unwashed, rather than a real analysis of the movement's identity and goals.[4]

Historians who have accepted these findings, findings that hold much value for parts of the American South, have tended to disassociate the Lost Cause movement from late-nineteenth-century farmers' protests. Charles Reagan Wilson, for example, noted that Confederate commemoration celebrated agrarianism but that "the agrarianism of the Lost Cause was aristocratic and conservative while the agrarianism of Populism was democratic and reformist." Gaines Foster sees a similar dichotomy, insisting that Bourbons "proved themselves masters at evoking the Confederate tradition and did so in order to defeat the Populists."[5]

An examination of South Carolina's agrarian protest movement reveals that "the planter-Confederate South" of the Lost Cause interconnected with the movement of agrarian protest, revealing the antibourgeois nature of South Carolina's romantic conservatism. Woodward himself noted that the spokesmen for the agrarian movement "would never have overcome their handicaps had they not been able to appeal to a great body of native southern tradition and doctrine."[6] This "great body" of tradition included an attachment to the ideal and reality of the freehold that structured an organic society where white men practiced virtue, understood after 1865 as Confederate virtue. White man's virtue could only be practiced within a framework of hierarchical social relationships that placed black and female Carolinians in subordinate social spaces.

The rise of a farmers movement in South Carolina coincided with a slow, but perceptible, disillusionment with the Bourbons. Hampton served as governor until 1879 and was followed in office by such loyal representatives of the old regime as Johnson Hagood and Hugh Thompson. In the 1880s, as economic depression and the continuing effects of war and emancipation shattered white man's world of land and hierarchy, frustrated Carolina farmers turned to the conservative ethos. Expressing their acceptance of hierarchy grounded in virtue, they often turned to leaders who embodied the Lost Cause to challenge banks, railroads, and the gold standard. Hampton seemed to show little understanding of these issues and exercised little control over the Bourbon Democrats in the 1880s. William J. Cooper writes that Hampton had "virtually abdicated" leadership of the South Carolina Bourbons by the 1880s.[7]

The organizational predecessor of the South Carolina Farmer's Alliance, the state Grange, had its roots in the economic frustrations and property-loss so prevalent during Reconstruction. D. Wyatt Aiken, a former Confederate general, member of the legislature, and an adamant opponent of all things northern, became the founder and leading figure of the South Carolina Grangers, embodying the state's southern conservatism, Confederate memory, and devotion to agriculture. Aiken had, like many Carolina planters, lost everything in the war and his view of his own economic difficulties drew directly on his Confederate experience. "I inherited two fortunes," he said in the spring of 1871, "One ended in smoke when Sherman's army passed through South Carolina, the other feathered its wings with the Emancipation act and flew away." Aiken's politics would give the movement a much more activist identity than it exhibited in many other southern states where the Grange functioned, according to McMath, as a continuation of the "genteel antebellum agricultural societies." South Carolina's Patrons of Husbandry, in contrast, acted in conjunction with the Ku Klux Klan and the rifle clubs to coordinate efforts to overthrow Reconstruction and to solve "the labor question" by forcing the freedpeople to work the land of their former masters.[8]

The use of coercion and violence against the freedpeople aimed at the restoration of the *status quo antebellum*. The rule of the independent white patriarch, holding sway over his own fifty- to one-hundred-acre fiefdom, remained the southern conservative ideal, and the Grange movement hoped to ensure the possibility of that ideal in the midst of the economic and political dislocations of Reconstruction. Grange educational efforts centered on the region's becoming less dependent on staple production, while still using various kinds of unfree labor, thus allowing white farmers to act as independent patriarchs in the postwar period. The Grange's clarion call for scientific agriculture promised a return to the independent past by increasing production through the use of guano and other fertilizers. Grangers thus faced the irony of needing a secure economic base from which to practice their independence while feeling anxious that moneymaking itself might undercut virtue and liberty. One doggerel poet from Barnwell County urged Carolina farmers to withdraw from the market in the face of an agricultural apocalypse:

Our Hands and Feet securely Bound
We'd Toil for Middle Men all Around
For Speculators and Spinners
A Vampire Crew-Saints or Sinner
Who Care not how the cotton blooms
So long as it feeds futures and looms[9]

Anxious over the fate of liberty and virtue amid the "vampire crew" of emerging American capitalism, the leadership of the Grange could be surprisingly optimistic about the postbellum world. Aiken actually believed that war and emancipation offered more promise than peril in assuring the continuance of southern conservative ideals. Speaking to the Barnwell County Agricultural and Mechanical Society in January 1871, Aiken charged that antebellum planters had not "attached themselves to the soil" because cotton and slavery yielded enormous profits if the planter engaged in an "exhaustive system of agriculture," left his depleted Carolina soil behind and moved to "the wild west." Engagement in capitalist agriculture, Aiken insisted, led again and again to "the abandonment of home." In something of a rhetorical sleight-of-hand, Aiken suggested that failure to engage in scientific agriculture came about because of a desire on the part of the planter to "enrich his pockets" and a lack of recognition that agriculture had spiritual dimensions. Even as he praised agricultural advances of the modern world, the former Confederate colonel asserted that "the spirit of the noisy nineteenth century where the developments of science had emboldened man" tempted the farmer from his high calling of "private worth and social virtue."[10]

Aiken's promotion of scientific agriculture that made the farmer more productive, expressed simultaneously with warnings about the dangers of profitable agricultural, exposed faults in Granger ideology. The Granger ideology seemed to suggest that enterprising farmers should pursue profit, but only if it represented more than simple financial gain. Aiken darkly contrasted what he called "the utilatarians" of the age with the South Carolina farmer whose devotion centered, not finally on profit and productivity, but rather on the "venerable homestead." Aiken exhorted the Barnwell farmers to make use of "every creditable device . . . to create local attachments." Showing the continued influence of a romantic conservatism on South Carolinians, Aiken urged that "the resting places of the dead should be frequented" so that farmers would have a sense of ancestral obligation to the lands they farmed.[11] Scientific agriculture, in Aiken's view, tied the farmer close to his land and his ancestors rather than freed him to become a bourgeois agrarian capitalist. Yet production allegedly expanded when the farmer put into practice scientific methods, granting the farmer "private worth." Anxious over the dangers of profits and markets, the Grange and, later, the Farmer's Alliance never encouraged a true subsistence agriculture and a disavowal of profit-taking. Just as in the antebellum era, turning a profit could serve as the handmaiden of liberty.

Attachment to home included attachment to a tight web of social relations structured by assumptions about paternalism and hierarchy rather than by the Thirteenth Amendment. The problem of labor, Aiken averred, could be solved by the continued use of what he called the "inferior race" that still inhabited South Carolina. Aiken wrote that while the "inferior race" could no longer be enslaved, all agreed that "they must be guided by superior intelligence." The Grange put such a high priority on the continued use of black labor that the cover of the *Rural Carolinian*, the organ of the state Grange, featured a field worked by black laborers, while the fruits of scientific agriculture flourished wildly about the edges. Cotton retained an honored place in this cornucopia but shared its throne with corn, wheat, potatoes, beans, and watermelons.[12]

The role of white women remained central to the creation of "a venerable homestead"; they served in a clearly subordinate position while surrounded by an elaborate mythology that made them a symbol of loyalty to the South and a kind of agricultural muse that served as a metonym for the life of "private worth and social virtue" that grew from liberty and property. Agricultural reformers, adapting to the realities of the postemancipation world, presented a southern lady unashamed to aid her husband on the farm. This did mark a change in attitude toward white women's labor, but should be placed in context of the changing roles of women in the larger American society. The *Rural Carolinian* often groused bitterly about the changing role of women in American society, believing that such demands constituted an attack on nature and Providence, undercutting the "attachments to home" they believed so important. One 1870 writer, familiar with some of the more radical demands of northern feminists, suggested that with the calls for "female suffrage, female doctors and female clergymen" might be added a call for "female women."[13]

The Grange, thus, not only concerned itself with the protection of property but also sought to shore up a construction of southern manhood centered on the idea of mastery and, allegedly, service as a force for social harmony. Agrarian leaders, in their war with industrial capitalism, constructed an image of southern masculinity not unfamiliar to Carolina yeomen. The Grange drew heavily on southern conservatism's devotion to a hierarchical social order in which independent white men mastered the labor of their families, "white and black." Such had not been the case in the movement's first years. The spread of the national Grange into South Carolina sputtered at first, because its charter allowed women to join local chapters, an element of the organization that led some critics to calls it "a women's rights institution." D. Wyatt Aiken, however, made it quite clear that the movement strengthened male independence and the patriarchal family he ruled, calling the Grange a place where "the father's manhood" and "the mother's devotion are cemented."[14]

Aiken's mention of devotion to ancestral graves and shrines shows that he had deeply imbibed Carolina's version of romantic conservatism, an ideology that reimagined the past to support structures and social arrangements in the present. The Confederate past, the heroic age of South Carolina, played this role among the discontented farmers. The aesthetic of the Lost Cause played a central role in giving legitimation to the white farmers' independence, his liberty from impersonal economic forces. The Confederate war effort, in the ideology of South Carolina Grangers, represented the paradigmatic attempt to secure liberty for white men and to protect organic social institutions from the assaults of modernity. The Grange represented another effort, and the sometimes subtle blending of the two emerges in the pages of the *Rural Carolinian,* with articles about the best way to whiten a straw hat or build a strong farm gate appearing in the same issue with tributes to Wade Hampton and popular Civil War poetry. In March 1871, Confederate General Johnson Hagood received a laudatory tribute in the *Rural Carolinian,* both for his "praiseworthy service to the state," resisting Yankee incursions into the low country during the war, combined with the fact that he "planted no lands without the use of manures." Hagood represented the Granger ideal; he used scientific methods, properly fertilized his fields, and raised his own draft animals so as to be "independent of the world."[15] Confederate virtue made for good farming.

Sectionalism and the issues of Reconstruction remained a prominent feature of the Grange movement in South Carolina, linking the agrarian protest to a revised edition of Confederate nationalism. An 1884 address by Benjamin F. Perry revealed the continued depth of sectional feeling. Speaking to the Pendleton Farmer Society, an antebellum survival that had important connections to both the Granger movement and, later, to the Farmer's Alliance, Perry suggested that the problems of "the agricultural interest" grew from white Carolinians being "heavily and oppres-

continued section / animosity

sively taxed . . . to protect northern manufactures." Perry, in fact, compared the 1880s to the days of "radical rule," when "audacious rogues
and ignorant scoundrels" pursued a policy of "ruinous taxation."[16] Perry
clearly shifted blame for the woes of the farmers from state Bourbon
policies to national policies and interests, while taking up the cudgel of
agrarianism against the "manufacturing interest" that had played a role
in South Carolina politics since Calhoun's crusade against the tariff.

Similar concerns appeared in 1879 in a failed third-party effort by a
party that attracted those who felt that 1876 had not created the desider-
atum it had seemed to promise. Feeling that the Redeemer government
took too little interest in the plight of Carolina farmers, J. Hendrix
McLane, of Fairfield County, used his leadership of the local Grange
to create the Greenback-Labor party. South Carolina "Greenbackers,"
as they quickly became known, focused heavily on national issues of
tariff and currency rather than on animus against the Bourbon regime.
McLane, a Confederate veteran and a straight-out Red Shirt in 1876, used
his Greenback platform to proclaim a strange brew of class enmity, a republican suspicion of concentrated economic power, and an Aristotelian
attitude about "the sterility of currency." McLane made few inroads in
1880, failing to recruit D. Wyatt Aiken to the tiny party's standard,
largely because Aiken disliked McLane's open calls for fusion with the
Republicans. The Greenbackers also faced the charge that they sought to
create a movement similar to William Mahone's "Readjuster" movement
in Virginia that had rallied blacks and whites around the concern of free
common schools and debt.[17]

discontent w/ Bourbon rule, too

The year 1882 offered the Greenbackers a more significant opportunity, in part because of discontent hinged on the miserable harvests of
1881 and, they hoped, because the Abbeville County movement allied itself with former Confederate general E. B. C. Cash. Cash seemed a strange
choice as a party standard-bearer for a number of reasons. First, he had
had personal and political links to Martin W. Gary, who had died in
1880. Gary, though devoted to the notion of economic reform to ensure
economic independence, could likely never have given his blessing to a
party that openly courted black votes. Cash did seek the votes of black
Republicans in a way that enraged his former Red Shirt compatriots, including Benjamin Tillman, and provoked a round of violence and assassination. A dark specter passed over the minds of many Carolina whites,
the frightening possibility of native whites at war with native whites and
the end of their organic social order.[18]

Cash seemed an odd choice for a struggling third party also because he had become, in 1880, the center of one of South Carolina's greatest controversies. A supporter of the Hampton campaign, steeped in antebellum notions of aristocratic manhood, Cash had challenged the railroad lawyer William Shannon to a duel, believing Shannon to have impugned his dead wife's honor in a legal matter. Shannon repeatedly refused (the antidueling laws adopted by the 1868 constitution remained in place), but Cash finally goaded him into granting satisfaction. Cash, reportedly a dead shot, killed the older man and, seemingly to his surprise, found the Democratic Party's leadership split over his actions.[19]

Stephen Kantrowitz has argued that the Cash-Shannon duel exposed the differing conceptions of manhood in the postbellum South Carolina upcountry. The controversy certainly suggests a changing view of southern manhood, in which a bourgeois conception of handling conflict militated against the older notions of the code duello. The controversy also served as a flashpoint for differing conceptions of South Carolina's social order. Martin W. Gary supported Cash, as did many of his maverick followers, who tended to take the popular side of issues such as the usury law and the homestead exemption. Matthew Butler, now a United States senator, challenged Cash's actions, even as he decried the state's adoption of a usury law, and often spoke for corporate interests that the fallen duelist, William Shannon, so often had represented.[20]

Cash failed to lead the Greenback-Labor party to victory, or to even a substantial showing in 1882. The party's failure came about both because the Red Shirt companies did their old work of voter intimidation and, perhaps more important, because Cash fractured his own fragile coalition. Though often speaking out against violence toward black Carolinians, he made it clear that be believed that whites would remain the ruling race, and blacks would serve as a subordinate labor source. One of the primary arguments made in his stump speeches urged whites to practice moderation toward black Carolinians, not because they deserved equal protection before the law, but rather because violence would drive them out of the state and deplete Carolina's labor supply. The Greenback-Labor party of South Carolina, not unlike the Democrats, affirmed a hierarchical social order in which white men enjoyed liberty based on property ownership, and black Carolinians provided labor for the most backbreaking undertakings. Greenbackers like Cash differed from the Democrats in their belief that South Carolina had a long way to go to reach this ideal and in their assertion that white farmers, themselves, were gradually slipping out of their "place" within the social hierarchy in ways that threatened racial mores and raised the possibility of class warfare.

The failure of the Greenbackers did not end the feeling among South Carolina white men that their ordered worlds were not secure. The South Carolina Farmer's Alliance, pushed into existence by continuing economic turmoil, served as a rallying point for the forces of conservative reaction to social and cultural transformations sweeping through the upcountry. The events of 1876 and the return of a Confederate Carolinian to the statehouse had not turned back the tide of change, nor silenced the "noisy nineteenth century." The Farmer's Alliance, like the taxpayers movement, the Ku Klux Klan, the Red Shirts, and the Grangers, represented an organized effort by southern conservatives to reinstitute the mores of the antebellum world, or at least a purified form of that world. The Farmer's Alliance in South Carolina resisted the emerging New South worlds of railroads and banks and eschewed the more radical path taken by the left wing of the national Farmer's Alliance.

The Southern Farmer's Alliance had its genesis on the prairies and in the cross-timber settlements of West Texas. The movement spread quickly throughout much of the old Confederacy in the late 1880s, absorbing the Patrons of Husbandry and a similar organization known as the Agricultural Wheel. The Farmer's Alliance stressed unity among agricultural workers and the building of cooperative stores, and used a germinal language of class warfare directed at merchants, bankers, and lawyers. Born on the Texas frontier, the Alliance expressed the concerns of landowning farmers throughout the South who faced the prospect of declension from freeholders into laborers, independent patriarchs into dependent tenants. The Alliance arrived in the southern seaboard states in the 1880s with particularly strong organizations in North Carolina and Georgia.[21]

The Farmer's Alliance in South Carolina had its origins in the low country, in 1887, but quickly spread, "like a summer wildfire," according to historian Walter Edgar, throughout all the upcountry counties. In 1888, the first year in which a strong state organization existed, Alliance membership exploded from three thousand to twenty thousand members, with 754 suballiances and 31 county alliances. L. L. Polk, the leader of the North Carolina Alliance and a national figure in the movement, wrote to South Carolina's secretary, J. W. Reid, to praise the spread of the order, noting that South Carolina had 870 suballiances, and "still they come." Robert McMath and Stephen Kantrowitz conclude that the South Carolina Alliance never became fully independent of Benjamin Tillman's movement, unlike in other southern states where the Alliance often swallowed earlier farmers' organizations. The Alliance and Tillman's organization did share membership and even some organizational structure, but in the late 1880s the Alliance clearly acted as the senior partner.[22]

The ideology of the Farmer's Alliance focused heavily on the Granger's goal of independence tied closely to antebellum conceptions of southern manhood. Spokesmen for the movement made an argument familiar to the ears of Carolina yeoman of the 1850s and 1870s, calling upon them to assert their manhood in the face of faraway centralized powers that sought to destroy their worlds of private worth and social virtue. J. William Stokes, editor of the Alliance *Cotton Plant* and later state Alliance president, warned that "northern financial interest" sought to "sap your manhood." In April 1889 a resolution of the Anderson County Alliance made clear their objective to "stand together as a solid phalanx for the maintenance of our honor and manhood."[23]

Agricultural distress had substantially worsened in the 1880s owing to a combination of several years of drought that blasted successive crops, and national trends that affected farmers in the North and West as much as the South. National policies, such as high tariffs (the ancient enemy of southern cotton producers), the rising power of Wall Street speculation in cotton futures, and currency contraction caused by the demonetization of silver, struck staple-producing southern farmers with special force. Emancipation had not only destroyed the South's primary capital investment, but the end of the slave economy had set off a wave of southern bank failures that added to the problems occasioned by shrinking currency. Furthermore, in both North and South, agricultural change moved in the direction of large-scale operations and away from small farmers, toward tenancy and away from ownership, away from the age of the independent yeoman and toward a bourgeois future. The possibility of profit raised by the years of high cotton prices in the late 1860s pushed the small farmer into making a few extra bales on acreage on which he could have grown corn. Falling into indebtedness in an effort to expand production with more land and equipment, Carolina farmers found themselves caught in what Gilbert C. Fite has called the "agricultural trap." Small unproductive farms represented independence from the market, but nothing resembling the possibilities of profit inherent in large-scale operations or the in new, consumer lifestyles being proffered in the pages of the Sears catalog that turned up in parlors and outhouses all across the South, beginning in the 1880s.[24]

The Grange had attempted to respond to these difficulties by its call for a scientific agriculture that would preserve southern conservative ideals of liberty and hierarchy in the midst of agricultural distress. Its great limitation, in the eyes of many Carolinians, inhered in its tendency to blame the farmers' behavior for the farming crisis. National issues, rather than simply repetitive calls for a more scientific agriculture, required the attention of a united farmers movement. Moreover, South Carolina farmers felt that the national Grange had diluted its purpose in the North by making peace with banks, railroads, and Wall Street, that the organization had been pirated by "men whose capital was invested in enterprises inimical to the farmer." [25] In contrast to the Grange, the Farmer's Alliance seemed the instrument fit for the purpose, as it combined calls for scientific agriculture with a profound critique of the reunited nation's emerging bourgeois economy.

The first meeting of the state Alliance made it clear that the troubles facing the farmers of the state grew from national issues. Tillmanism, which had become quiescent after the Edgefield firebrand's speech in 1885, also stressed the maliciousness of faraway trusts but made much more of the wickedness of Bourbon "rings" (corrupt political networks made up of former Confederate generals) and the impractical young aristocrats being produced by South Carolina College and the Citadel. The Farmer's Alliance would eschew such a language of class, instead voicing traditional southern conservative fears about the centralization of power and the consequent dangers to liberty. Alliancemen who met in 1888 passed a resolution asserting that the order had grown so quickly because of the need "to avert the ruin which must result from the continued centralization of money and political power." One address at the meeting of the state Alliance voiced the fear, shared by South Carolinians since the Jacksonian era and fully developed by Calhoun, that the government had turned "the National Banking system into a great money trust." A call for the farmers of Lexington County to organize declared that, "the whole class of farmers are kept down" by what the Alliance organizer referred to darkly as "the money power." [26]

The Farmer's Alliance in South Carolina had an agenda much broader than discussions of proper fertilizing techniques or even challenges to the "monopolies and trusts" that stalked the landscape of the Gilded Age. The Alliance also acted as a watchdog for community mores and helped to structure the meaning of resistance to the emerging world of the New South. The spotty records kept by county and suballiance cells of "rejections and expulsions" reveal an organization committed to a patriarchal ethos, and a critique of the emerging town milieu. M. P. Player, of the Bear Creek suballiance in Chesterfield County, was expelled for "whippen his wife"; A. Cox found himself ejected from the order for what was obscurely called "improper conduct." Other expulsions or rejections from the order followed the Alliance's commitment to the interests of the farmer and expressed a challenge to the new, professional town elite. In Spartanburg, the Cairns suballiance suspended J. W. Alexander for "going into mercantile business," and J. J. Bennet for "reading law." In this way, the Alliance performed a function similar to that of the antebellum evangelical churches that had desired to shape into an organic social ideal the often recalcitrant wills of South Carolinians. The chaplains of each suballiance who opened the meetings with prayer surely underscored the interconnections between evangelical faith and Alliance membership and discipline. Ironically, the Alliance continued to practice "discipline" against its members even as the practice began to decline in the Carolina churches of the 1880s and '90s.[27]

The Alliance saw its mission as shaping a social and economic world in which independent men could profit from agriculture, and thus bring about D. Wyatt Aiken's dream of "private worth and social virtue." Their producerist ideology, which viewed agricultural labor as the truest form of labor and saw the professions as parasitical elements in society, led them to reject lawyers, merchants, and bankers as members of their fellowship. At the same time, the southern conservative ideal of an organic society sublimated the growth of hard-and-fast class lines. For example, in the Spartanburg County report in which Alexander and Bennett received their suspensions for entering the merchant class and studying law, respectively, a note scrawled at the bottom of the official report sought to make the state secretary understand that both were "honorable young men nevertheless," suggesting the notion that participation in the southern culture of honor carried more weight than Alliance membership. The constitution of the South Carolina Farmer's Alliance further illustrates this wary attitude toward class warfare. Though modeled on the constitution of the national Alliance and those of its sister southern states, the Carolina Alliance excluded the platform's call for the "unity of action on the part of the laboring classes," an idea included in, for example, the Virginia Alliance's constitution. At the third annual meeting of the state Alliance in Newberry, Alliance president William Stokes used his address to praise "the local honest merchant" and placed the onus for the Alliancemen's financial straits on northern "financial despots." The enemies of the southern organic social order, this fact suggests, were regional rather than tied to any specific occupation.[28]

The commitment of the Farmer's Alliance to challenging the emerging corporate culture of America did not suffer from their lack of sympathy with a particular model of class struggle. Sectionalism, a deep distrust of concentrated political and economic power, and a culture of dissent drawing on the aesthetic of the Lost Cause pushed the Carolina Farmer's Alliance to openly challenge the increasingly bourgeois ideals of the late nineteenth century. The romantic conservatism of the Lost Cause gave added weight to the critique of profoundly unjust economic conditions. The dream of ordered worlds challenged the social Darwinist assumptions of the world emerging from the "incorporation of America."[29]

A conservative agrarian critique of Gilded Age America formed a crucial element in the ideology of the Lost Cause throughout the South. The roots of this dissent grew out of the antebellum identification of concentrated economic power with northern society. South Carolina had its own Cato the Elder, virulently criticizing the "industrial interests" and their corruption of civic virtue, in the form of John C. Calhoun. Calhoun, in his opposition to the tariff during the 1832–33 Nullification Crisis, had linked a consolidated and centralized government with economic despotism by suggesting that the Federal government used the powers of taxation and regulation to create new financial classes that would support the Leviathan state. Calhoun, writing in his 1830 *Exposition and Protest,* expressed the fear that a powerful Federal government linked to business interests would transform the republic into a "great joint stock company." Calhoun had darkly warned the North that once southern republicans "are exhausted, the contest will be between the Capitalists and the Operatives . . . under operation of the system wages will sink much more rapidly than the prices of the necessaries of life." By the time of the Civil War, the image of the Yankee embodied for South Carolinians all the heartless, accumulative, entrepreneurial vices of unbridled capitalism. Meanwhile, as Charles Reagan Wilson has convincingly argued, Confederate heroes and their warrior virtues became the spiritual ideals of the Lost Cause movement, symbols that stood in sharp contrast to the getting and spending of America's Gilded Age. Such a powerful critique of the emerging world of economic modernity strengthened the Alliancemen's view of postbellum America.[30]

The Alliance, like the Granger movement before it, leaned heavily on the Lost Cause movement. Links between the Lost Cause aesthetic permeated the South Carolina Farmer's Alliance, both in its rhetoric of resistance and in its leadership, with prominent figures in the Lost Cause celebration taking an active role in the Farmer's Alliance. For example, from 1895 until 1897, George B. Lake served as commander of the Abner Perrin Camp of the United Confederate Veterans, in Edgefield, while also serving as a lecturer for one of Edgefield County's suballiances. Lake's entire family took an active part in Lost Cause commemoration, with his teenage daughter serving as camp sponsor to a United Confederate Veterans reunion in 1897. M. C. Butler described Lake as being quite poor, though "poverty could not cow him." Butler also praised the Alliance lecturer as being an enemy of both "radical Reconstruction and sham reform," suggesting that Lake became one of Benjamin Tillman's agrarian opponents in the 1890s.[31]

John J. Dargan, who had close familial connections with Wade Hampton, became one of the most outspoken proponents of agricultural reform, viewing the national policies of the Republican Party and the "manufacturing interests" of the North as the great evils preying on southern farmsteads. Dargan traced the woes of the South Carolina farmer from Appomattox, telling one northern audience in 1886 that "the war . . . for the liberation of the black man has given birth to another form of slavery for the white man." Dargan singled out the protective tariff as an especially heinous example of northern perfidy and, for good measure, blamed the North for the international slave trade. A struggle against the tariff and for reform in national politics, Dargan asserted, represented a struggle "for South Carolina's honor." Linking the struggle against the capitalist north on behalf of the "unprotected classes" to the Confederate war effort, Dargan told a Brooklyn audience that the people of South Carolina still wept "tears of deepest affection on the graves of the gallant Confederate dead." Any who enter the struggle for "liberty in America," Dargan crowed, "will find the Palmetto flag advanced over the front rank."[32]

Colonel D. K. Norris, of Anderson County, also combined devotion to the Lost Cause aesthetic and the Farmer's Alliance movement. An officer in the Second South Carolina Artillery, Norris received severe wounds at the Battle of Bentonville, the Army of Tennessee's final stand against Sherman, in 1865. Not only an important figure in upcountry Lost Cause celebrations, Norris serves as an example of continuity from the antebellum agricultural societies to the Granger movement and finally to the rise of the Alliance. Norris served as the president of the Pendleton Farmer's Society, an organization with roots reaching back to the 1830s. Norris, following the war, used the organizational structure of the society to create a successful Granger movement in Anderson County. Norris himself rose within the ranks of the Alliance to serve two consecutive terms as state president and to run in 1890, according to one observer, "as a farmer's candidate."[33]

Most significantly, prominent leaders in the Lost Cause movement played crucial roles in the organizational structure of the Alliance. S. L. Ready and W. S. Allen, of Edgefield, led a committee of the Edgefield County Farmer's Alliance in an effort to establish an Alliance Cooperative Bank in January 1890. Both Ready and Allen also served in prominent roles in the Edgefield County Confederate veterans movements, serving, for example, as delegates to the dedication of the Chickamauga National Military Park in 1895 and on a committee to erect a monument to Abner Perrin, an Edgefield Confederate general. Joel Hough, meanwhile, acted as the secretary of the Kershaw County Farmer's Alliance while acting as adjutant general of the Richard Kirkland Camp of the United Confederate Veterans. W. F. Reid, another Confederate veteran in Camden, played a prominent role in the county Alliance's executive committee. In Lexington County, cooperation between the Farmer's Alliance and the Ladies Memorial Association became so close that the memorial association used the county Alliance meeting as a fundraising event, serving barbecue and ice cream to raise money for a Lexington County Confederate monument.[34]

A shared leadership between the farmers movement and Lost Cause organizations could simply suggest that the South Carolina elite joined veteran and Alliance organizations as equivalent expressions of civic concern. However, the language of the Lost Cause appeared to be the rhetoric of the Farmer's Alliance as it marched out to face "Yankee trusts." William Stokes, too young himself to have fought in the Confederate army, used part of his speech at the Spartanburg gathering of the Alliance to invoke Robert E. Lee and his devotion to the southern cause as a model for the Alliancemen who prepared for "the coming conflict" of the 1892 election cycle. In Abbeville County, an Alliance lecturer with the liberty-loving name of Patrick Henry Adams, traced much of the South's agricultural distress to the failure to prevent emancipation. Placing the burden for Carolina's farming woes on "the northern capitalist," Adams described the Alliance struggle as another chance to exhibit "southern manhood and southern heroism."[35] The Alliance organ in South Carolina, the *Cotton Plant,* frequently included discussions of the wartime heroism of its leaders. In 1890, for example, the paper featured an article on state Alliance president E. T. Stackhouse that focused on his service in the Eighth South Carolina under E. B. C. Cash.[36]

The continued commitment of Carolina Alliancemen to the Lost Cause also emerges in their relationship to the national Farmer's Alliance and its goals. The national Alliance stressed sectional reunion, the necessity of the agricultural classes of South, North, and Northwest binding together against their common enemies in Washington and Wall Street. South Carolina's farmers, in contrast, continued to make use of a Lost Cause aesthetic in the form of references to Confederate heroism and the evocation of agrarian protest as a continuation of the southern war for independence, militated against the ideology of sectional reunion prominent in the national order. The occasional willingness to express solidarity with other sections of the country reveals the issues important to the Alliancemen. The 1891 meeting of the state Alliance, presided over by Joseph Keitt, son of Ellison Keitt, passed a resolution against the Federal election law proposed by Henry Cabot Lodge, known throughout the South as the "force bill." Included in the resolution was an appeal to the farmers of the North and Northwest to join South Carolina in rejecting this renewed "bayonet rule." Clearly, white Alliancemen in South Carolina would rejoin the Union only so long as they could preserve their paternalistic white supremacy and continue to resist incursions on their social arrangements by the Republican Party.

The Carolina state Alliance members sometimes expressed support themselves for their northern allies, though often on issues that had a resonance for conservative Carolina's resistance to Federal intervention in local institutions and arrangements. The fifth annual meeting of the state Alliance in 1892, for example, expressed sympathy for the northern railroad workers who had taken part in the violent Homestead strike in Pennsylvania. Eager to express their distrust of government action, the Alliancemen evoked old republican fears of "standing armies" to excoriate governmental action against the strikers. Their concern for the outcome of the strike rested more on their horror of Federal troops' being used against the citizens of the United States, with the shades of Reconstruction that image invoked, than on the treatment of northern railroad workers.[37]

The Alliance grew in number and strength in the late 1880s. Oddly, many of South Carolina's Bourbon leadership seemed disengaged from the rising chorus of agricultural discontent. Hampton and M. C. Butler spent much of their time in Washington as United States senators during the 1880s and 1890s, a period of service that moderated their often virulent sectionalism. Hampton attempted to stay above the fray, and out of touch, with regard to many of the more controversial episodes of the 1880s in South Carolina. Hampton, who had ridden at the head of many of the men who led the agrarian protest, gave little indication in public pronouncements that he knew of the Farmer's Alliance existence.[38]

While Hampton transformed himself from a rebel warlord to a respectable senator, the South Carolina Democratic Party's political leadership successfully ran a number of colorless candidates for governor. They all tended to express sympathy with the farmers' plight but seemed stultified by even the simplest request for aid, such as for the creation of agricultural experimental stations or that more priority be given to the study of agriculture at South Carolina College. Such somnolence with regard to "the basis of all wealth" cannot be explained with simple reference to southern anxiety over an activist government. The state government did take an active role in structuring commercial and economic relationships in the state, but it was often a negative role. Willing to restrict and regulate railroads, few of the stingy Bourbon leaders believed that any activity should receive anything resembling a state subsidy, even agriculture.

The refusal of the Bourbons to deal forthrightly with the emerging crisis shows the beginnings of a new cultural ideal in South Carolina, an ideal that will be explored fully in the following chapters. Bourgeois notions of property-holding emerge in Bourbon rhetoric clearly at odds with both the antebellum ideal and the ideology of Grangers and Alliancemen that praised the white patriarch, whose liberty grew from land and who received protection from a tight web of dues and obligations between the ranks and orders of society. A study commissioned by the state board of agriculture in 1883, for example, suggested that South Carolina join what Aiken had called "the noisy nineteenth century." Too much land found itself bound by "artificial absurdities" inherited from "the dark ages and feudalism," the report suggested. The real problem, the state board argued, involved the inability of Carolina farmers to sell their property and turn to more profitable occupations in times when market forces turned against them. To break this cycle, the board suggested that new laws make land into movable property, "as convertible as titles to property in railroads and factories are through the medium of stocks and bonds."[39] Such a view could never please those who saw farming as the basis of "private worth and social virtue," and its defense as "the maintenance of honor and manhood."

Agricultural unrest in the state had found its champion, two years before the organization of the Alliance, in the person of Benjamin Ryan Tillman, of Edgefield County. In 1885 Tillman had used his time as a delegate to the annual meeting of the Grange to excoriate the Bourbon regime for its laissez-faire attitude toward agriculture. Following a line of attack that would become common among twentieth-century southern historians, Tillman melded planters, lawyers, and railroads into a single insidious "ring." In truth, Tillman himself had more of the scent of the brave new world of the postbellum South about him than did those he attacked. Early in his career, for example, Tillman received the aid and comfort of New South booster Francis W. Dawson, of the *Charleston News and Courier,* who agreed with the Edgefield firebrand that Carolina's conservative regime did nothing but "moon over the way it used to be."[40]

Tillman's attacks on the Bourbon regime drew their strength from his frustration over agricultural failure, the debt-ridden nature of South Carolina's single-staple economy, and the white South Carolinian's conceptual inability to deal with the full ramifications of a free labor economy. Tillman's rhetorical attacks on the Bourbons could find little purchase in their actual behavior. Though Tillman accused the Bourbons of a shady alliance with northern capitalists, Hampton, and his allies that had followed him in the governor's mansion, had done little to make themselves friendly to corporate interests. In fact, Bourbon leaders had appointed a railroad commission that sought to set equitable freight rates to aid the farmer. Furthermore, the Bourbons of South Carolina, quite out of step with much of the rest of the South, had refused to engage in the brutal practice of convict-leasing to railroads and other corporate interests. Popular outcry and the state legislature's response to this practice emerged because it both placed the largely black prison population outside the protective bounds of paternalism and gave aid to largely northern financial interests. D. Wyatt Aiken, with the help of Martin W. Gary, had successfully pressed for a "usury law" and a "homestead exemption" that preserved traditional rights of property and did much to protect Carolina farmers from their perpetual indebtedness. If the Bourbons did little to aid the farmers in their plight, the fault lies with their ignorance of the emerging bourgeois order rather than simple greed and maleficence.[41]

The aura of Confederate service combined with the more recent success of 1876, prevented a full-scale challenge to Bourbon rule in the 1880s. In fact, Tillman's attack on the "rings" that allegedly ran South Carolina threatened to founder in the late 1880s, despite the support lent him by Charleston's powerful *News and Courier.* Tillmanism did not die the early death so many Conservative Democrats heartily believed it would. The organizational strength of the Farmer's Alliance would, ironically considering later events, grant Tillman immeasurable help. The one-eyed farmer from Edgefield, who sprinkled his fiery speeches with allusions to classic English novels, southern country colloquialisms, and an angry language of class and racial warfare would soon watch his political movement rise from the dead. Tillman would ride the crest of the wave of the New South, trumpeting a strange brew of white supremacy, progress, and bourgeois rationalism. Confederate veterans, men who had ridden at night, marched with Hampton and joined the Grange and the Alliance to form "a solid phalanx for the maintenance of honor and manhood," would throw their support behind the Tillmanite juggernaut and soon find themselves in a world they never wanted.

CHAPTER EIGHT

Headless Soldiers and Sham Duels

The Rise of Tillman

In the early summer of 1882, a bolt from the heavens decapitated the
South Carolina soldiers monument. A contemporary wrote that "a light-
ening flash, guillotined our soldier and severed the body just above the
ankles." He added, probably unnecessarily, "the community was horror
stricken."[1]

White South Carolinians had taken great pride in the Confederate soldier's monument that stood in front of their statehouse. The statue seemed
a silent sentinel, representing Carolina white men's struggle against Yankeedom, both in 1861 and in 1876, the struggle against all the forces that
would undermine their independence. One observer especially praised
"the poise of the figure" that indicated "a vigorous and manly temper."
The South Carolina Monument Association agreed, describing the monument, in 1878, as "denoting much latent vigor" with a face that "denotes
full and manly strength."[2]

Surprisingly, the replacement head for Carolina's Confederate *David*
bore little resemblance to the original. The former head from the statue
had found its way to the Museum of the Confederacy, in Richmond, but
the new sculpture represented anything but "manly strength" to many
observers. The gentle, pudgy features of the new statue, combined with
its wavy and full locks of hair, resembled the cherubic guardians that
flourished around the borders of Victorian-era greeting cards more than
a battle-hardened warrior of Carolina. Mrs. A. T. Dargan, a member of
the original monument committee, voiced the criticism that "in point of
manly strength and beauty the new face and figure is not the equal of the
original."[3]

The gentle cherubic head that replaced the "manly features" of the
Confederate soldiers monument gave witness to a changing cultural ethos
in the South Carolina upcountry, a change already apparent by the 1880s.
Formerly shaped by the conservative ethos common to slaveholding

republics, the intrusions and demands of capital combined with new attitudes toward gender and the meaning of "respectability" clashed with, and overcame, Carolina's cultural traditions. This transformation heralded the embourgeoisement of the South Carolina upcountry, the rise and triumph of the middle class as a new economic reality.

The changes brought to South Carolina by the 1880s can be attributed, in part, to the emergence of a textile mill culture in the upcountry. The new economic structures of the upcountry, however, did not by themselves generate the new middle-class ideology that warred with the aesthetic of the Lost Cause. In this, South Carolina showed a similarity to the rest of the nation. Charles Sellers writes that the northern bourgeoisie "was constituted not by mode and relations of production but by ideology."[4]

The desire for political participation in a more proactive state, combined with a new ethos of personal self-restraint and economic success, heralded the rise of the middle class in the Western world. South Carolina began to experience just such a profound cultural change in the 1880s, mirroring larger changes in American culture. The southern conservative ideal, with its divinely ordained hierarchies, property-holding white men, and celebration of martial values in the Lost Cause, gradually gave way to the ideals of the middle class, the bourgeois values that had swept the North beginning in the 1830s. The state and its institutions combined with new forms of economic institutions began to play an unprecedented role in the lives of South Carolinians. White men rejected their culture of honor and came to emphasize the bourgeois values of restraint, self-control, and rationalized standards of behavior in both public and private realms. A new gendered identity replaced traditional versions of South Carolina manhood, even as women advanced from their role as dependent matrons and became domestic partners, empowered to use moral suasion to spread bourgeois values. Outward forms of southern cultural expression, such as the Lost Cause movement, remained vibrant but now glossed new cultural values and social realities, eschewing confrontational and aggressive attitudes toward the North and acting as societies of nostalgia.[5]

Benjamin R. Tillman, and the forces he unleashed as a leader of the farmers' movement of the 1880s, in his long tenure as governor, and, finally, as a United States senator into the twentieth century, acted as crucial catalyst for this profound transformation of Carolina's conservative culture. To rally his mass movement in what Stephen Kantrowitz has called "a shotgun wedding of reform and white supremacy," Tillman brought together an antiaristocratic reform agenda and appeals to white supremacy. His combination of fiery oratory and political acumen struck a series of blows against the somnolent Bourbons who took for granted that the best men would rule the state as they had since the colonial period. They understood little of the changed realities of the 1880s. The hierarchy of white men had always been in delicate balance, slavery serving as its cornerstone. Slavery's destruction had both destroyed the power base of the ruling class and sent shock waves through the state's economy, making unstable property ownership, and thus liberty and independence, for multitudes of the state's farmers. Tillman successfully allied himself with this discontent, appealing especially to the upcountry and its long-standing resentment of low-country aristocrats.[6]

Tillman would appear an unlikely agent of bourgeois values. His national reputation as "Pitchfork Ben"—a crude, wild champion of the farmer—stayed with him, from the beginning of his movement in Edgefield County to his long years as a United States senator. An examination of Tillman's background suggests that he represented a much more complex cultural ethos than his admirers and enemies have understood, that he in fact became the perfect instrument of a bourgeois revolution. Tillman hailed from southwestern South Carolina, where a bourgeois class had begun to develop in the 1870s, entrepreneurs who operated small farms combined with capital investment in an increasingly consumer economy. Edgefield and Aiken Counties, linked to prosperous Augusta, Georgia, through railroad, telegraph, and, eventually, telephone lines, became the centers of this "new departure." Randolph Werner, in an excellent article on this process, has described how the traditional break between town and country, a dichotomy often used as a rhetorical tool by Tillman, increasingly ceased to be a reality in Tillman's home region. For example, local Edgefield notable Oscar F. Cheatham operated a profitable dairy farm in the 1880s while running one of Edgefield's most successful mercantile firms.[7]

Tillman had firm links to this new class of entrepreneurs and their revolutionary ideology that suggested basic changes in South Carolina agriculture, modes of production, and work habits. In 1884 Tillman, Cheatham, and several other Edgefield leaders issued a joint statement urging South Carolinians to "take a new departure." The statement, prepared in the context of the progressive Edgefield Agricultural Society, reminded recalcitrant South Carolina, "we live in the nineteenth century. Let us show that we realize it and keep abreast of the times."[8]

Tillman never detected the irony of using the same vocabulary of "progress" as had been used by the Radical Republicans of Reconstruction whom he had tracked down and murdered in the 1870s. Murder, as much as "reform," had long played a role in Tillman's agenda. Tillman's base of operations, Edgefield and Aiken Counties, had a dark and bloody history. The region that incubated bourgeois social change had been among the most violent in South Carolina during Reconstruction. Tillman himself participated in the Ned Tennant Riot of 1874, and while serving as captain of the Sweetwater Sabre Club, he had played a major role in the Hamburg riot and massacre of 1876. Getting his first taste of racist terrorism in the Hamburg massacre, Tillman apparently took part in the cold-blooded execution of seven black Republican militiamen captured after the melee, joining other rifle club members afterward for a breakfast celebration of "barbequed shoat, coffee and corn pone."[9]

The contrast between Tillman and the Bourbon conservatives emerged most clearly in their attitude toward progress. D. Wyatt Aiken spoke darkly of the "utilitarian values of the noisy nineteenth century"; white supremacist Tillman joined with the 1868 constitutional convention in praising the advantages of modernity. Such an ideology of progress, especially Tillman's version that tied improvement to economic change and development, constituted the heart of bourgeois liberalism in the late nineteenth century. Eric Hobsbawm has written that the principles of the bourgeois liberals assumed that "irrational behavior and institutions" hindered the "pervasive individualism" in which they so deeply believed. A heavy emphasis on individualism, at least on economic individualism, did not prevent the chief theorists of liberal thought, like the utilitarian Bentham, from suggesting that an important degree of "state management" would aid in the sweeping away of "irrational" institutions. Such a utilitarian view, Hobsbawm notes, "provided the sharpest of radical axes with which to chop down traditional institutions."[10]

Tillman assumed the possibility of progress, if only the "dead hand of history" would loosen its grip, and the South Carolina farmer would become a rational entrepreneur rather than practicing what Tillman called the "land butchery" of the past. Tillman's appeals for scientific agriculture sounded not dissimilar from those of the Grange, except in its purposes. Once farmers became free from the crop-lien and the one-staple economy, they would constitute a political force able to topple the ancien régime of old Confederate captains, the "patronizing Wet-Nurses" who had ruled the state since colonial times.[11]

The image that Tillman sought to project to South Carolina farmers combined the values of the Victorian bourgeois and his own commitment to violence and white supremacy. Tillman, unlike his Bourbon predeces-

sors, proclaimed that only through violence had white men saved South
Carolina from "monrgrelism and barbarism." The Tillman vocabulary
represented the world, in true bourgeois fashion, as a struggle between
savagery and civilization, with Tillman himself as the hero-deliverer of
besieged civilization.

A rags-to-riches tale of Tillman's life foisted upon the state by his admirers strengthened this picture of a bourgeois gentleman. A biographical
sketch of the governor prepared for his 1894 senate race told voters that
the scion of wealthy planters had been "a mere farm lad" who through
"common sense, an honest heart and tireless energy" rose to South Carolina's governor's mansion. Tillman's refusal to engage in personal habits
anathema to bourgeois values, such as heavy drinking, smoking, or chew-
ing tobacco, completed his image.[12]

The nineteenth-century bourgeoisie moved from the contemplation
and cultivation of the self to the crafting of new institutions with which
to rationalize society. Tillman's role as a New South innovator and an
agent of the values of bourgeois liberalism emerges in his commitment
to creating new centralized institutions of control and surveillance, his
alliance with the forces of middle-class hegemony, and his attempt to
tie bourgeois notions of racial purity to the increasingly powerful state.
Tillman and his movement called on upcountry farmers to wage war on
low-country Bourbons, insidious trusts, and "black beasts." Giving their
wholehearted support to Tillman's rhetoric of white manhood and honor,
these farmers consented to a Faustian bargain with the very forces that
would strip them of all the accoutrements of manhood and honor. Tillmanism introduced bourgeois values to South Carolina through the back
door of his agrarian rhetoric, fundamentally reshaping South Carolina
on behalf of the "farmers."[13]

Educational institutions would provide Tillman with bases of support
for his program. South Carolina's first common-school system, serving
black students and white students, was the most important legacy of
Radical Reconstruction; certainly it was the primary positive contribution
made during that period of the state's history. After 1876 Wade Hampton
had supported a revivification of these common schools, viewing them as
a way to educate Carolinians in civic virtue and to prepare them for participation in the political realm. Hampton believed that a proper education,
which included a grounding in the classics, formed citizens whose wisdom and virtue strengthened republican institutions. Under the Hampton administration, and into the 1880s, the state spent approximately the

same amount on white education as on black, funding white schools at $168,516 in 1879–80, and black schools at $182,899.[14]

Tillman and his agrarian entrepreneurs, on the other hand, viewed education as an option for whites only, seeing it as a tool to rationalize and restructure the economic character of the state and its white people. During the Tillman era, local newspapers touted the building of public schools not to create educated citizens and social harmony, but because of a perceived link between a practical education and the building of textile mills. The *Anderson Intelligencer,* for example, editorialized that public schools attract "people who buy and improve property."[15] Tillman himself argued that the antebellum ideal of the educated gentleman who had imbibed Cicero and Shakespeare must give way to a "practical and technical education." South Carolina "could never compete with the North" unless such a pragmatic approach to education took root. Moreover, Tillman's accusations of "extravagance" hurled at the Bourbons often centered on the support of black schools, arguing that those who paid little, or no, taxes should not receive a free education.[16] The Bourbons believed that black Carolinians could enter the body politic if educated into their inferior position—Tillman's solution was to reject the idea of a biracial state altogether and to create instead a white supremacist paradise by main force.

The hope that common schools might inculcate bourgeois values into a new white laboring class seemed to have confirmation in several of South Carolina's industrial experiments of the 1890s. In Anderson County, in the late 1890s, the mill town of Pelzer began turning cotton bales into textiles, and Carolina farmers into a respectable working class. Pelzer embodies a general trend in the South Carolina upcountry, and throughout the Carolina piedmont, of entrepreneurs coming to a region attracted by the cheap fund of labor produced by the agricultural crisis and the increasingly complex railroad network. Like many of the entrepreneurial patriarchs, they ruled over their industrial "families" and sought to make their property as productive as possible. The sheer size of these "families," unlike their antebellum precedents, made the entrepreneurs' oft-expressed familial concern a heavy-handed metaphor, and more important, ties to their charges were the cords of the cash-nexus rather than of organic obligations of custom, history, and religion.[17]

Pelzer itself was not an incorporated town. Its owner, "Captain" Ellison A. Smyth, proudly told northern interviewers that it was his "private property." This corporate entity functioning as "private property"

gave Smyth latitude to force a number of regulations on the farmers who
sought relief from the crushing debts of tenant farming, regulations that
allegedly ensured that "order and peace uniformly prevail." The captain
did not allow liquor to be sold or imbibed in his industrial utopia; neither
did he allow the perennial companion of South Carolina men, the hunting
dog, to be kept. Children were forced to labor in the mill and to attend
the common schools, schools that Smyth owned.[18]

Interested in changing the cultural ethos of the farmers as well as in
making money, Smyth openly spoke of his desire for "the elevation of
the working man" and the creation of "useful citizens." The common
schools represented the most concerted effort to accomplish this goal,
though Smyth hoped to influence Pelzer's adult population of six thousand by building a lyceum that contained "approved standard literature."
He also invited middle-class ladies to engage in the "systematic teaching
of cooking and other housewifely arts" to the mill town's women. Such
blatant intrusions into the homes and values of these failed farmers were
the price they paid to escape the system of crop-lien and tenantry that
gradually swept over the Carolina upcountry. Nevertheless, the desire for
independence and liberty never left these farm families, and criticisms of
Smyth's industrial panopticon seep through the generally laudatory (and
generally northern) descriptions of the experiment. One woman decried
the common schools her children had to attend, telling an interviewer that
"she never knew no educated man who waren't a rascal." A common
complaint among men raised in the southern conservative ethos centered
on the reality that "there can be no home ownership" in Smyth's system.
No matter how hard they worked, these former rural tenants would always be industrial tenants, unable to become "masters of small worlds."[19]

The example of Smyth and his industrial experiment shows that Tillmanism alone did not transform the former slaveholding republic into
a bourgeois state. However, the Edgefield coterie, and Edgefield County
generally, did play an important role in the coming of upcountry capitalism. Tillman's old captain from the Red Shirt days, A. P. Butler, served
as the state commissioner of agriculture and distributed a pamphlet that
called for an end to "feudalism" in South Carolina and the transformation of land into moveable property. Daniel H. Tompkins, a scion of
an Edgefield antebellum slaveholding family, became the great promoter
of industrial development in South Carolina. Educated at the Rensselaer
Polytechnic Institute in New York, Tompkins served an apprenticeship at
the Bethlehem Steel Works, then returned to South Carolina as an advocate of industrial development and the sworn enemy of child labor laws.

He worked to create textile schools associated with Tillman's Clemson College and North Carolina State, in Raleigh, hitching his wagon of industrial development to the new system of education that Tillmanism had created. These schools would in turn ally themselves closely with upcountry manufacturing interests. Indeed, as Allen Tullos notes, "their purpose was to supply technical workers, engineers and managers" for the ever-expanding web of capitalist interests. In turn, mill owners donated funds and equipment to these schools and sat on their boards of trustees.[20]

The growth of a protoindustrial society in the upcountry disassembled the patriarchal family and, ineluctably, reshaped gender roles and relations. Tillman's support for a transformation of South Carolina's school system included the possibility of higher education for women; practical training would transform them into a ready work force in the state's changing economy. During his rabble-rousing days in the 1880s, Tillman had infuriated conservatives by suggesting that the Citadel, South Carolina's storied military academy, become a technical training school for women. The farmer's wife, he insisted, had a role to play in the restructuring of South Carolina and needed a practical education similar to that of her husband. Tillman also supported the creation of the Winthrop Normal and Industrial School for Women, in Lancaster County, in hopes that it would serve this purpose. Speaking at the laying of the school's cornerstone in May 1894, Tillman thanked those who had provided the funding for Winthrop by extolling a laundry list of bourgeois values, praising "those whose pluck, self-reliance and business instincts had made them winners." Tillman assured his listeners that Winthrop Normal and Industrial, along with Clemson, would encourage formerly aristocratic South Carolina toward "labor and self-reliance." "Knowledge of books is good," Tillman admitted, "but knowledge of things is better." Perhaps, Tillman suggested in an argument that surely sent chills up the spines of many Carolina conservatives, the women of South Carolina would someday resemble the women of the northern laboring class in their "dress, demeanor and evident prosperity."[21]

Tillman's support for a new kind of education, one that would function as a means of state coercion, raised the hackles of his most ardent supporters. Many of the farmers, the men for whom Tillman allegedly spoke, resisted the building of common schools, because of their indigenous hatred of high taxes and their fear that such institutions would represent an intrusive presence in their households and family structures. The patchwork pattern of South Carolina's school districts reflected this conflict, with many districts skirting isolated communities where farmers actively resisted the schools. One upcountry editor agreed that Tillman's plan to create common schools in rationalized school districts might provide "better schools and roads" but would ultimately impose the "New England Town meeting system" on South Carolinians. Brushing all such criticism aside, Tillman used a speech at the 1895 constitutional convention to call for a rationalization of the state's patchwork patterns of school districts and the centralization of state powers to crush all resistance. "Let us levy the taxes," Tillman demanded "and not leave it to an ignoramus or any set of ignoramuses who want to breed up ignoramuses.' " A new school system could transform aristocratic dudes into bourgeois gentlemen, and yeoman farmers into frugal, practical workers. Tillman believed that other new institutional structures could inculcate the state's people with the values of restraint and self-discipline. No effort proved more controversial in this regard that the creation of "Tillman's baby," the state dispensary.[22]

Tillman, the triangulating politician, presented the idea of a dispensary in 1892. With his plan for county dispensaries operated by the state, Tillman hoped to quiet growing conflict over the issue of prohibition. The plan would quiet temperance advocates' concerns about the soul-killing, home-destroying effects of barroom sociability, keep whiskey in the hands of thirsty farmers, and provide Tillman himself with a vast patronage machine reaching into every county in the state. Tillman failed spectacularly in his attempt to please his various constituencies, and the dispensary ultimately proved the greatest political mistake of his life. The plan did provide the governor with new institutional machinery with which to ensure his control over local government. A state board of control, made up of Tillman and two hand-picked officials, appointed yet more county-level bureaucrats to run the dispensary with the help of a constabulary to enforce its monopoly. Tillman's willingness to use his special constabulary against the farmers, for whose independence he claimed to speak, reveals even more ironies in his mercurial career. Though Tillman often invoked his own part in the struggle to end Reconstruction, his dispensary plan duplicated the invasive behavior of the Federal revenuers who had hounded whiskey-making South Carolinians throughout the 1870s.

Tillman's administration further transformed South Carolina by increasing the power of state government in ways that would have been anathema to earlier generations of South Carolinians. During his administration, taxes rose to levels the state had not seen since Reconstruction, yet white South Carolina tended to acquiesce. Seemingly, these former members of the taxpayer's movement now agreed with Tillman's assertion in his December 1890 inaugural address, when he proclaimed that "the people will pay even more taxes . . . if they know those taxes are wisely expended and for their benefit." Tillman had tapped into a primary theme of nineteenth-century bourgeois liberalism—the state as repository and caretaker of human communities and their values. Michel Foucault refers to this trend as modernity's "myth of social happiness," which leads the state to construct various "prisons of moral order."[23]

In fact, Tillman did manage to appeal to a new trend in South Carolina life, a tendency to assume the necessity of "prisons of moral order" in the construction of a respectable society. Tillman and the capitalist coterie shaped the economic base and the institutional arrangements for the middle-class state; other groups spread the ideology of the bourgeoisie. The emergence of the Women's Christian Temperance Union (WCTU) in South Carolina, for example, became an important force in replacing rural patterns of life and changing southern conservative mores regarding liberty and its relationship to the state. The WCTU, which had created a strong organization in the Northwest, beginning in the early 1870s, did not enter the South until the mid-1880s. It grew quickly, if not without controversy, and tended to join with older evangelical suspicions of the world and its pleasures.[24]

Nevertheless, it faced important challenges in the South Carolina up-country from critics who attacked it with appeals to the state's older conservative tradition. Presbyterian minister David Frierson, always an enemy of Leviathan-like modernity, preached a sermon entitled "Christianity and Women" to his Anderson County congregation in 1888. In it he characterized the Old South as replicating the patriarchal domesticity of the Old Testament, sharply contrasting its gender relations to "modern schemes of social and religious improvement." Frierson hauled in the WCTU for specific criticism, suggesting that this organization with northern roots sought "to make man and woman competitive in the struggle of life," an unthinkable proposition for a deeply conservative man who regarded any challenge to a paternalistic social organism as pernicious.[25]

Beset with critics, the WCTU also had important allies. In fact, Sallie F. Chapin, an organizer and early leader of the WCTU, gave the increasingly influential organization a link to Ben Tillman. Chapin admired Tillman and seemed to believe that his ideology of bourgeois progress combined with a continued commitment to white supremacy would herald a new day for South Carolina. Chapin looked to the state's powerful governor as a source for what Foucault calls "normalization." The creation of new, rational institutions in public life and the cultivation of the private bourgeois self would regularize South Carolina life in the wake of the unstable boundary conflicts of race and gender created by war and reconstruction. The conservative hierarchy, with its delicate balancing of dues and obligation, its paternalist compromises, would come tumbling down. In its place, white South Carolinians would have Tillman's stark contrast of savagery and civilization, the protected white middle-class self warring with the contagion of blackness, the threat of what Tillman called "mongrelization."

A domestic novelist, Chapin wrote a highly didactic work, *Fitz Hugh St. Clair: The South Carolina Rebel Boy, or It Is No Crime to Be Born a Gentleman*, in 1873, a work she later sent to Ben Tillman inscribed, "Take Fitz, dear boy, as your model for your state sadly needs men grown from such boys." The hero of the novel, though coming from an aristocratic low-country family, has little of the southern aristocracy about him. Chapin describes the youth as "the best boy in town. No one ever saw him with a cigar in his mouth or heard him use profane language." St. Clair acquired this rather unaristocratic mien by a proper training in bourgeois values. He learned from his parents, Chapin says, not to have "extravagant tastes" and to control his temper "by strong effort and unceasing watchfulness." [26]

Having described St. Clair as anything but the "South Carolina gentlemen" she insists he is, Chapin next has the young man leave his home state, overrun with carpetbaggers, and go North to seek his fortune. Studiously avoiding the severe temptations of gambling, the circus, and Sabbath-breaking, St. Clair receives, in a true rags-to-riches style, help from a wealthy northern patron whom Chapin uses as a mouthpiece of New South economic ideology. If only "southern boys" would become "intelligent scientific mechanics," St. Clair's protector urges, the South could find its salvation in "manufacturers and manufacturing towns." Marrying his patron's daughter, St. Clair restores the fortunes of his family—with the help of northern capital from his father-in-law. [27]

Chapin's tale reflects a desire for reunion with the North made possible by economic cooperation and a laissez-faire northern attitude toward southern racial mores. Though evoking the Lost Cause by praising the honor of the Confederate soldier, the book breathes little spirit of defiance. Chapin dedicated her work to "the children of the southern Confederacy," as if to make clear that the war-waging generation's time has passed. The children of the South, Chapin writes, should honor their father's sacrifice by "doing nothing to disgrace their names." Such "disgrace" came by failing to live up to middle-class values rather than by failing to continue the veterans' war with northern perfidy. Chapin transforms the veteran from a warrior for a traditional society into the very model of bourgeois respectability. Look up to "the brave Confederate boy," urged Chapin, as her work closed, "neither befogged with tobacco or drunk with whisky."[28]

Increasingly, the WCTU throughout the South received the support of the Evangelical churches. Such churches had always preached temperance, understood as moderate drinking. Moreover, only a small number of antebellum Evangelical ministers ever came to believe in coerced prohibition. Attitudes toward alcohol hardened in the 1880s, in part because of the influence of such groups as the WCTU, and likely because alcohol represented a source of disorder and riotous behavior in a society that white southerners felt had had enough of chaos and instability. The Evangelical churches had always attempted to create order and stability in the face of the backcountry's often libertine spirit by strengthening the bonds of husband and wife, master and slave, and by shaping a Confederate religion that united white southerners in the holy cause of secession. Emancipation, the rise of Tillman, a changing ethos of southern manhood, and disputes over the meanings of the Lost Cause drove churchmen to search for new ways to create order. Reigning in "demon alcohol" offered a very simple means of expressing that concern for order.

Ironically, the practice of Evangelical church discipline declined precipitously in the 1880s and 1890s, even as Evangelicals took a more active interest in using the coercive levers of state power to accomplish Gospel order. One Greenwood Baptist layman wrote to Furman University's Harvey T. Cook in the 1890s complaining about a number of changes in Evangelical culture, including that "the churches no longer discipline." Meanwhile, churches in the upcountry, and throughout the South, accepted many of the ideals of an increasingly professionalized mass culture. The ecstatic revivalism that had marked the early emergence of Evangelical faith gave way to a much more regularized spirituality in which revivals became organized seasonal events rather than charismatic moves of the Spirit. Simultaneously, Evangelical congregations found themselves led by ministers who saw themselves as a professional class and employed the techniques of scientific management to congregational life. These changes even reached far northwestern Oconee County, a mountain county carved out of Pickens District in the postbellum years. The Reverend A. W. McGuffie, asked in 1884 to write a series of "religious reminiscences" for the local Oconee County paper, used his column to launch a jeremiad against upcountry Christians for how they had allowed their sacred world to disappear since Appomattox. "Gospel discipline in the churches was strictly observed" in the Old South, he reminded his readers, and "there was no thousand dollar salaries for preachers." McGuffie insisted that these outward changes reflected an inward spiritual degeneration, because in the churches of the New South "there is not much worship of God in spirit and in truth."[29]

Changes in religion mirrored other changes in South Carolina's conservative culture. The combined strength of middle-class reform and Tillman's harangues against the "aristocratic" values of South Carolina had a slow, degenerative effect on the cultural ideology of South Carolina, including its ideology of southern manhood. The southern culture of honor had bound white Carolina men together since the days of the militia muster brawl. The duel between aristocrats had stood at the apex of the state's system of manly honor, with former South Carolina governor John Lyde Wilson literally writing the book on the practice. Wilson's 1838 *Code of Honor* served generations of South Carolina men as a guide to proper manly behavior in moments of social conflict.[30]

The University of South Carolina, formerly South Carolina College, had a long history of affairs of honor. Since 1808 the institution had functioned as a training ground for South Carolina's ruling class, training that included the inculcation of the nascent southern aristocracy's code of honor. In one antebellum example, J. Marion Sims prankishly pulled a chair out from under his roommate, Boykin Witherspoon. Sims quickly found himself entangled in the elaborate ritual machinery of the duel, apologizing profusely until his own masculine honor could stand it no more, and he finally accepted Witherspoon's demand for satisfaction.[31]

The transformation of this ethos in the 1880s becomes evident in what must have been for many a startling episode. Two students at the University of South Carolina did the unthinkable in 1881; they fought a sham duel. Perhaps inspired by the deadly Cash-Shannon duel of the same year, the pranksters went through all the public rituals necessary to the code duello, with an exchange of challenges, the picking of seconds, and loud demands for satisfaction. Choosing pistols at dawn, the two met on the Columbia campus, but, reported an amused classmate, "the cartridges were blanks and the blood was red ink." Laughing together, the two companions and the rest of the student body enjoyed their elaborate practical joke enormously.[32]

Bertram Wyatt-Brown identifies the southern system of "honor and violence" with the older notion of "primal honor" that reaches far back in the history of the Western world. Wyatt-Brown defines "primal honor" as "an ethic almost entirely external in nature. It was easily comprehended and was considered physically demonstrable without resort to abstraction, without ambivalence or ambiguity."[33] The willingness of two of South Carolina's elite to mimic the dual, to introduce the elements of "ambivalence and ambiguity" into a time-honored ritual, suggests a subtle yet important change in South Carolina's white conservative culture. Romantic cavaliers were becoming bourgeois gentlemen.

Tillman helped to facilitate the trend away from the *affaire d'honneur*, refusing repeatedly to answer the challenges he often received following the verbal barrages he directed against political opponents. Dueling had been outlawed by the 1868 constitution, and, ironically, as justification for his refusal to duel, Tillman often pointed to that document, whose writers he had helped throw out of office. Just as often, Tillman evoked the bourgeois ideal of "manly restraint" as his reason for refusing to answer such challenges. Surprisingly such justifications worked for Tillman, even though his opponents continually impugned his courage. Stephen Kantrowitz has suggested that Tillman shifted South Carolina's ethos from an emphasis on individual honor to the collective honor of white men. Pointing to the Redemption struggle of '76 , but seldom back to a war in which he had not participated, Tillman assured his followers of the honor of white supremacy in this new bourgeois world.[34]

Tillmanism never eschewed violence, even if duels between white men became rare in the 1890s. Bourgeois politics through the fin de siècle Western world sought to restrict and contain violence on the part of the masses, leaving the state as the sole custodian of deadly force.[35] Tillman followed the same program, becoming the critic of "lynch mobs," although he enlisted such mobs as agents of the state, and attacks on African Americans became increasingly savage in their frequency and ferocity. Rejecting the idea of individual honor, Tillman made clear in his public statements and actions that the honor of the white race would remain unstained. When white fourteen-year-old Mamie Baxter claimed to have been assaulted by a black male in the spring of 1893, the lynching of the primary suspect, Henry Williams, seemed imminent. Stephen Kantrowitz, writing about this episode, shows that Tillman attempted, successfully, to link his notion of the power of the state to launch violent assaults on black bodies with his simultaneous demagogic appeals to the mob. Tillman wrote to S. G. Mayfield, the Barnwell County senator, urging the "process of law"; at the same time, he assured Mayfield that the men of Barnwell County had the support of the state for any violence they wanted to mete out on "the would-be ravisher." Kantrowitz writes that both Tillman and his crony Mayfield "sought to appear gravely law-abiding while they arranged a lynching."[36]

Tillman appealed to the deeply rooted fears and anxieties of South Carolina white men that had been evident since the experience of war and emancipation. The psychosexual aspects of the white South's assault on black bodies serves as an especially egregious example of how, to use Foucault's terms, the "symbolics of blood" ally with "the analytics of sexuality."[37] Black males came to be regarded as "black beasts" when latent fears regarding emancipated slave men as sexual threats intertwined diabolically with a newfound concern with racial purity. This fascination with a kind of racial hygiene marked a departure from antebellum racial attitudes in which black Carolinians, while assumed inferior because of their enslaved status and cultural background, were viewed as having a place within the hierarchical social relations of the South Carolina. Joel Williamson has described this "conservative outlook" by noting that it sought to "save" the emancipated slave "by defining and fixing his place in American society." The new racism of South Carolina, defined and bounded by bourgeois attitudes toward sexuality and identity, did not allow that blacks had any "place" within the social organism.[38]

Such a change in attitude found its perfect expression in the Tillman movement's effort to drive black Carolinians from the public sphere in every arena. Tillmanites used legal statute backed by mob violence to keep black men from both the ballot box and white women. In these attitudes, South Carolina, rather than dissenting from American culture as it had often done in the past, reflected larger influential trends in scientific racism. Prominent thinkers of the 1890s, such as Nathaniel Shaler, dean of the Lawrence School of Science at Harvard University, propounded the theory that African Americans would naturally "retrogress" to a lower state of nature with slavery, and referred specifically to the dangers they presented to white women. "The Negro is sexually a very brutal creature," the former Union artilleryman wrote, "who cannot be trusted in contact with white women." Meanwhile, statistician Frederick L. Hoffman published a study in 1896 that claimed to show that black Americans had been gradually declining to a state of savagery throughout the nineteenth century, with the pace of declension accelerating after emancipation. Hoffman suggested that the sexual immorality of black males had been responsible for this degeneration, even proposing that black men had become especially pernicious disease agents, "spreading scrofula, syphilis and consumption." These supporters of scientific racism had strong bourgeois credentials. Shaler became a regular contributor to the

Atlantic Monthly and other magazines popular with the northern middle class; Hoffman worked for the Prudential Insurance Company and published his racist study under the auspices of the American Economic Association. Unwary of the source of such twaddle, South Carolinians accepted similar notions of black people. In 1889, James R. Sparks, a former rice planter and agricultural reformer, wrote of the "contagious diseases" carried by a new generation of black Carolinians.[39]

South Carolinians imbibed these ideas, but the crisis in masculinity produced by Confederate defeat likely had much more to do with the horrendous nature of lynching in the state than imported northern "scientific racism." This crisis had been allayed by the Red Shirt crusade of '76, when South Carolina men had ridden with their Confederate captains to the cheers of Carolina's women. Into the 1880s, as South Carolina farmers lost their independence and went from mortgaged farms to tenantry, concerns over the loss of manhood revived with a vengeance. Inability to control land and labor cut to the heart of male self-conceptions, making liberty and property an antique dream. A new generation of black men, many separated from the dying hierarchies that had structured work and social space since the early part of the century, became targets for the dark and savage obsessions of South Carolina's embittered white farmers. Public spectacles like the Hampton campaign, with its iconographic representations of blacks and whites building a biracial South Carolina, became unthinkable, replaced by the spectacle of the lynch mob and a bizarre iconography of violence and sexual obsession.[40]

The Tillman administration attempted to lift this complex of ideas out of the minds of white South Carolinians and into the realm of state power. Tillman assured his supporters that he himself would lead the lynch mob against any black man who dared view white women as a sexual object. Black desire for white women, and the attraction in the other direction, became a special concern of South Carolina. Such relationships had always been policed, often violently, by local communities and, more frequently, by folk mores. The rising middle class of the 1890s apparently felt that it needed more protection from contagion than folk mores afforded. One of Tillman's supporters in the WCTU suggested that the state take racial discipline and surveillance one step further, calling for Tillman to use the same constabulary that enforced the dispensary laws to police racialized sex. The state, she suggested, in its effort to ensure racial purity, could keep lists of mulatto children and the women who bore them.[41]

Not satisfied with stamping out demon rum and the baneful effects of interracial conjugation, the ladies of the WCTU also pressed for the protection of white bodies through the teaching of "physiology and hygiene." In 1894, the Tillmanite legislature passed a law requiring the teaching of hygiene in South Carolina's new school system. Many rural school districts, slow to accept bourgeois standards of antiseptic cleanliness, quietly resisted this requirement until after the turn of the century. Tired of such passive resistance, the WCTU brushed aside objections in 1903 and used the coercive power of compulsory attendance to inflict on the rural children of Spartanburg County a series of lectures and exhibits on "hygiene . . . and the effects on the human system of alcohol and narcotics."[42]

The opponents of Tillman and of the forces that allied with him did not remain silent in the 1890s. Often summoning the Lost Cause to legitimate their challenge, a diverse collection of aristocratic clergymen, old Bourbon leaders, and Confederate veterans with Farmer's Alliance sympathies, attempted to prevent South Carolina's slide into what they derisively called "Tillmania." Though sharing assumptions about black racial inferiority, many conservatives schooled in Hampton's paternalistic ethos found themselves sickened by the mob spectacles and anxious over the danger to social harmony such violent actions presented. N. G. Gonzales, editor of the conservative organ the *State* and a close political ally of Wade Hampton, asserted throughout the 1890s that Tillmanism had stirred the lynch mobs to life and that such violence would destroy the natural harmonies of society. John J. Dargan, an Allianceman, Confederate veteran, and duelist who had declared that all those who fought for economic reform would find "the Palmetto flag advanced over the front rank," actively opposed Tillman. He showed enormous physical courage by speaking in favor of black suffrage and racial uplift in Grendel's lair itself, the town of Edgefield. Dargan did, in fact, find himself in a tussle with the crowd, which threatened him with tar and feathering before he took a train back to Columbia. Through the publication of his newspaper, the *Freeman*, Dargan attacked Tillman, praised the Farmer's Alliance, and published articles in praise of the bravery of Confederate soldiers, including the text of speeches delivered at monument dedications by the likes of Wade Hampton, M. C. Butler, and Ellison Capers.[43]

Ellison Keitt, one of the upcountry's symbols of Confederate heroism, also actively opposed Tillman, using the Lost Cause as the basis of his challenge. Keitt openly asserted that fellow Newberry County resident and Tillman lieutenant Samson Y. Pope had shown cowardice in battle, a charge that led to physical combat between Pope and Keitt in the streets of Newberry. Keitt made special appeals to his fellow members of the

Farmer's Alliance, insisting that the war against Tillman constituted a struggle "for Christianity and civilization."[44]

The most subtle, and surprising, argument that Keitt made against Tillmanism portrayed this movement of white farmers led by respectable bourgeois entrepreneurs as a force more dangerous to the state than the black Republican government of Reconstruction. Tillman had committed a crime "as base as that of Cataline," according to Keitt, by attacking the men who led South Carolina in the Confederate War effort. Though he had made numerous campaign speeches for Hampton in Newberry County, Keitt asserted that "even the Negro legislature that held high carnival in the state between 1868 and 1876" compared favorably with Tillman, whom Keitt referred to as "a vile dog." Writing vociferous editorials against Tillmanism in both the *Charleston News and Courier* and the *State,* Keitt made particular appeals to his fellow Alliancemen. Ironically, and somewhat awkwardly, Keitt appealed to some of the same instincts that roused the Tillmanite lynch mobs. "Men of Carolina," he wrote in 1890, "rouse yourselves and save . . . the sanctity of your homes and your chaste mothers from pollution."[45]

The Lost Cause offered fertile ground for Tillman's opponents, because Captain Tillman himself had not participated in South Carolina's first great effort to secure property and independence from the centralizing forces of the age. Suffering from a cranial tumor in 1863–64, the teen-aged Tillman lost his left eye and remained wretchedly ill to the end of the conflict. Whatever his excuse, Tillman's Confederate opponents attempted to present him as cowardly in his refusal to fight for the South, a cowardice reiterated in their own minds by Tillman's refusal to duel. Conservatives seemed most troubled by Tillman's attacks on former Confederate leaders whose wartime service, Lost Cause celebrants tended to believe, created a sacred legitimation for these leaders that should not be challenged. In the 1892 gubernatorial race, Leroy Youmans attacked Tillman for being "flat on his back" during the war years and then heightening his crime by, "casting discredit" on Confederate heroes and suggesting that "the followers of Lee and Jackson should be retired to the rear."[46]

Tillman answered these criticisms by portraying the former Confederate leaders as outdated remnants of an outdated struggle. His own legitimacy, Tillman claimed, came from his integral involvement in the struggle of 1876. Tillman preached Martin Gary's version of '76, insisting that it be seen as a white man's struggle. In an 1892 speech in Anderson, Tillman actually took credit for making the red shirt the symbolic uniform of Hampton's supporters.[47]

The dispensary plan and the Tillmanite constabulary especially angered conservatives, largely because of power of the constables to intrude on private property in search of illegal whiskey. Ignoring objections, the governor insisted in his public statements that "the right to search private houses on a warrant is as old as the law itself." Tillman also waved aside objections that the dispensary enlarged state power; "How can the state government, which is the representative of all the people . . . be said to create a monopoly?" In Tillman's view, the sovereign state represented a sovereign people whose rights inhered in the state's capacity to exercise power on their behalf.[48]

Tillman's misunderstanding of this issue came very close to creating civil war within the state and actually did provoke violence in the 1894 Darlington Riot. Located in northeastern South Carolina and referred to as a "hell-hole" of anti-Tillman sentiment, Darlington became a maelstrom of violence when the governor's order for constables to search private homes resulted in a shoot-out between townspeople and the state authorities. One white Darlingtonian died in the melee, and the Tillman constables fled for their lives. In angry response, mounted troops of Darlington's militia began searching the countryside in search of constables, in the words of one observer, "to hunt and kill."[49]

Tillman responded by declaring martial law in the state, personally assuming control of telegraph and railroad lines to prevent news of the resistance from setting off a firestorm. News that South Carolinians had, in the words of Darlington's mayor, "dared maintain their liberties" traveled quickly nonetheless. Anti-Tillmanite militias broke into armories in Columbia and in Chester County, and Ellison Capers gave a rousing speech to Columbia's Governors Guards, calling on them to remember their Lost Cause and challenge Tillman's tyranny. Tillman gathered loyal militia himself, and though he later claimed that "10,000 farmers" would have answered his call, only three hundred in fact did come to the governor's aid. Nevertheless, Tillman's forces restored order in Darlington, and Tillman, the consummate politician, managed to portray the riots to upcountry supporters as a struggle between town and country, even upcountry against wicked Charleston. The leading Tillmanite paper, the *Edgefield Advertiser,* crowed that Tillman's elimination of brawl-filled barrooms and wayside taverns had prevented the riots from turning into a full-scale rebellion. Sallie Chapin, without a trace of irony, wrote that Tillman's victory over the antidispensary forces represented a victory for "home protection." In the new world of the emerging South Carolina bourgeoisie, the home remained sacrosanct if free of strong drink, even with armed state constables bursting through the door.[50]

Tillman undoubtedly understood that his triumphs over an older South Carolina political tradition might be short-lived. His mercurial personality caused the rupture of many alliances he had formed by the end of his second term, including his relationship with his brother George D. Tillman, a former Confederate soldier, renowned duelist, and conservative agrarian. George Tillman had said of the dispensary system that he "would be damned" if he "didn't shoot the first spy who enters my residence and opens my package of goods."[51] Ben Tillman surely understood that his regime faced formidable opponents in men like his brother and from the continued power of the Lost Cause, the boundaries of which he had to navigate carefully. Hoping to solidify the alliance of entrepreneurs and discontented rural folk into a solid phalanx of white supremacy, he looked to a new state constitution to create a new power mechanism in the state.

Tillman's constitutional convention, at which Senator Benjamin Tillman presided like a grand mogul, met to create a white supremacist, bourgeois state. Creating an absurdly baffling system of voting that theoretically disenfranchised poor whites as well as black Carolinians, the convention also passed stringent miscegenation regulations; it attempted to define racial differences in scientific terms, coming to the conclusion that those carrying one-eighth a former slave's blood in their veins should be classified as Negroes. George Tillman, during one surreal discussion concerning the fine points of racial classification, stood up with exasperation to remind his colleagues that "there is no full-blooded Caucasian on the floor of this Convention." Though chagrined by a comment such as this from his own brother, Ben Tillman had his way in much of the convention proceedings, failing only in his attempt to have South Carolina accept a progressive divorce law or to at least recognize divorces granted in other states. In only this did the old order prevail.[52]

Conservatives denounced Tillman's action as, in the words of Johnson Hagood, "lawless and tyrannous." A private letter to Lost Cause movement leader Leroy Youmans praised a speech he had given in honor of Confederate hero L. Q. C. Lamar. The "splendid eulogy" had included much of the conservative's beloved references to classical history, but the letter-writer wondered "what's the use of brains when you can hire a ruffian for 25 a month to break open your trunk and shoot you if necessary in a hunt for whisky. . . . The outlook," he concluded, "is gloomy."[53]

The proceedings of the convention even proved troubling to those who looked at Tillman as their champion against "rings" and special interests. White Carolina farmers, a large minority of whom now labored on land belonging to others, watched an entire way of life slip away at the behest of their "agrarian rebel" hero. One angry farmer, the type who soon would be derisively labeled as a "redneck" by respectable town folk, expressed to a partisan *State* reporter his feelings about Tillman. A Confederate veteran, he reminded the reporter that the war had been "a rich man's war and a poor man's fight" but that he had gladly shouldered his musket for South Carolina. Nevertheless, he roared, "when they jerk my vote away from me because I don't live in Charleston and read Homer at night, I will bresh up on my military education and the blue blood . . . will run down the same gully as the red blood of the sand wolloper." The class-conscious farmer added, "I think I am voicing the sentiments of the ignorant classes."[54]

Tillman, in the eyes of some, had joined with the blue bloods. In truth, he had. Until his death in 1918, Tillman would serve as a United States Senator. Most of South Carolina's redneck class would delight to Tillman's theatrical representations of himself as Pitchfork Ben, endlessly prodding the Federal government on behalf of the laboring classes. Meanwhile, Tillman's closest friends and political allies in the Senate would become those from New England, who, in odd ways, shared his vision of a bourgeoisie America, a white man's civilization free of both a hoary past and a mongrelized present. During the 1910s, Tillman became a keen imperialist and supporter of the war in Europe. Upon his death, Tillman would be eulogized by none other than Henry Cabot Lodge.[55]

Conservative Democrats, attempting to maintain the ethos of southern conservatism in a changing world, often spoke in seemingly contradictory ways in response to the convention. The end of the convention brought the announcement of George Tillman's retirement from public life. He used the announcement to give general praise to the work of Negro disenfranchisement and to angrily tell the bourgeois entrepreneurs who supported his estranged brother that "we are not a free people . . . if we were free we would have Negro slavery instead of Negro suffrage. Instead of having the United States government, we would have the Confederate States government." Meanwhile, Wade Hampton spoke out against the convention from retirement, saying that he had "no fear of Negro domination—a cry used only to arouse race prejudice." Hampton seems to have assumed, with a less reactionary spirit than George Tillman's, that the old definition of race relations worked best—a hierarchy braced by paternalism and dependence.[56]

The use of violence in the 1870s that culminated in the '76 campaign attempted the impossible task of harnessing the ideal of social organicism to the wild horses of terror and mob violence. Ultimately an ideology that imagined a delicate harmony existing between property-owning white men and filtering down through paternalism to their dependents, the rather delicate and exotic flora of southern conservatism could not withstand the blasting heat of the popular mass movement that Tillmanism represented. Supported by bourgeois values that encouraged the utter transformation of public and private boundaries and the re-shaping of gendered and racial identities, Carolina conservatives found themselves in another losing fight. At last, even their lost cause deserted them.

CHAPTER NINE

The Lost Cause
We Cherished and Loved

The Travail of Southern Conservatism

The petrified man bobbed up out of the Saluda River on November 12, 1895. W. M. Buff, a Lexington County farmer who claimed he had discovered this prodigy while fishing, assured a reporter from the *State* newspaper that "it was a white man, judging by the moustache and the hair." Soon "medical experts" connected to the fall state fair would proclaim to South Carolinians that the Saluda River Petrified Man had been a British soldier, a link to South Carolina's glorious Revolutionary past, that all could view for the admission price of a nickel.[1]

Eager to cash in on the find, the State Agricultural and Mechanical Fair advertised throughout the Carolina midlands. A broadside appeared in the streets of Columbia, inviting the citizens of the city to view this prodigy and assuring them of the veracity of the story. A long list of "experts" signed their names to the bottom of the broadside in tiny print. More significantly, Farmer Buff's Confederate background figured prominently in the state fair's attempt to sell its curiosity to the public. The broadside describes Buff as living on land that had been his grandfather's, land that Buff had defended as a Confederate cavalryman. More important than the legitimacy conferred by forensic experts was the appeal to South Carolinians' respect for Confederate virtue to convince them that the Saluda River Petrified Man was no hoax.[2]

The discovery and commodification of this bit of bizarrerie occurred only days after the close of the 1895 constitutional convention. Significantly, the newspaper report of the petrified man immediately sought to give a racial classification to the find, asserting forthrightly that it could be only a white man. In this, the operators of the state fair shared the convention's fervor for defining racial identity. The showmen also invoked the Lost Cause to their aid, using it as a way to advertise their spectacle.

The memory of the Confederacy was slowly becoming the tool of carnival barkers. The Saluda River Petrified Man is a perfect symbol for the changing ethos of South Carolina; a public representation of racial purity, depoliticized and at the same time summoning a heroic Confederate past to press into the service of the entrepreneurial impulse. Like the petrified man, the Lost Cause increasingly became a hollow spectacle, hawked by vendors interested in financial gain rather than Confederate virtue.

The transformation of the Lost Cause celebration in South Carolina mirrored larger changes in Confederate memorialization throughout the South in the final decade of the nineteenth century. The rise of the United Confederate Veterans (UCV) in particular signaled a transformation in the uses of Confederate memory. Subsuming local organizations, the UCV would increasingly propound an ideology of reconciliation grounded in racist notions of imperialism and white supremacy. Rather than defending an organic society shaped and spanned by tradition and custom, the Lost Cause became an agent of bourgeois values throughout the South, joining with other cultural and ideological forces that pressed the region into the mold of a larger America.

The UCV grew out of a New Orleans meeting of representatives of Mississippi, Tennessee, and Louisiana veterans' groups. Gaines Foster has pointed out that of the eight original organizers, none had ties to the traditional southern elite. Instead these representatives of a new southern bourgeoisie had worked after the war as insurance agents, merchants, private building contractors, and railroad executives. John B. Gordon, Georgia senator, hero of the Lost Cause, and ally to New South business interests, lent his name and influence to the fledgling organization, helping to develop it from its small beginnings in 1889 into an organization of 850 local camps by 1896 and 1,565 camps by 1903. The *Confederate Veteran,* the official organ of the UCV, aided immeasurably in the spread of the organization. The cheaply printed, and cheaply sold, magazine related military history, half legendary tales of Confederate exploits, and campfire lore and humor from the bivouac. Appealing to the common soldier, the *Confederate Veteran* reached a larger audience than earlier Lost Cause journals that had focused on the intricate details of campaigns and spilled much ink over controversy among generals.[3]

In South Carolina, the UCV grew slowly in the early 1890s. Tillman's rise to power and the attendant upheaval perhaps accounts for the original difficulties the organization faced. In September 1893, S. S. Crittendon, of Travelers Rest, described South Carolina as "still behind most of her sister states in organizing Confederate veteran camps." Crittendon,

a veteran and virulent opponent of Reconstruction, had in the 1890s become a booster of the failed Atlantic, Greenville, and Western railroad
and of the UCV. In the late 1890s, Crittendon could look with pleasure
on a state that had, in the words of Gaines Foster, "a dramatically higher"
number of camps than other states of the old Confederacy.[4]

New South promoters like Crittendon may have celebrated the growth
of the new organization, but South Carolina veterans evinced a desire to
cling to local "survivors associations" rather than to allow themselves to
be subsumed in the national UCV. Anderson County's Survivor's Association of Orr's Rifles, for example, remained independent of the UCV
at least until 1904. A wary attitude toward the UCV's theme of reconciliation with the North influenced this recalcitrance, even after Carolina veterans joined the national organization. Partisanship in a controversy that rocked the national organization reveals the orientation of at
least one South Carolina camp. The Abner Perrin Camp in Edgefield was
guided through its early existence by Tillman opponent and Alliance lecturer George B. Lake. In October 1899 the members passed a resolution
giving their full support to S. A. Cunningham, the editor of the *Confederate Veteran,* in his running battle with J. C. Underwood. Cunningham charged that Underwood, who superintended the Confederate Battle
Abbey project, in which veterans sought to build a Richmond, Virginia,
reliquary for the Lost Cause, had not only used the project as a source
of personal gain, he had committed sacrilege against Confederate religion
by raising funds from northern financiers. Cunningham also likely proved
popular with South Carolina veterans because of his resistance to the idea
of holding a common Memorial Day observance with Union veterans.[5]

Increasingly, the UCV and its large annual reunions functioned as tools
for reconciling the South back into the Union and for transmitting the
values of the American middle class. J. L. M. Curry, a thoroughly recon-
structed rebel, used his speech at the 1896 reunion in Richmond to praise
the Atlanta Exposition, a forum for celebrating New South industrial
progress, and the "northern governors and troops" who attended. Curry
found these and similar events to be signs of "reconciliation and broth-
erhood between north and south." While praising the conquerors of the
South for their magnanimity, Curry lashed out at those agrarian southerners who had challenged the emerging corporate order through the
Farmer's Alliance and the People's Party. "Nothing can be greater folly
for the southern people," Curry insisted, "than to take up false or destructive issues, assaulting the foundations of private and public credit, weak-
ening financial integrity and rectitude." Curry used this speech, and others

SOUTH CAROLINA CURIOSITY
～～ THE ～～

PETRIFIED MAN

Found by W. M. BUFF, near Saluda River, five miles north of Columbia, in Lexington County, South Carolina, November 10th, 1895.

WILL BE ON EXHIBITION IN

We have one of Edison's Latest Improved PHONOGRAPHS and all who visit the Exhibition can listen to a free tune.

ADMISSION TEN CENTS.

...man, supposed to be a Crickee Sei..., ...ed duri... over a hundred years ago, and supposed to be 25 or 30 years of age at death. He is 5 feet 9 in. high and weighs in his present condition 313 lbs.

Mr. Buff, who found the body, is well known in Columbia and Lexington County, S. C. He was born and reared, as was his father before him, on the land adjoining the creek, in the bed of which the body was found. He bears a good reputation, is a veteran of the late war and did several years' service on James Island. He was a member of the Fifth South Carolina Cavalry.

Hundreds of physicians have examined the body and pronounce it, beyond all doubt, to be really a petrified human body. It is well worth seeing and there is no doubt as to its genuineness. While in Columbia, the body was carefully examined by Dr. Birney, the State Chemist, who, with the aid of a microscope, found traces of hair in the eyebrows and other parts of the body. When found lips were tightly shut. On chipping the lip, three teeth are thus exposed and are perfect. All gentlemen of the medical profession are invited to examine the body.

THE EXHIBITION IS OPEN TO LADIES AND CHILDREN, WHO MAY ATTEND AT ANY TIME.

We the undersigned Physicians, have examined the body and pronounce it a genuine specimen of petrifaction of the human body:

F. D. Kendall,	M. D.	Columbia, S.C.	R. M. Galloway D.D.S.	Lancaster, S. C.	E. C. Smith	M.D.	Richmond, Va.
L. K. Philpot,	"	"	R. C. McManus	M.D.	" "	R. D. Brooker	"	" "
J. M. Quattlebaum, D.D.S.		"	J. F. Atkinson	"	Richburg, "	B. F. Webster	"	Norfolk, "
C. E. Leaphart	M.D.	Lexington,	W. D. K. Wylie	"	"	J. W. Thomas	Chemist	" "
D. M. Crosson	"	Leesville,	M. J. Walker	"	Yorkville, "	G. S. Ramseur	M.D.	Blacksburg, S. C.
M. J. D. Dantzer	"	Elloree.	W. G. White	"	"	S. B. Crawley	"	Gaffney, "
A. S. Mydrick	"	Orangeburg,	S. W. Campbell	"	Clover, "	W. A. Fort	"	"
W. G. Houseal	"	Newberry,	J. H. Sage	"	Sharon, "	O. S. Fall	"	Clifton, "
J. M. Kibler	"	"	J. C. Montgomery	"	Charlotte, N. C.	W. A. Smith	"	Glendale, "
W. H. Young	"	Clinton,	J. W. Byers	"	"	G. H. Jones	"	Cashville, "
L. M. Bailey	"	"	W. H. Wilson	"	Gastonia, "	W. M. Drummond	"	Woodruff, "
Hugh K. Aiken	"	Laurens,	C. E. Adams	"	"	H. T. Templeton	"	Enoree, "
J. A. Barksdale	"	"	J. G. Hord, M.D., King's Mountain, "		S. P. Neal	"	Greenwood, "
J. P. Carlisle	D.D.S.	Greenville,	J. L. McKay	"	"	R. B. Epting	"	"
Thomas Earle	Chemist	"	A. S. Whitaker	M.I.	Biltmore, "	J. P. Ducket	"	Anderson, "
J Nott Moore	M.D.	Spartanburg,	John H. Williams	"	Asheville, "	W. C. Bomer	"	Belton, "
C. E. Johnson	"	"	B. A. Cheek	"	Marion, "	J. M. Caldwell	"	King's Creek, "
W. F. Strait	"	Rock Hill,	W. A. Marler	D.D.S.	Hickory, "	J. H. Roberts	"	Ehrhardt, "
Jas. P. Crawford	"	"	J. C. Whitesides	M.D.	Newton, "	W. F. Mitchell	"	Blackstock, "
F. M. Storks	"	Branchville,	A. E. Ledbetter	"	Greensboro, "	G. M. Jordan	"	Rodman, "
S. C. Miller	"	Chester,	A. B. Robertson	"	Chapel Hill, "	J. A. Hancock	"	Carlisle, "
S. M. Davega	"	"	R. V. Barksdale	"	Danville, Va.	J. B. Delvaux	"	Paris, France.
J. G. Going	"	Union,	H. W. Cole	Chemist	" "			

In the 1890s, the Lost Cause lost its tone of defiance and became, in the hands of some, a commercial phenomenon. Hawkers of the Saluda River Petrified Man, placed on display at the 1895 South Carolina State Fair, insisted on its legitimacy by underscoring the Confederate service record of W. M. Buff, the alleged finder of the curiosity. Courtesy of the South Caroliniana Library, University of South Carolina, Columbia (SCL).

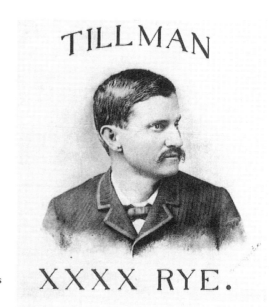

The dispensary plan—"Ben Tillman's baby"—ignited controversy between bourgeois reformers and Bourbon conservatives. (SCL)

Famed Confederate Cavalry general Wade Hampton became the titular head of South Carolina conservatism. (SCL)

An aging Hampton remained a symbol of South Carolina's Lost Cause until his death in 1902. Here he speaks at a Confederate monument dedication sometime in the 1890s. (SCL)

Monument dedication, Edgefield, South Carolina. (SCL)

given throughout the South, to memorialize the Confederate soldier and to expound his view that state-supported public education would civilize the ignorant, and possibly dangerous, masses. During his days as a Harvard student, Curry had been influenced by Horace Mann's view that education should act as a bulwark of bourgeois order.[6]

South Carolina hosted two UCV reunions in the 1890s, and both events reveal the changes wrought on Confederate memory by the ideals of the bourgeoisie. Charleston, rather than the upcountry, hosted these events, both because of Charleston's symbolic value in connection with the war and because local boosters successfully attracted and profited from the event. Instead of being planned by local veteran groups or UCV officials, the 1899 reunion had been organized by "a committee composed of the representative professional and business men of the community." At a cost of thirty-five thousand dollars, the city council erected Thomas Hall in the downtown area specifically for the two reunions; local entrepreneurs used the souvenir guide distributed to the veterans as advertising copy. Edward P. Guerard, of the Mutual Life Insurance Companies of New York, helped pay for the printing and distribution of the 1896 guides.[7]

In keeping with an event partially funded by a New York insurance firm, little of the spirit of rebel defiance crept into these reunions. The UCV, now preaching reconciliation with their former foes, promoted a new Americanism in which rebels formally pledged allegiance to a United States if only Yankees would agree to recognize that they had shown valor on the battlefield and had committed treason in good faith. Promotional literature for the 1899 reunion asserted that "whether men fought on one side or the other" the remembrance of the war that Charleston would provoke "must ever excite the martial spirit." Seeking to inflame this "martial spirit," the planners of the 1899 reunion prepared a number of tourist events, including a trip to the ruins of Fort Sumter and a tour of the U.S. Cruiser *Raleigh* that could be seen "by small boats and cheap rates."[8]

The desire for reunion, rather than an effort to keep alive the issues of the war, drove the impulse to tell "the true history" of the conflict and to defend the South against the charge of treason. A special concern of the 1899 reunion was that "the truth be told" about secession as the veterans would tell it, not "as some would-be historians would write it." The truth about southern valor on the battlefield, and the constitutional right of secession, would, the UCV promoters asserted, bring "perfect reconciliation between the North and South." Addressing a South Carolina UCV reunion in November 1901, C. S. Vedder, a Presbyterian minister, chose a similar theme. Vedder seemed too pleased by half that Theodore Roosevelt had praised Robert E. Lee as a great commander. In arguing that the South had fought for its constitutional rights, rather than for slavery or for an illegal secession from the Union, Vedder assured the veterans that "these things are not recalled to open old wounds but to show that these wounds were honorably earned." In a moment of supreme irony, Vedder told the UCV gathering that what northerners referred to as "the War of the Rebellion" actually "is part now of the priceless heritage of the whole American people."[9]

South Carolina Confederate veterans did publish several histories of the war in the 1880s and '90s, hoping, they claimed, to tell its true history. Occasionally the authors of these reminiscences served the purpose of sacralizing their nouveau riche identity in the older traditions of the South. Colonel David Cardwell, who became the adjutant general of the South Carolina UCV in the 1890s, wrote one such account, a history of Pelham's battery. Cardwell seems to have been the UCV official that S. E. May described as one of the "incorrigible skulkers" in Lee's army, although a biographical sketch by University of South Carolina historian Yates Snowden has him fighting in every major battle on the eastern front.[10]

Sometimes the "true" history of the war, or at least a version of the conflict less pleasing to southern bourgeois sensibilities, did make it into the pages of these memoirs. J. B. E. Sloane, often a lecturer to audiences on his role in the Battle of First Manassas, paid for the publication of a history of Greenville County's Fourth South Carolina Regiment, written by Private J. W. Reid. Reid had been one of the few South Carolinians to work in manufacturing before the war, moving from a cotton factory in Laurens County to Vardry McBee's small Reedy River factory in 1838. His brief history, based on his correspondence with his wife, tells the tale of what he called "our glorious and old 4th regiment" and includes stories of Confederates carousing, drinking "popskull," and engaging in criticism of the conscription bill by calling Jefferson Davis a tyrant and the Confederacy a military dictatorship. Reid had received money from Sloane after writing to his old colonel with a tale of sickness and impoverishment. "I am unable to do much work," Reid had written to his colonel, "I have lost my wife and is going from pillar to post as best I can." Sloane surely saw the financial gift he made to Reid for the publication of his book as a show of paternalism and concern for a fellow Confederate. Though there exists no record of the response to Reid's utterly honest history of the working class Confederate's life and attitudes, it likely ruffled many a bourgeois feather in its telling the "true" history of the war.[11]

A harsh demographic fact further explains the interest in publishing histories of the war. Several of the most prominent leaders of the generation who had fought the war had, in one way or the other, passed from the scene by the late 1890s. Martin W. Gary had died in the early 1880s, following his failed bid for governor against Hampton ally Johnson Hagood. William King Easley had died by the time Redemption came in '76. D. Wyatt Aiken had passed away in the 1880s without seeing his beloved Grange become a much stronger movement in the Farmer's Alliance. Other Confederate or conservative leaders passed into the shadows, even as Tillman's sun rose in the late 1890s. Ellison Keitt seems to have gone into semiretirement by the last decade of the century, writing an unpublished memoir of his life in 1900. Keitt's memoir came to an abrupt end before the rise of Tillman, as if the war and the 1876 campaign had represented the only events worth recording now that "Christianity and civilization" had been overrun by Tillman's "barbarian hordes." S. E. May left the state for Florida after the beginning of the Tillman aegis.[12]

Wade Hampton, the lodestar of Carolina's conservative culture for almost thirty years, disappeared from the scene after his humiliating defeat by Tillman lieutenant J. L. M. Irby in the 1891 senatorial race. A shady and inept character, Irby would eventually alienate his own political allies as he descended into what Stephen Kantrowitz calls "an alcoholic confusion and paranoia." Irby represented a new political generation in South Carolina that cared little for the conservative invocation of the past, causing Hampton to lament in 1890, "Good God! The memories of '61, of '65, have they been obliterated?" Irby himself had been only seven years old at the time of Lee's surrender.[13]

Meanwhile the UCV camp gatherings reflected the growing realization that the generation that had fought the war now faced its own mortality. The Confederate Survivor's Association of Augusta, in which a number of veterans from western South Carolina participated, began their 1893 meeting with a recitation of "Confederates of rank and prominence who died since our last meeting." The officers mentioned several leading members of South Carolina's Hampton Legion and South Carolina's wartime governor A. G. Magrath, all of whom had "entered into the realm of shadows." Edgefield County's Abner Perrin Camp of the UCV transformed itself into a burial society in February 1897, when it passed a resolution that each member should pay a dollar into a general fund for the burial of veterans. The Edgefield veterans realized that their own position in South

Carolina society had changed as they entered their golden years; they were forced to pass a resolution in 1895 condemning an editorial writer who had called for aged veterans to be placed in a state-run poorhouse. An invitation to the veterans to the 1899 Charleston reunion seemed eager to shuffle them off the stage as quickly and as melodramatically as possible. "Feel the presence of the hosts of shadow forms that gather," the advertisement copy purpled, that "beckon their weary companions across the river and into rest under the shade of the trees." At the turn of a new century, many believed the time to fold the banner of the Confederacy had truly come. In urging a grand celebration in Charleston, one piece of promotional literature noted, "it has been suggested that as the war began in Charleston, it would be a fitting conclusion to the whole martial period if it should end in Charleston—or rather that the Confederate reunion of 1899 might very well be the last." [14]

Sic transit gloria mundi seemed the most common sentiment among Confederate veterans of all ranks in the 1890s. J. W. Reid, writing to his old commander for financial help, appears to have been propelled to write his history by the feeling that his life, and the celebration of the Confederacy, had drawn to a close. In "a few verses" of what Reid admitted to be "badly composed poetry," the working-class Reid gave voice to the feeling of many veterans of the Confederate generation. "I was alone in my cabin," Reid said, "thinking of where I was just thirty years ago and thinking of the difference between that time and the present:

> But thirty years are now gone by
> How Few I now can see
> That heard the dying man's sad cry
> That fought that day with me
> Theay are gone to mansions upon high
> Whear I hope sometime to go
> And join the Band that I stood by
> Just Thirty year ago. [15]

Even as the UCV camps took on the tone of funeral societies, new organizations sought to take up the mantle of Confederate memory and to redeploy it in the interests of middle-class ideals. The United Daughters of the Confederacy (UDC) became the most successful of these efforts, acting as an agent for the new southern bourgeois, even as they expressed their new values in the language of filial piety. The Daughters had their origin in Nashville, Tennessee, a town that, like its Georgia cousin Atlanta, had quickly bought into the gospel of the New South. Caroline

Meriwether Goodlet, the wife of a prominent Nashville lawyer, founded the organization. Goodlet made good her bourgeois credentials by serving as vice-president for the Tennessee Humane Society, a member of the board of managers for the Protestant Orphans Asylum, an advocate for prison reform, and the driving force behind the state's first compulsory-education law. Goodlet and the women who formed state chapters of the group would ensure that their members brought with them bourgeois credentials as well. A welcome address at the 1896 third annual reunion of the Daughters insisted that the doors of the organization stood open "for all those in whose veins flowed one drop of patriotic blood." In truth, that patriotic blood had to flow at least a bit blue. Membership requirements included obtaining the sponsorship of two current members; individual chapters could reject women of "objectionable character," even if they proved themselves true Confederate daughters. Status anxiety played such a central role in the organization that it almost tore itself apart when Goodlet's claim as founder of the group faced a challenge from Mrs. A. M. Raines of Savannah. In 1900, a committee to decide which woman had been the founding member tried to reach a compromise, but neither party seems to have been mollified. Goodlet had the last word, literally, by having the words "Founder of the U.D.C." carved into her tombstone.[16]

Following the turn of the century, the UDC would go so far in their drive for middle-class respectability as to seek to change the words of the soldier's beloved song "Dixie." The "Negro dialect" of the song, some suggested, did not match the "chaste and refined" image that the southern people allegedly could claim. Through a closed circle of membership, composed of women who sometimes had little relationship to the horrors of the war and the larger meanings of the Confederacy, the UDC perpetrated an absurd "moonlight and magnolias" view of the South and became a bulwark of bourgeois racism into the twentieth century.[17]

The South Carolina UDC did not emerge until 1896 and seems to have grown quite slowly. Like the men's organization, it may have emerged late because of the continued strength of local groups, particularly the Ladies Memorial Association. The greatest strength of the South Carolina UDC seems to have been in Charleston, with a Mrs. Augustine T. Smyth organizing the original chapter. Smythe's leadership of the fledgling organization ensured that it would become an agent of middle-class values. Mrs. Smyth was the wife of a prominent attorney, state senator, and stockholder in the Anderson Phosphate and Oil Company. Her brother-in-law was Ellison Smyth, the "Captain" who had created the "model industrial experiment" in Pelzer, South Carolina. Under the leadership of Smyth and other Charleston grande dames, the UDC presence would slowly move across the state, not really taking fire until 1900. Just as elsewhere in the South, the Carolina membership would draw primarily from the wives of the town elite.[18]

The South Carolina UDC would soon come to play a role in the state's Confederate home in Columbia. Part of a larger movement to provide homes for indigent Confederates, and to place them on public display as both images of a lost past and examples of bourgeois virtues, the movement for a Confederate home in South Carolina did not begin until 1900, and a home itself did not open until Confederate Memorial Day, 1909. R. B. Rosenburg, who has written an excellent history of the Confederate soldier's homes, finds no easy explanation why the birthplace of secession came so late to the movement. In part, lack of interest in the home surely came from veterans themselves who shared the Abner Perrin's Camp's hostility to the notion that elderly Confederates could be placed in "the poorhouse."[19]

The home that finally opened in Columbia represented Foucault's "prison of moral order," in which the veterans were forced to adhere to middle-class notions of temperance and hygiene. One Abbeville County veteran found himself expelled for hiding a bottle of whiskey; then, having no means of support, he faced the shame of begging for a second chance and agreeing to "try to comply with the rules and regulations." One group of veterans who slipped out of the Columbia facility for an all-night drinking and fishing frolic forced the home to build walls and hire night watchmen to prevent another escape. The UDC would eventually lead inspection teams into the homes to monitor the behavior of the elderly veterans, becoming so intrusive that several male superintendents resigned in protest.[20]

As the Confederate generation aged and went to their graves in the 1890s, increasing numbers of monuments were built in South Carolina. One motive behind the creation of these memorials was the sacred aura of Confederate sacrifice that had pervaded the earliest efforts to preserve Confederate memory; other, more complex motives related to realities of life in the New South. When the older generation of Confederate leaders took part in the dedication of these monuments, they often took the opportunity to express a clear anxiety that the values of southern conservatism had been eroded by the ways of the New South.

The unveiling of the Greenville County monument in September 1892, for example, drew on older themes in the celebration of the Lost Cause, even as the celebrants pondered the changes coming to their state after the first two years of Tillman's governorship. Bishop Ellison Capers lent the aura of Confederate religion to the occasion, and the monument's model was James Blackman Ligon, a Greenville resident, the first man to enlist in the Saluda Volunteers of the Fourth South Carolina. A parade and marching band attended the dedication ceremony, but a sense of palpable gloom pervaded much of the proceeding, including the inscription on the monument itself, which read in part, "All Lost, But by the graves / Where Martyred Heroes Rest / He wins the most who honor saves." James Hoyt, a leader in anti-Reconstruction violence and a vehement opponent of Tillman, expressed in his speech the hope that Confederate memory might inspire new generations as the New South world of commerce and entrepreneurship intruded on the conservative values of South Carolina. "The Lost Cause" had been "purer and holier," Hoyt intoned, "because of the woes attending its sepulcher." Hoyt hoped that in the future, as the marble Confederate soldier looked out on the "mart of trade," children of the New South would recall the warrior values of the past. A woman "visiting the home of her ancestors" will bring her child to see the stone Confederate, Hoyt predicted; this symbol of a lost place and time would awaken in the young "an earnest desire to know more of the deeds of his forefathers, rescuing the story so familiar to this generation, but now fast dying away with the men who have borne the honored title Confederate survivor." Hoyt's hope for a revival of Confederate virtue in some far off future would never come. In the 1920s Greenville would move the soldier from the "mart of trade" on North Main Street because it interfered with the new reality of automobile traffic. In 1924 the city council moved the monument to its present location in the city's Springwood Cemetery, underscoring just how "lost" the cause had become.[21]

Other South Carolina upcountry monuments at the turn of the century drew heavily on the aspirations and nostalgia of American middle-class culture. The Greenwood County monument, erected in 1903, represented a monument to the prominent Waller family rather than to the Confederacy. Creswell Archimedes Calhoun Waller, whose substantial name matched his substantial holdings in Greenwood real estate, provided most of the thirty-five hundred dollars necessary to build the monument, a marble figure modeled on his brother Robert A. Waller, who had died at the Battle of Antietam in 1862. C. A. C. Waller, described by one chronicler as a man "whose influence was felt in all areas of Greenwood life," seems to have hoped to use the Lost Cause to give his New South wealth the patina of hoary antiquity, just as he engaged in absurd genealogical speculations in which he became a direct descendant of William the

Conqueror.[22] A similar attempt to substantiate New South fortunes occurred in York County. The Fort Mill Confederate Park, which contained
monuments to faithful slaves, the women of the Old South, Catawba who
had served the Confederacy, and Johnny Reb, resulted from a financial
partnership between local notable Samuel Elliot White and John McKee
Spratt. Spratt represented a new generation of South Carolina leaders; a
child during the war, he used family connections in the 1880s to become
a land magnate, lumber baron, and cotton mill owner.[23]

The turn of the century would see businesses such as the McNeel Marble Company of Marietta, Georgia, actually launch efforts aimed at encouraging UDC chapters to begin monument building campaigns. They
urged the Daughters into various financing schemes with the argument
that their being dependent on contributors (as were the Ladies Memorial
Associations) slowed the process of monument building. Increasingly, this
commercialization of Confederate virtue showed in the pages of Cunningham's *Confederate Veteran,* in which more and more pages were devoted
to advertisements with the legitimating mantle of the Confederacy. One
issue contained an advertisement for "E. W. Averell: Practical Jeweler,"
which contained the Confederate battle flag and described Mr. Averell
as "a member in good standing of Cheatham Bivouac, UCV." The many
South Carolina veterans who joined their Confederate sympathies with
the Farmer's Alliance must have been appalled by the advertisement for
"Jennings Business College: The Most Practical Institution of its kind in
the World," which bragged of being endorsed by "leading merchants and
bankers."[24]

Changes in the celebration of Confederate memory reflected changes
in South Carolina, an adjustment to the zeitgeist of a new age. The Lost
Cause had offered South Carolinians a body of tradition that recreated
patterns of deference, republican notions of liberty for property-holding
white men, and a hierarchical society believed to reflect a transcendent
order. The 1890s had seen the unseating of the leaders of the Old South
by a bourgeois vanguard preaching a virulent white supremacy connected
to a watery progressivism. Men like Tillman supporter W. H. Timmerman, of Edgefield, elected to the state senate in 1890, represent this new
class. Organizer of the Farmer's Loan and Savings Bank in Edgefield, an
upstanding member of the Baptist Church, and a stockholder in the Edgefield Oil Mill, Timmerman helped press through Tillman's "white's only"
progressivism. Most of the new leadership in South Carolina had similar
biographies. William J. Cooper's study of the professional backgrounds of
leading Tillman supporters compared with those of the leaders among the

Bourbon Democrats found that, despite the Tillmanite harangues against rings and corporation lawyers, more lawyers gave their support to Tillman than to the old regime. Even more telling, almost twice as many merchants, the real power base of the changing South Carolina economy, gave their support to Tillman's agenda than to the conservatives'.[25]

The rise of this new leadership class coincided with the decline of the independent yeoman farmer and the creation of a new working class of South Carolina whites, whose point of reference became the cotton mill rather than the cotton farm. By 1900, six out of every ten farmers worked as tenants or sharecroppers, all the while paying a fertilizer tax to support Clemson College so that the sons of landlords could learn "scientific agriculture." For the farmers, this transformation meant both a loss of independence and a loss of identity, as Confederate virtue and allegiances to local notables that had been so important in rural farming communities gave way to the new relationships created by mill and town. Increasingly, new railroad lines and the availability of waterpower in the upcountry transformed much of the state northwest of Columbia into a region that, linked with western North Carolina, became the cradle of a southern industrial revolution. The dream of entrepreneurs and politicians who wanted a New South free of cotton fields, stubborn mules, and stubborn Confederates came to fruition as Greenville, Spartanburg, Oconee, York, Lancaster, Greenwood, Fairfield, and Chester Counties became the center of the textiles revolution. In 1880 South Carolina had fourteen cotton mills; sixty-one mills would be built in the state between 1895 and 1907. One hundred and sixty-seven mills employing forty-seven thousand former farmers and farm wives would make the state second to Massachusetts, its ancient enemy, in textile production by 1910.[26]

Transforming the economic base of South Carolina, the rise of the cotton mill also transformed the nature of work. The population of the wage-earning class increased from 2,053 in the 1880s to 48,079 in 1920. David Carlton argues that such a basic change in the economic structure of the state inevitably created a class system that reordered traditional rural patterns of behavior and resulted in a growing distinction between town people and mill people. The town merchant became the fulcrum of the town's economy, subordinating agriculture to the demands of crop-lien and credit. Carlton's investigation of upcountry Anderson revealed that before 1860 the town had 44 residents running small business concerns. By 1881, 188 worked as shopkeepers. Such changes represented "a fundamental shift in economics and social power."[27]

The new elite seemed no longer interested in the values of the older southern order, and reconciliation in the interests of bourgeois ideals quickly became the order of the day. In the case of South Carolina, if a Woodwardian "great compromise" between southern politicians and northern capitalist occurred, it happened in the 1890s rather than in 1877. Tillman, for example, showed little interest in regulating South Carolina business, except for the phosphate industry in the low country, which likely would have moved on to the more profitable Florida deposits without the help of Tillmania. Landlords and merchants who found themselves pleased with Tillman's governorship had few qualms about lending their support to Tillman when they saw that he had no intention of changing the crop-lien law. Tillman helped pass a law limiting the textile mill workers' week to sixty-six hours, a law made after consulting with the South Carolina piedmont's new captains of industry rather than with what Tillman referred to as "the damned factory class."[28]

South Carolina's new leadership class continued to give a respectful nod to the Lost Cause, but their Lost Cause represented a dead past to be honored rather than a living ideology of defiance. Increasingly, reconciliation with the North became a theme of even the Lost Cause celebrations. Wealthy landlords, railroad interests, textile mill owners, and the ladies of the UDC could find little reason to refight the issues of the war. This new ideology found expression in Confederate monuments as well. The town of Camden, in Kershaw County, for example, dedicated a decorative drinking fountain to Richard Kirkland, a South Carolina soldier who had taken water to the suffering wounded in both blue and gray after the battle of Fredericksburg. Rather than symbolizing Confederate virtue, this monument, built with money raised by some of Tillman's public school children, honors the turn-of-the-century sentiment of reconciliation. An inscription describes Kirkland as "moved by Christlike compassion" for the northern soldiers he aided, a sentiment at odds with the warrior virtues praised by the earlier Lost Cause celebration. As if to stress the changed meaning of this particular Lost Cause monument, the Humane Society of New York City provided the design for the structure.[29]

Reaction in South Carolina to the Spanish-American War in 1898 reveals the growing strength of reconciliation sentiment as part of the popular mood, but it also reveals the wariness with which some segments of the state resisted the impulse to fight on behalf of their conquerors. Interpreters of the Lost Cause have accurately seen attitudes toward the Spanish-American War as a bellwether for southern attitudes toward reunion. Charles Reagan Wilson notes that southern attitudes at the turn of the century made it "the key period of reconciliation." Upcountry sentiment certainly showed a marked change toward northern and national ideals. Greenville's upper-middle-class First Baptist Church hosted Philadelphia's Peter H. Goldsmith, a hawkish Baptist minister, in May 1898. Goldsmith almost seemed to invite the congregation to reunion with the North on the basis of a notion of "national destiny" that promised to crush the forces of disorder and radicalism. Goldsmith, alluding to the recent May Day antiwar strikes in New York, praised the city for "killing a few anarchists" and thus proving that America could be "a vast incinatory for evil." Goldsmith praised the South as "the mainstay of the republic," and his sermon concluded with the singing of "America" and "God Bless Our Land." [30]

Newspaper editors, often voices of middle-class and New South sentiment at the end of the nineteenth century, became the most vociferous proponents of involvement in the war. The editor of the *Gaffney Ledger,* writing for a region that had been a hotbed of anti-Reconstruction violence in the 1870s, suggested in 1898 that "sectional prejudice is fast becoming a thing of the past." The *Greenville Mountaineer* certainly evinced this desire for reunion on the basis of an American imperialism, reporting with glee the success of county enlistment officers. Both newspapers unwittingly reveal a lack of enthusiasm in some quarters. Though reporting on the alleged decline of "sectional prejudice," the *Gaffney Ledger* also admitted that recruitment in South Carolina had been quite slow. Although the *Mountaineer* crowed about heavy enlistments in Greenville, its editors criticized Spartanburg County for "not sending any troops to the front at this time" and noted a "real lack of military organization" throughout the state. [31]

Michel Foucault has written that historical eras do not disappear as discreetly as geological epochs. Older notions of southern conservatism and its relationship to the Lost Cause continued to appear in the midst of a changing cultural ethos. An aged Wade Hampton occasionally spoke with some of his old fire, seemingly freed to become an unrepentant Confederate warlord once his senatorial days had passed. Hampton sounded as if he were speaking in 1866 or 1876 when he exclaimed at an 1896 UCV reunion, "I would still be fighting had the flag not ceased to wave!" The few Bourbon state legislators who had survived the Tillman onslaught spoke up for a conservative state paternalism that limited the depredations of capital on the people and institutions of the state. J. Q. Marshall, a Richland County Bourbon, presented the state's first child labor law in 1903; Tillman ignored the issue, and Ellison Smyth, of the Pelzer experiment in progressive capitalism, called the evils of child labor "imaginary and greatly exaggerated."[32]

Leroy Youmans, until his death in 1906, continued as an outspoken critic of the new age dawning. Youmans had embodied the ideal of the elite southern warrior; twice he was elected to the South Carolina legislature, in 1862 and 1864, and returned to lead his cavalry command at the end of each session. A leader of the conservatives in 1876, Youmans had been outspoken Bourbon. His attachment to Confederate virtue appears in his November 1895 address to Confederate veterans. Showing none of the age's obsession with reconciliation, Youmans referred to the army that had plundered Columbia as a "mob" headed by "the vandal of the century." Confederate memory, he asserted, could serve as a point of reference in a world of change, even in the face of the "juggernaut of progress." Youmans asserted that such an ancient landmark seemed especially necessary in this "utilitarian age" in which "shrewdness has taken the place of principle." Nor would Youmans accept South Carolina's growing American nationalism. An address Youmans delivered on Washington's birthday, likely in 1900, criticized the United States' willingness to intervene in Cuba and the Philippines. Calling such incipient imperialism "a cloud, foretelling danger," Youmans believed that such adventurism represented "Yankee meddling" all over again, with the Federal government now seeking to "spread its laws and usages around the globe."[33]

Youmans and other outspoken critics of the new regime represented voices crying in the wilderness, listened to respectfully for past service and bravery and then happily ignored. Youmans's private musings reveal a man obsessed with a bygone era, fully aware that a new era was upon him. The old Bourbon's private scrapbooks are filled with pictures of Wade Hampton, M. C. Butler, Jefferson Davis, and Robert E. Lee. Keeping his mind active by tracing out the odes of Horace, in Latin and from memory, the Edgefield lawyer also occasionally versified about the lostness of the Lost Cause. Youmans heard "Echoes of olden voices / Phantom delights long dead" and took the measure of contemporary South Carolina when he wrote sadly of "fortunes broken / Vandals in forum and mart." In Youmans's eyes, the Barbarians had beaten down the gates.[34]

Southern conservatism certainly had a voice to raise in protest to the new order, but these voices sometimes seemed as aged and decrepit as the Confederate veterans themselves. No event better reveals the degree to which South Carolinians had forsaken the southern conservative values of the Lost Cause than the controversy surrounding the meeting of the Farmer's Institute at Clemson College in 1903. The Farmer's Institute, which met yearly at what some called "the old homestead of John Calhoun," embodied much of Tillman's dream for a capitalist agricultural revolution. Preaching the gospel of scientific agriculture and an end to what Tillman had called "land butchery," the Clemson faculty and reform-minded speakers throughout the state induced a number of South Carolina's landlords to make a yearly pilgrimage to the event. Senator Tillman had himself served on the original planning committee that attempted to reconfigure traditional South Carolina agriculture by offering lectures on fertilizers, dairying, and beekeeping, with keynotes regarding the supreme importance of continuing agricultural education.[35]

Upcountry South Carolinians had often combined their celebrations of agriculture and the Lost Cause. The state fair, a project of the South Carolina Agricultural and Mechanical Society, had functioned as an agricultural showcase and as gathering of veterans to hear speakers such as Hampton or to do the organizational work of, for example, the Ladies Memorial Association. Thus, Anderson County's Survivor's Association of Orr's Rifles, one of the few remaining groups that had not been subsumed by the UCV, planned to hold its reunion in conjunction with Clemson's Farmer's Institute. Much to the surprise of the veterans, Clemson's board of trustees informed them that they would not be allowed to meet with the Institute.

The reasons for this decision are not clearly explicated in the minutes of Clemson's Board of Trustees, and the controversy seems not to have made it into local newspapers. The board apparently acted in conjunction with a Farmer's Institute committee regarding the veterans' application to attend. The board approved an earlier action of the committee, "declining to allow organizations, societies to meet at the college" that did not have an "agricultural or mechanical purpose." This seems a specious reason for refusing to allow the veterans to meet, particularly since the college later allowed an upcountry minister's conference to meet in conjunction with the Institute.[36]

The attitude of Tillmanism toward the ethos of southern conservatism offers a more plausible explanation for the refusal. Tillmanism represented an upheaval of South Carolina life, an upheaval in which the merits of the Old South and the centrality of Confederate virtue had to give way to the practical goals of progressive reform and, more important, capitalist development. Though Tillman's attitude of rabid sectionalism complicated his attitude, the class and generation whose interests he represented tended to view the Confederacy and its veterans as being out of

step with the new, progressive age. The new generation of political leaders that he represented certainly had little connection to the Confederate
experience or to the values of southern conservatism. The chairman of
Clemson's board, R. W. Simpson, serves as a case in point. Though born
in 1840, Simpson had limited experience in the Confederate army after
having been "detailed for special duty" because of illness. Following the
war, Simpson advocated that the state shift from "a classical education"
to "a more practical one." Like Tillman, Simpson had been a leader in
an upcountry Red Shirt unit and thereafter adopted and used the title
of "Colonel." In the 1880s Simpson was Tillman's ally and served as
the executor of Thomas G. Clemson's estate, likely urging him to donate
Calhoun's plantation to the state so that it could become the land grant
for Clemson College and Tillman's new power base. Even members of
the board who had a clearer relationship to the Lost Cause than Simpson
often had their role in the Confederate struggle downplayed. Clemson
College honored board member D. K. Norris for his role as "a leader and
a decided success" and for being in the "front rank of industrial leaders."
Although the college noted that Norris had been a "consistent Christian,"
no mention was made of his service to the Confederacy.[37]

The veterans of Orrs' Rifles responded with frustrated anger. One veteran reminded his fellows that "fully 90 percent of our few comrades left
to meet and celebrate these our annual reunions are farmers and have
proved their loyalty to the state." Impotent in the face of this decision,
the men of Orr's Rifles could only pass a resolution expressing chagrin
and surprise, telling the board that "we disapprove of the action of the
chairman of the Board of Trustees in refusing to allow us to meet at the
time and place so near where our services were dedicated to our beloved
state and the lost cause we cherished and loved."[38]

Tillman's bourgeois world shattered the aesthetic of the Lost Cause, at
least in its function as a grand narrative for the southern social order. The
Confederate veteran had a place within South Carolina society but had to
stay in that place once Tillman's bourgeois revolution had shivered apart
the older conservative ethos. Shuffled off to soldier's homes and relegated
to a lost past, the veterans received, ironically, much the same rhetorical
treatment as the "faithful old-time Negro." Like the former slave, the
Confederate veteran found himself on the margins of society, patronized
as representative of a world that no longer existed, a world that did little
but justify the antiquarian interests of middle-class ladies. Replaced by
the ethos of a new generation in whose ears echoed the clatter of textile
mills, Confederate virtue became the talk of doddering old men. Money,

mills, and railroads would combine with segregation, lynching, and the profound economic inequalities of tenantry to create the new bourgeois state.

The more prescient of the veterans had known that such a world would come. In November 1895, George B. Lake wrote in protest to the Tillmanite *Daily Register*. The *Register* had urged veterans to recognize that "changed conditions exist" and to "bring to the resolution of present questions hearts ever young," lest they be "relegated to the rear." Lake, who in his day had fought Yankees as a Confederate, Republicans as a Red Shirt, and trusts and monopolies as an Allianceman, now challenged Tillman as a southern conservative. Invoking the names of Hampton, Butler, and "old Joe Kershaw," Lake asserted that Tillmanism had brushed aside the old leadership and its values. "There is no use beating about the bush," he wrote to the New South boosters at the *Register*. "You and a good many people of your way of thinking would like to relegate the Confederate soldier to the rear, but there are those yet to come, generation after generation, who will say Shame! Shame! Respectfully, Geo. B. Lake."[39]

In the spring of 1903, South Carolina had perhaps its largest Confederate reunion. Columbia filled with thousands who turned out to see the parade of elderly veterans and the floats that bore the last living signers of the Ordinance of Secession. Of as much interest to a new generation, many of whom had not been alive at the time of war, were the "balls and receptions . . . entertainment, parades, decorations and meetings" that at times had little clear relationship to the Lost Cause. The grand parade and review along Main Street to the statehouse contained not only veterans but students from South Carolina College, two hundred public school students, the Cotillion Club of Columbia, the Metropolitan Club, the local Elks Lodge, and all the "merchants, manufacturers and other businessmen" who had given time and money to "elaborately decorate their stores and businesses."[40]

Slightly off-key in the uproarious celebration was the unsaddled white horse led by an elderly African American. The horse had belonged to Wade Hampton, who had died in 1902. John Johnson, Hampton's former slave and his constant companion following the war, led the dead general's horse behind the parade's grand marshals, where Hampton himself had ridden at reunions and monument dedications in the past. Katherine Dupre Lumpkin, a child and an observer of the parade, called the riderless horse a "somber note" in the midst of the celebration. "I do not remember seeing him ride at the head of the columns," she said of earlier reunions, "though I may have. Vaguely I can recall the great funeral, the vast throng; and clearly the many times in ensuing years when our family would troop in reverent pilgrimage to his always flower-strewn grave after Sunday services at Trinity."[41]

The Great Train Robbery

On May 6, 2000, the Confederate army gathered to defend the South Carolina statehouse against new "vandal hordes" threatening the southern way of life. This army, however, arrived in SUVs and mail-order-catalog uniforms, with the tradition they sought to defend involving neither slavery, nor a genteel conservatism. They did not even come to protect the liberty and virtue of property-holding white men. They had come to fight for their flag, and the "unconquered banner" would soon again be dipped in defeat, as it had been in 1865.

The South Carolina legislature raised the Confederate battle flag in 1961, apparently as both a commemoration of the Civil War centennial and a statement of defiance against a Federal government that had hesitantly begun to support the integration of public schools, voting rights, and equal protection under the law for black Americans. Ironically, the symbolic gesture of raising the flag of the Confederacy would constitute one of the state's few acts of defiance during the civil rights era, as community and business leaders agreed on what one historian has called "a conspiracy of peace" that would allow the state to move to desegregated public facilities and a unitary public school system.[1]

The battle flag raised in defiance of the black freedom struggle had far more to do with the racist ideology of the turn of the century than with Confederate memory. The southern struggle to defend Jim Crow, rather than representing a last stand of the southern conservative ethos, represents the continuing declension of the paternalist values of Hampton and the older southern elite. By defending segregation, white southerners buttressed a system born of the changed conditions of the 1890s, a system inextricably linked to the New South world of mill and town rather than to the conservative's world of farm and plantation. Segregation constituted a rejection of structured paternalism. In South Carolina it was a rejection of Wade Hampton's dream of social harmony, in which all the state's citizen received equal protection before the law while living in a hierarchical society bounded by custom and tradition. The twentieth-century southerners who supported segregation, and who supported extreme violence whenever Jim Crow was challenged, roundly rejected these ideas, preferring the Tillmanite nightmare in which society became a perpetual racial warfare that pitted white civilization against black savagery.[2]

The role of Tillman in shaping a discourse of terrorist white supremacy calls for a substantial revision of southern Bourbonism. William J. Cooper has suggested that, at least in South Carolina, Bourbon rule varied "considerably from the Woodward portrait." Cooper made the case that in both political and economic culture, Bourbon hegemony had represented a continuing survival of southern conservatism across the chasm of the Civil War.[3]

Cooper's study focused overwhelmingly on political and economic culture, ignoring South Carolina's culture of the Lost Cause. The Lost Cause in South Carolina functioned as an aesthetic representation of cultural ideology—public spectacles, monuments, narratives, and religious experiences that allowed postbellum South Carolinians to dream of lost southern worlds; it energized them to struggle for these worlds against what they saw as the predatory forces of modernity. I have argued that this public aesthetic did not operate as what scholars have called a "civil religion," as Charles Reagan Wilson argued in his groundbreaking study. "Civil religion" helps us to explain the meaning of the Lost Cause only if we expand that contested term to include movements that emphasize conservative traditionalism as well as liberal inclusion.[4]

This Lost Cause aesthetic represents a true American conservatism. This claim does not include the assumption that the Carolina conservatives actually managed to shape a world of organic social relations that would have stood up to some abstract litmus test for a conservative society. In fact, the triumph of Tillmanism underscores that conservatives celebrated their aesthetic of the Lost Cause in a world in which social relations were in flux, a transitional moment in the history of the South and of the nation. The conservatism of South Carolina did not survive the tides of change, the social transformations it so rightly feared.

The claim that a region in the United States could produce, for a short time, a conservative tradition will be met by skepticism in some quarters. Allen Guttmann has argued that conservatism in the United States has largely been an intellectual exercise, because the structures of American society and the shape of American culture have been overdetermined by the liberal ideals of the Enlightenment. Guttman views American conservatism as very much an isolated, even a "literary," phenomenon, kept alive by a faithful illuminati who have largely written for one another.

The experience of defeated South Carolina offers a different model, while suggesting that the "literary," or, better, aesthetic, definition of southern conservatism serves an interpretive purpose. The widespread celebration of the Lost Cause in South Carolina provided conservative thinkers with a cultural omnibus within which to trumpet their ideals of hierarchy, organic social relations, and prescriptive tradition. The South's peculiar racial experience provided a grammar of hierarchy for southern conservatives unknown in the rest of the nation. Postbellum southern conservatives, particularly in the heartland of secession, would not have to complain of being "ignored" by their contemporaries, as had antebellum conservatives.[5] Instead, they would be invited to speak at monument dedications and veterans' gatherings to crowds of farmers and townsfolk. The bravery of the South Carolina yeoman farmer charging at Gettysburg and Shiloh provided these conservatives with a model for resistance to modernity. An aesthetic of the Lost Cause thus became the vehicle for southern conservatism.[6]

The struggle in South Carolina to create, and then to defend, a society whose structure emerged from an aesthetic of the Lost Cause provides us with a model of the possibilities of conservatism in the American context, a conservatism that looked much more like that of Schlegel and Novalis, filtered through Carlyle, than the conservatism of Thatcher, Reagan, and Gingrich. The Romantic ideal of the organic society, structured by property and the southern male identity, attempted to escape the clutches of possessive individualism, the denigration of the human being into the atomized monad that represents the final product of capitalist economic relations. Southern conservatives, resisting to the last the emergence of the new corporate order, evoked in their Lost Cause aesthetic what Stephen Vincent Benet poetically rendered as "the America we have never been."[7]

The alacrity with which the culture of South Carolina turned bourgeois would seem to belie the reality of a true conservative ethos in South Carolina, and perhaps in the South generally. In fact, this rapid change reflects conservatism's fate in America. J. Clinton Rossiter describes the 1890s as "the Great Train Robbery" of American conservatism, when an older conservatism "sank into lonely disrepute," and the American Right adopted the vocabulary of liberalism in an effort to legitimize laissez-faire capitalism and economic individualism. Much of the confusion over the meaning of American conservatism, and much of the doubt that such a thing exists, has its origins in this era when the term became a deeply contested one.[8]

The conservative aesthetic in South Carolina died with the triumph of Tillman. The ancien régime did not live again. Indeed, some of values of that regime would likely have seemed "socialistic" to the Sunbelt capitalists of the late twentieth century. The late-nineteenth-century Carolina conservatives, especially with their attitudes toward agrarianism and property, would look peculiar to the cowboy entrepreneurs who pass for conservative in the twenty-first century. This fact, more than any other, underscores the difficulty of defining an ideology as complex as conservatism.

The study of conservatism has too long languished on the rack of theory, the profound tensions within this ideology frustrating varied attempts at its definition. A focus on aesthetic issues enables us to see conservatism in action rather than as a static phenomenon. Such an interpretation allows us to move beyond debate over whether the Old South represented a capitalist society, a neofeudal society, or a slave society living parasitically in the world market. Each side has been able to draw blood with quotations from appropriate passages of Marx's *Capital;* those engaged in this conflict generally talk past one another by their use of different meanings attributed to capitalism.

The present study has suggested that scholars bypass some of those debates, that we instead see southern conservatism primarily as a function of culture and a lived ethos, bodied forth in political speeches, sermons, novels, monuments, relationships among neighbors, oddities, songs, ownership of property, and public rituals. These disparate materials are the mechanics of southern conservative life, fragile machinery, the flesh on ideological bones. This interpretation does not ignore the basic role of economics in the creation and destruction of ideology, but it has instead attempted to integrate economic change into the process of cultural transformation.

Imprecision in name and definition has become an inherent problem in defining southern conservatism. Past interpreters of the postbellum South have too quickly invested the entrepreneurial New South Boosters with the title of "conservative," when in fact that designation appears as contested ground in the 1880s and 1890s. A romantic conservatism, firmly attached to a mythical Old South and representing what Bernard Crick calls "a violent breach with the actual course of history," emerged in the postbellum South. The celebration of the Confederacy in the Lost Cause movement provided a vehicle for this romantic conservatism. Ultimately, the aesthetic of the Lost Cause fought a losing battle with the emerging New South and the new southern middle class it represented.[9]

Reasons for the rapid disintegration of this aesthetic are easy to find at the end of the nineteenth century. The emergence of a politics of class in South Carolina, perhaps more than any other force, sundered the conservative vision of an organic society. Charles J. Holden has argued that the 1880s saw the beginnings of conflicts over the meaning of the Lost Cause, the emergence in South Carolina of cultures of the Lost Cause that failed to unify the white populace as the struggle against the North in the 1860s and 1870s had succeeded in doing.[10] Holden fails to note how a traditional southern conservatism played a role in the emergence of a South Carolina farmers movement. Elements of this movement resisted Tillman as strenuously as did Hampton, and those usually adumbrated the Bourbons. Furthermore, the South Carolina Farmer's Alliance, headed by Lost Cause figures such as Ellison Keitt, provides a different picture of Lawrence Goodwyn's "movement culture." Rather than from a progressive movement culture, the Carolina farmers' protest emerged from the Lost Cause and the conservative values it embodied. Benjamin Ryan Tillman, perhaps the most influential political figure in South Carolina history, derailed the farmer's alliance movement that would likely have ended in revitalizing, rather than destroying, South Carolina Bourbonism in the 1890s, perhaps turning South Carolina's struggle with the twentieth century into a clash over agrarian values rather than over the phantoms of race and segregation.

A changed understanding of the meaning of race further transformed the conservatism of the Palmetto State. The paternalist ethos that had developed among South Carolina planters by the 1850s heavily influenced the Bourbons, and especially Hampton, in their attitude toward the role of African Americans in the social order. Indeed, black South Carolinians had a crucial role to play in the conservative vision of an organic social order; they would serve as the peasant class, a voting and legally protected peasant class whose faithfulness would buttress the power of the planter elite. This neofeudal vision of society, many believed, better represented the conservative ideal of organic social relations than had the institution of slavery.

Tillman offered white South Carolinians freedom from racial questions altogether. The 1895 constitution would marginalize African Americans politically, and the bourgeois world being shaped in the upcountry would marginalize them culturally. Implicit in Tillman's rhetoric and actions was a call to violence, the literal destruction of African American people through lynching, beatings, and the intervention of the state. In South Carolina in the 1890s, neither the Bourbons nor Tillman offered black men and women a vision of a just social order and black liberation. Blacks, hemmed in by their political disempowerment, watched as a proponent of racial savagery replaced the planters who wanted them to be peasants.

Finally, the destruction of the conservative vision of order emerged from the experience of mourning itself, an element in the aesthetic of the Lost Cause that, ironically, gave it such power. Literary theorist Idelbar Avelar, writing about the task of mourning in postdictatorial Latin America, writes that mourning "is always, in a sense, the task of *actively forgetting*." Avelar argues that mourning loss can become purely passive in a society, like modern Latin America or like South Carolina at the turn of the century, that is increasingly industrialized and commodified. Consumer societies have little use for memory; in fact, Avelar writes, "the erasure of the past as past is the cornerstone of all commodification."[11]

Increasingly, South Carolinians erased their past, as their society underwent profound social and economic change. Mourning no longer constituted an act of defiance against modernity, or even against the North, but instead became a passive act, engaged in by a society no longer deeply moved by the drama of Confederate virtue. The new middle class, marking its identity with racial classification and consumption, behaved very much as triumphant bourgeoisie in much of the rest of the Western world.

Some may protest the idea that South Carolina had forgotten its past with the coming of Tillman, noting that Lost Cause celebrations continued and, in fact, revivified during the late twentieth century. The United Daughters of the Confederacy, for example, remained a powerful organization, and Confederate memory continued to influence everything from racial mores to the writing of textbooks of South Carolina history. The raising of the Confederate battle flag in the 1960s certainly suggests that few in the Palmetto State were ignoring Confederate imagery.

Avelar writes, however, that the past can live on in a consumer society as "an anachronistic, obsolete commodity, the recycled gadget." Images of the past can provide anchors for a society that lives in what Avelar calls "a perpetual present"; imagery can endure and does endure in a society that mourns through the ironic act of active forgetfulness. The continued use of Confederate symbols, the continuing strength of Lost Cause organizations, did not represent yearning for the lost past as much as it did an effort to buoy up the present, to refuse the past with its horrors and loss.[12]

White South Carolina had watched almost a third of its men killed in a war that ended in humiliating defeat. The virtual destruction of their capital city, and of the symbolic city of Charleston, left them stunned. Reconstruction turned their social order upside down. The defeat of the Confederacy, a political movement that evangelical religion had transformed into a sacred ideal, constituted a spiritual crisis as much as a military failure. The widespread loss of land, the free fall into dependence, finally untethered the white yeoman farmer. The living past seemed to offer only a tale of death, destruction, and abandonment by God. Some few stomached the harsh indictment of history, meditated on ruins, and actively remembered the Lost Cause, actively yearned for elusive worlds of organic order its ideals promised. Tillman offered a simpler path, one in which the power of the state closed off the era of defeat and humiliation, one in which whiteness equaled status, and the demons of the past could be exorcised by mob violence. The new middle class, which collaborated in this cultural project, ignored the ruins all around them, except when they needed those ruins to legitimize their "perpetual present."

These cultural trends continued into the twentieth century. The political menagerie that followed Tillman into the governor's mansion and to positions as representatives of the state in national councils duplicated much of his style and continued to impose on the state his brand of reformist racism, his chosen instrument of forgetfulness. Often these figures represented fun-house images of Tillman, voicing a rancid racism and a bitterly class-conscious rhetoric that even disturbed Tillman himself. Coleman Blease, a former Tillman lieutenant, represented this new kind of politics, which combined Tillman's racial savagery with the politics of class envy and hatred. Constructing himself as the defender of the "lintheads" (a term of abuse used for millworkers), Blease took the prejudices of the new South Carolina industrial class and voiced them in stump speeches renowned for their obscenity and calls for violence. Unbelievably, South Carolina historian Walter Edgar calls Blease "one of the most misunderstood figures in South Carolina history" and has written that "Blease really did strive to set his people free—to restore to them the individualism, the dignity and the sense of worth they had lost when they deserted their farms for the mills." [13] It is quite unclear how "Coley," as working class whites affectionately called their demagogue, restored "dignity" and a "sense of worth" to these people by stirring them into lynch mobs. Moreover, how can we misunderstand someone who plants the fingers of lynched African Americans in the garden of the governor's mansion? Edgar correctly notes that Blease has been "dismissed as a demagogue," but understanding the Blease phenomenon does not mean we have to deny that, as would so often happen in the twentieth century, poor white South Carolinians elected a leader that embodied all of their racial pathologies. When these monsters finally shambled off the scene, businessmen, real estate brokers, members of chambers of commerce, and the army of the civic-minded replaced them. The task of actively forgetting reached its zenith.

The death of southern conservatism resulted from a death of memory, from a decision to mourn by forgetting the horror of history. A visit to the May 2000 Confederate Memorial Day celebrations in Columbia, South Carolina, made this willing amnesia abundantly clear. To an observer walking along the quiet side street that runs beside Trinity Church, "dear old Trinity," as many Carolinians came to call the cathedral after it survived the torches of Sherman's conquering army, it was obvious that numerous Memorial Day participants had used the cathedral parking lot. They made their presence known with their harmless but deadly-looking muskets leaning across the backseats of Volvos and luxury SUVs. Regardless of the stereotype of pick-up-truck-driving, frothing-at-the-mouth "rednecks," these Confederates seemed yuppified and suburbanized, proudly displaying both Sunbelt prosperity and Confederate identity. A Lincoln Navigator sported a bumper sticker that read, "I am a proud descendant of a Confederate Veteran."

The rally itself featured marching reenactors, a speech by an elderly, brittle-looking Confederate daughter from Charleston, and interestingly enough, a prayer ascribed to Bishop Ellison Capers. The gathering, billed as nonpolitical, as are all the activities of the Sons of Confederate Veterans, centered on the defense of the Confederate flag while exhibiting little certainty about why the display of this symbol mattered. The anger over the displacement of Confederate symbols has been matched only by the utterly meaningless role this iconography plays in the lives of even the most dedicated of neo-Confederates. Flags, monuments, and memorial days—all have become floating signifiers, wrenched out of context by time, change, overuse, and misuse.

The Lost Cause, this work has argued, served as an aesthetic embodiment of southern conservatism. The assumption throughout has been that the aesthetic impulse threaded together a variety of phenomena, providing modern scholars with access to the intellectual world of southern conservatism. George Santayana, describing aesthetic expression of all kinds, has written that "mind grows self-perpetuating only by its expression in matter."[14] The mind of the South, so eagerly sought by interpreters of the region, can perhaps best be understood by examining the artifacts of its culture.

Anyone who has read Tony Horowitz's *Confederates in the Attic* knows that Confederate symbolism no longer serves such a purpose. In fact, these symbols now seem meaningless, signs that have no significance beyond a vague dis-ease over the meaning of southern identity, the fear among southern yuppies that their cultural ethos has dwindled to a drawl and a taste for fried foods. Southern historian James Farmer has pointed out that the white southerners who vociferously demand public space for Confederate symbols seldom, if ever, structure their lives around the more challenging values of the Old South, such as a rejection of capitalism, an agrarian simplicity, and a high standard of personal and public honor.[15] Even more important, none have experienced the trial by fire of wartime South Carolinians, white and black, who ended the war with loved ones dead, homes and farms in ruins, and a world having to be remade. Hampton offered one vision of what that world could be, a world grounded in an aesthetic vision of society as a social organism. Tillman and the entrepreneurial elite who supported him offered a different vision, and South Carolina chose it because it was simpler and easier, even if it was also ugly and wrong.

The choice the South made, and the consequences of that choice, ought to be kept in mind when tallying our historical estimation of the Bourbons. Reactionary and looking bewildered in the light of postbellum realities, the South Carolina Bourbons nonetheless should not be blamed for the savage violence that rocked the South in the 1890s and into the twentieth century. This ruling elite has not been considered as the varied group that it is, clearly including what can only be called an agrarian wing in the 1870s, '80s, and '90s that nevertheless saw in Tillmanism the rise of barbarism and a betrayal of the Lost Cause. Though some Bourbons, such as Hampton and Butler, seemed largely out of touch during the 1880s and '90s because of age and their experiences on the national stage, other local notables, such as Ellison Keitt and John J. Dargan, remained vital and interesting thinkers, attempting to find conservative solutions to their state's agrarian crisis. These solutions involved neither lynching nor Jim Crow but rather policies that confirmed traditional attachments to land and systems of credit and currency that favored those who worked from the land.[16]

Modern South Carolina lowered the Confederate standard on July 1, 2000. The lowering of the flag came about as a result of a compromise adopted by the South Carolina legislature in response to the national media attention from the NAACP boycott and the issue's being raised in the presidential primaries. The compromise called for the removal of the flag from the statehouse dome and for a new Confederate banner to be placed by the Sons of Confederate Veterans at the South Carolina Confederate Memorial. The NAACP, eager to replenish the group's dwindling political capital in the black community, had refused an earlier compromise proposal that would have displayed the flag in a historical monument park, in a setting that would contain, along with a brief description of the issues and causes of the Civil War, a copy of the Emancipation Proclamation and a monument to achievements in black education. Refusing this option led to the banner's being placed at the corner of busy Main and Gervais streets, "off the dome and in your face!" as some flag supporters chanted on the day of the ceremony.

Rival rallies represented two views of Confederate memory. On the north side of the statehouse, black choirs sang the sad songs of the South and newer anthems of hope and racial pride. "We have come treading our path through the blood of the slaughtered, out of the gloomy past," sang the choir of the historically black Benedict College. Later a silent march of black South Carolinians, dressed in white robes as if going to a mass baptism, filed by the statehouse. Flag supporters raged at the passing throng, "If you don't like this state, go back to your own continent!" one white woman screamed, waving Lee's banner maniacally.

Fittingly, the loudest and most unpleasant group of flag supporters huddled around the bronze statue of Ben Tillman that stands in a prominent place on the statehouse grounds. Literally red-necked men in muscle shirts were accompanied by scantily clad, hard-faced women, spitting racial invectives and insults at the dignified NAACP marchers. Clad in Confederate bandannas and bikinis, likely having driven from the bedraggled trailer parks that dot the South Carolina midlands, they represented a different outcome of the Sunbelt than those fresh-faced SCV reenactors who had the money to purchase Confederate uniforms and muskets. One warehouse worker, dressed in a Confederate flag T-shirt and face smeared with fake blood, blamed the NAACP for the lowering of his flag in language that would have made Tillman proud. "They're all in with the big money people," he said of the NAACP, "they're all interested in the Almighty Dollar."[17] These sons and daughters of the South, living in the shadows of the Sunbelt, were angry without knowing why and convinced that black Carolinians had something to do with it. These were the children of Tillman and Blease and "Cotton Ed" Smith, the children of progress and industrial development, the children of modernity, the children of the New South.

Hundreds of confrontations accompanied the lowering of Lee's banner. A young African American artist, Darien McCloud, confronted long-haul trucker James Custer in front of the South Carolina Soldier's Monument the day the flag came down. Thrusting a finger at the trucker's "Confederate heritage" T-shirt, McCloud tauntingly said, "It's over, it's done." "No, no, no," Custer angrily replied, "It's not done." State police, who had assembled at the ceremony complete with water hoses and riot gear, moved in to separate the two angry South Carolinians. As a white policeman strong-armed McCloud away, he angrily screamed at Custer, "You're over man! Your days are gone! You're like a dinosaur!" [18]

NOTES

INTRODUCTION. South Carolinians Never Surrender

1. A discussion of Page and his role in valorizing the Old South and the Confederacy in the midst of Reconstruction appears in Weaver, *Southern Tradition at Bay,* 267–73.

2. "Ethos" might suggest to some an all-embracing ideology, but I use it to mean a cultural mood among white conservatives, expressing itself in specific cultural forms. On the peculiarity of South Carolina's antebellum political culture, see Genovese, "South Carolina's Contribution to the Doctrine of Slavery in the Abstract," 146.

3. Wilson, *Baptized in Blood,* 15, 79–99, 13.

4. Foster, *Ghosts of the Confederacy,* 8.

5. Herberg, *Protestant, Catholic, Jew.* See also Wilson, *Baptized in Blood,* 12–13.

6. Hegel, *On Art, Religion, and the History of Philosophy,* 38; see Langer, *Philosophy in a New Key,* and Percy, "Metaphor as Mistake," 64–82.

7. Burke, *Reflections on the Revolution in France,* 96. English conservatism's romantic elements have been ignored, except by Kirk in *Conservative Mind,* 260–79. England, as opposed to Germany, has been viewed as the home of what might be called common law conservatism, which grounds itself in the unwritten English constitution. Scholars have not always noted the elements of romanticism in that idea.

8. Straka, "Influence of Thomas Carlyle in the Old South." Biographical material on Carlyle comes from his best contemporary biography, Heffer, *Moral Desperado,* 105, 236, 325. Carlyle's own "cultural alienation" comes out in his reaction to *Uncle Tom's Cabin,* which, according to Heffer, he "loathed." The popularity of the abolitionist tract on both sides of the Atlantic only proved to Carlyle that the public was little more than "Gadarene Swine" following one another over the cliffside. Heffer explores material that defeats the attempt to portray Carlyle as a liberal social reformer.

9. Hunt, *Politics, Culture, and Class,* 12.

10. Braudel, *History of Civilizations,* 9; Edgar, *South Carolina,* 8, 9.

11. Hatley, *Dividing Paths,* 3, 4; on the role played by trade in contacts between Indians and Europeans, see Morris, *Bringing of Wonder.*

12. Ibid., 60ff, 80–81.

13. Pratt, *Imperial Eyes.*

14. Woodmason, *Carolina Backcountry*, 6, 15.

15. Edgar, *South Carolina*, 205.

16. Weir, *Colonial South Carolina*, 214–15; on the results of the Cherokee War and a full discussion of the Regulators, see 269–89.

17. Ford, "Republics and Democracy," 121–45.

18. Genovese, *Southern Tradition*, 80–86; Genovese and Fox-Genovese, "M. E. Bradford's Historical Vision."

19. Edgar, *South Carolina*, 252–53; Niven, *John C. Calhoun*, 331.

20. Ford, *Origins of Southern Radicalism*, 5–14; Sinha, *Counterrevolution of Slavery*, 11.

21. Edgar, *South Carolina*, 271–74; Ford, *Origins of Southern Radicalism*, 13, 14.

22. Klein, *Unification of a Slave State*, 157–58.

23. Robertson, *Red Hills and Cotton*, 98–99; Editorial, *Keowee Courier*, July 31, 1858.

24. Ramsay, quoted in Weir, *Colonial South Carolina*, 232.

25. McCurry, "Two Faces of Republicanism," 1245–64; see especially 1246, 1251. See also McCurry, *Masters of Small Worlds*, 209–38.

26. Sinha, *Counterrevolution of Slavery*, 1–7; on the "republican" notions used by South Carolina secessionists, see Ford, *Origins of Southern Radicalism*, 340–73.

27. Young, *Domesticating Slavery*, 5–14; "Last Will of Henry Hortman," June 25, 1861, Hagood Papers, South Caroliniana Library, hereafter referred to as SCL.

28. Batson, *History of the Upper Part of Greenville County*, 588; Sinha, *Counterrevolution of Slavery*, 5.

29. "Home Productions," *Keowee Courier*, November 26, 1859.

30. Freehling, *Prelude to Civil War*, 17–21; Ford, "Republics and Democracy," 123.

31. Sellers, *Market Revolution*, 4, 5. Sellers himself suggests that land-hunger, the drive to hold property in land, became a revolutionary force in antebellum society. When Sellers writes that "subsistence culture was doomed by its own population dynamics," it is another way of saying that the drive for property played a central role in the emerging market economy.

32. Klein, *Unification of a Slave State*, 50.

33. Batson, *History of the Upper Part of Greenville County*, 107, 133, 350.

34. Edgar, *South Carolina*, 279.

35. Sease, *Aunt Kate 100 Years Dear*. Genealogical data such as the Sease work has been generally ignored. This is unfortunate. A vast amount of material has been excavated by amateur enthusiasts, material that should not remain unanalyzed by professional historians.

36. *Carolina Spartan*, May 15, 1849.

37. Oakes, *Ruling Race*, 42; McCurry, *Masters of Small Worlds*, 112–13.

38. Weir, *Colonial South Carolina*, 211–12.

39. Faust, *Ideology of Slavery*, 1–20.

40. Woodward, *Origins of the New South*, 429.

41. Peter Bardaglio notes that "the rise of individualism and contractual social relations in the north" symbolized for southerners the dangers of radical autonomy, in particular the danger such autonomy represented for "the southern domestic order." See *Reconstructing the Household*, 116–21. Radical autonomy had a resounding effect in the world of politics and culture, one best described by Isaiah Berlin as "a new and restless spirit, seeking violently to burst through old and cramping forms, a nervous preoccupation with perpetually changing states of consciousness, a longing for the unbounded and the undefinable, for perpetual movement and change . . . a passionate effort at self-assertion both individual and collective, a search after means of expressing an unappeasable yearning for unattainable goals." See "Joseph De Maistre and the Origins of Fascism," 91–174.

42. Edwards, *Gendered Strife and Confusion*, 8.

43. See Fields, "Ideology and Race in American History," 144–45, 150. Fields's insistence that the economic base trumps the influence and reality of cultural forms remains influential among historians, despite the work of Stuart Hall. See Hall's interpretation of cultural forms and economic base in "Problem of Ideology," 25–46. Hall offers a set of Marxist analytical tools without the weight of traditional Marxism's creedal statements on class structure or its teleological enthusiasms. See also Geertz, *Negara*, 135.

CHAPTER ONE. A Spirit amongst These Hills

1. Elizabeth Fox-Genovese has made the most convincing argument regarding differences between northern and southern households in *Within a Plantation Household*, 37–82.

2. In *Cradle of the Middle Class*, Mary P. Ryan describes the growth of a bourgeois class in the North, a class in part structured by new gender relations. The material on Liza and Benjamin Perry appears in Carole Bleser's study of their correspondence, "Perrys of Greenville"; Steven M. Stowe, in *Intimacy and Power in the Old South*, describes the rituals of the planter class as exhibiting "an attention to limits . . . joined to social relations which the elite assumed were part of the natural world and not open to change" (8).

3. December 1864, Letters File, Hagood Papers, SCL.

4. Ford, *Origins of Southern Radicalism*, 64–66.

5. "Manufacturing at the South," *Carolina Spartan*, June 28, 1849; *Greenville Southern Patriot*, October 23, 1856.

6. James Oakes takes a similar view when he insists that the "primacy of individual rights" played a central role in the planter class's view of the world and

links this "slaveholding liberalism" with capitalism, defined as "the rationalized pursuit of sustained profit." *Slavery and Freedom,* 40–79; Blackbourne and Eley, *Peculiarities of German History,* 89–90, 148.

7. This position has been argued eloquently by James Oakes in *Ruling Race.*

8. "Powder," *Keowee Courier,* December 3, 1859.

9. An examination of the Pickens County tax lists of 1866 reveal that upcountrymen, after the economic desolation of the war, willingly spent a substantial amount of their cash income paying taxes on hunting dogs "over and above one per dwelling." These are not venture capitalists. Pickens District of South Carolina Tax List, 1866 (compiled by Peggy Burton Rich and Margaret Gibbs Ogle, 1991), South Carolina Department of Archives and History, Columbia, S.C., hereafter referred to as SCDAH.

10. Genovese and Fox-Genovese would not go this far. Fox-Genovese seems reluctant to view the slave as absolute property in the antebellum slave system. See Fox-Genovese *Within a Plantation Household,* 53.

11. William W. Freehling calls farmers and planters who flooded the backcountry "an entrepreneurial army." *Road to Disunion,* 28.

12. Braudel, "History and the Social Sciences," 145–74.

13. Franklin, *Militant South.*

14. Ira Berlin suggests this distinction between "societies with slaves and slave societies." A slave society is one, he argues, in which "slavery stood at the center of economic production, and the master-slave relationship provided the model for all social relations." See *Many Thousands Gone,* 7–13; South Carolina's version of conservative republicanism contains real similarities to the political theories of Renaissance civic humanism. Machiavelli's discussion of the role of an armed militia in an ordered society appears in *The Prince* and, in a more analytical form, in his *Discourses on Livy,* 172–78. A good, if at times eccentric, discussion of Machiavelli's view of arms in the history of conservative republicanism appears in de Grazia, *Machiavelli in Hell,* 289–92.

15. "Muster at Hunt's Ground," *Keowee Courier,* August 22, 1857; Easley receives a laudatory description from his political opponent Benjamin F. Perry in his *Reminiscences of Public Men* 74–76. See also "The General Muster" *Keowee Courier,* September 18, 1858. Wilson, *Exercise and Instructions of Field Artillery,* 57; my interpretation of this quote relies heavily on Joel Williamson in *Rage for Order,* 24. Williamson sees such rituals of subordination as part of a southern symbolic complex of "Swords and pistols, love, sex and violence, women, blood and death." Flynn, *Militia in Antebellum South Carolina Society,* 127.

16. *Greenville Southern Enterprise,* August 10, 1855.

17. Gettys, "Mobilization for Secession in Greenville District," 34ff.

18. Ibid., 38.

19. "The University Riflemen," *Greenville Southern Enterprise,* July 31, 1856.

20. Hunt, *Politics, Culture and Class in the French Revolution,* 56; Gettys, "Mobilization for Secession in Greenville District," 34ff; "The Fourth," *Greenville Southern Enterprise,* July 7, 1859.

21. Racine, *Piedmont Farmer,* 99; Edgar, *South Carolina.*

22. Horowitz, *Confederates in the Attic;* "Speech of O. M. Dantzler, October 24, 1851, in Columbia, South Carolina," SCL.

23. Genealogy Folder, Folder 10, Box 1–10, Easley Papers, SCL.

24. Biographical material on Easley comes from Perry, *Reminiscences of Public Men,* 74–76; secessionist speeches and orations on other public occasions come from the Easley Papers, SCL.

25. Files 1–17, Easley Papers, SCL.

26. Ibid.

27. Gettys, "Mobilization for Secession in Greenville District."

28. Files 1–17, Easley Papers, SCL.

29. Rollin G. Osterweis has traced the influence of Carlyle on southern intellectuals in *Romanticism and Nationalism in the Old South,* 33–36. Carlyle became the conduit for Herder, Goethe, and Schlegel in the American South. Easley evinced a special knowledge of Goethe and the German intellectual milieu. See his "Speech at Walhalla," in the Easley Papers, SCL. On Burke's influence in the South, see O'Brien, introduction to *All Clever Men.*

30. "1848," *Carolina Spartan,* April 10, 1849, August 9, 1849.

31. Channing, *Crisis of Fear,* 56, 57.

32. Krick, "Maxcy Gregg," 3–4.

33. "Speech to Vigilance Committee," 1860, Files 1–17, Easley Papers, SCL.

34. "North and South," Norris and Thomson Family Papers, SCL.

35. "Meeting of Rifle Companies on Hall's Muster Ground," *Keowee Courier,* January 12, 1861.

36. Ibid.

37. J. Sloan to J. E. Hagood, February 6, 1861, Letters File, Hagood Papers, SCL.

38. Batson, *History of the Upper Part of Greenville County,* 28.

39. Crusy (?) letter, September 5, 1861, Letters File, Hagood Papers, SCL.

40. Edgar, *South Carolina,* 370.

41. Reid, *History of the Fourth Regiment,* 8.

42. Hester letter, August 1864, Letters File, Hagood Papers, SCL.

43. Reid, *History of the Fourth Regiment,* 73; P. E. Maxwell letter, Warren Papers, SCL; "Collection of letters, part of the war record of Captain John R. Jefferies," Jefferies Family Papers, SCL.

44. David Y. Allen notes how European conservatives disregarded early features of romantic conservatism late in the nineteenth century, specifically the theme of "cultural alienation." "Modern Conservatism," 597.

CHAPTER TWO. We Have No Head but Christ

1. Minutes of Big Creek Baptist Church, Anderson, S.C., November 31, 1861, microfilm, Manuscripts Division, SCL.

2. Snay, *Gospel of Disunion,* is the best work on the role of evangelicalism in shaping Confederate identity. See especially 214ff. It should be noted that while maintaining his strong thesis, Snay allows for a significant degree of ambiguity regarding the role religion played in the sectional crisis. Drew G. Faust cites the crucial role of southern religion in shaping a sense of Confederate nationalism in *Creating Confederate Nationalism,* see especially 22ff.

3. The *via media* of the Anglican tradition did not prevent the southern Episcopal Church from taking on many of the characteristics of southern evangelicalism. Sam Hill writes that "southern Episcopalians have had more in common with the popular churches than either their theological heritage of higher social status would seem to suggest." See *Southern Churches in Crisis,* 74. Also, 20–39, on the homogeneity of southern religion. "Sermons," bound volume, Frierson Papers, SCL.

4. Max Weber, in *Sociology of Religion,* 2–19, made the classic statement of the move from the "charisma" of the prophet to the "routinization" of the institution, a paradigm he finds common in all religious experience. Bernheim, *History of the German Settlements and of the Lutheran Church,* 352.

5. Lacy K. Ford notes, however, that such ecumenism did have clear limits. Baptists and Presbyterians looked askance at the Methodist emphasis on human free will. The question of "open communion" in the Lord's Supper at the revivals also troubled Baptist leaders, whose churches practiced "closed communion." See Ford, *Origins of Southern Radicalism,* 26–28.

6. Ibid., 31. Sparks, *History of Padgett's Creek Baptist Church,* 4–8.

7. See Hill, *Southern Churches in Crisis,* 78. Hill puts the matter well when he describes how the southern religious experience has tended to slight both theological form and sacramental structure in favor of "immediate psychic experience." "Sermon Book," bound volume, Wilkinson Family Papers, SCL.

8. Isaac, *Transformation of Virginia;* Matthews, *Religion in the Old South;* and Heyrman, *Southern Cross.*

9. Minutes of Milford Creek Baptist Church, Greenville District, 1856–66, microfilm, SCL; Minutes of Padgett's Creek Baptist Church, Union District, 1864–67, microfilm, SCL.

10. A different view of the continuing importance of church discipline appears in Ford, *Origins of Southern Radicalism,* 33–43.

11. Minutes of Big Creek Baptist Church, February 6, 1864, SCL. The pre-bourgeois nature of rural openness about sexual matters has been discussed by Charles Sellers in *Market Revolution,* 240. Peter Gay has argued that the sexual experience of most bourgeois couples in the nineteenth century was much spicier than our impressionistic ideas regarding Victorianism imply. Gay does note, how-

ever, that the nineteenth-century bourgeois ideal "kept the door of the bedroom firmly closed." Upcountry evangelicals did not allow for such cautious privacy in their war against personal sin. See Gay, *Pleasure Wars,* 238.

12. Minutes of Milford Creek Baptist Church, SCL.

13. Minutes of Padgett's Creek Baptist Church, SCL.

14. Genovese, *Consuming Fire,* 109–16; Farmer, *Metaphysical Confederacy,* 222–28.

15. *Records of the Session of Hopewell ARP Presbyterian Church, Chester County, S.C., 1832–1897,* 17, SCDAH.

16. Minutes of Big Creek Baptist Church, SCL.

17. Landrum, *History of Spartanburg County,* 96. The connections between temperance, evangelicalism, and the making of the northern bourgeoisie are made clear in Johnson, *Shopkeeper's Millennium; Greenville Southern Enterprise,* August 21, 1856.

18. Michaux, quoted in Cecil-Fronsman, *Common Whites,* 197; Racine, *Piedmont Farmer,* 88, 149–51; Minutes of Neals Creek Church, Anderson County, 1866, SCL; Minutes of Padgett's Creek Baptist Church, SCL.

19. Minutes of Padgett's Creek Baptist Church, SCL.

20. *Records of the Session of Hopewell ARP Presbyterian Church,* 17, SCDAH.

21. "Sermon Book," bound volume, Wilkinson Family Papers, SCL.

22. T. L. McBryde, "A Sermon for the Times," *Keowee Courier,* January 26, 1861.

23. "Yankee Heresy," *Confederate Baptist,* November 11, 1863; "The First Abolitionist," *Keowee Courier,* March 30, 1861.

24. "Address on Education—Laying the Cornerstone of Newberry College," Newberry College Archives, Newberry, S.C. Special thanks to Gordon Henry, college archivist, for unlimited access to these materials; Zettler, *War Stories and School Day Incidents.*

25. McCardell, *Idea of a Southern Nation,* 202; King, *History of South Carolina Baptists,* 220–21, 239.

26. "Collection of Letters," Jefferies Family Papers, SCL; "A Sermon for the Times," *Keowee Courier,* March 15, 1862.

27. "Minutes of Big Creek Baptist Church, Williamston, S.C., 1861–86," microfilm, SCL.

28. "Work for All," *Confederate Baptist,* November 11, 1863.

29. Elmore, *Heritage of Woe,* 79, 80.

30. J. M. C. Breaker, "Revivals," *Confederate Baptist,* October 28, 1864.

31. Ibid.

32. Taylor and Conner, *South Carolina Women in the Confederacy,* 156. Writes Machiavelli, "Where there is religion, arms can be introduced, and where there are arms and not religion, the latter can be introduced only with difficulty." *Discourses on Livy,* 35.

33. Sease, *Aunt Kate 100 Years Dear*, 18.

34. Elmore, *Heritage of Woe*, 94.

35. "Dear Mary," letter, Youmans Papers, SCL.

36. Emma Leconte, *When the World Ended*, 46, 60; Elmore, *Heritage of Woe*, 87.

37. Simms, "Humiliation Spreads Its Ashes," 346; Elmore, *Heritage of Woe*, 87; Minutes of Big Creek Church, May 6, 1865, 38, SCL.

38. Krick, "Maxcy Gregg," 3–5.

39. Edgar, *South Carolina*, 378–79.

40. Meynardie, *Amy Oakley*, 216–17, 220–28.

41. An example of these ribbons, in poor condition, is contained in the Youmans Papers, SCL. Youmans, a Confederate cavalryman, received this honor. "In Memoriam G. W. Holland," 44.

42. Biographical sketch of Capers in Snowden, *History of South Carolina*, 259. The best discussion of Capers as a Lost Cause figure appears in Charles Wilson, *Baptized in Blood*, 55, 56.

43. Kurt O. Berends has argued that the Confederate soldiers who experienced conversion during the war assumed a new identity that combined Christianity and the ideal of southern manhood. Berends sees this as a departure from antebellum southern attitudes that identified Christianity with femininity. See Berends's "Wholesome Reading Purifies and Elevates the Man."

44. See Bellah, *Broken Covenant*. Charles Wilson notes the differences when he writes, "In their religion, southerners stressed 'democracy' less than the conservative concept of virtue." *Baptized in Blood*, 13. See also John F. Wilson's *Public Religion in American Culture*, chaps. 6–7.

45. John Crowe Ransom has some fascinating observations on the connections between orthodox religion and conservatism in an agrarian society in his wonderfully peculiar little book, *God without Thunder*, 116–38.

46. Bellows and Connelly, *God and General Longstreet*, 14. See also Charles Wilson, *Baptized in Blood*, 58–78.

47. Shipp, *History of Methodism in South Carolina*, 499, 500.

48. Perry, *Reminiscences of Public Men*, 75–76.

49. Percy, "Stoicism in the South," 83–101.

CHAPTER THREE. No Tears of Penitence

1. "Speech at Ladies Memorial Association," 1866, Easley Papers, SCL.

2. Ibid.

3. Edwards, *Gendered Strife and Confusion*, 169.

4. Leland, *Voice from South Carolina*, 16.

5. Edgar, *South Carolina*, 383–84.

6. Eugene Genovese has argued that southern conservatives, taking their cue

from Carlyle, sometimes expressed the hope that slavery might evolve into a ne-ofeudal relationship of *villeinage. Consuming Fire,* 117.

7. Williamson, *After Slavery,* 245.

8. "The Jefferies Pioneers," Jefferies Family Papers, SCL; De Forest *Union Officer in Reconstruction,* 28, 29; Reconstruction Scrapbook, 1865–77, SCL.

9. "Outrages at Abbeville," *Newberry Weekly Herald,* August 2, 1865.

10. "State News," *Anderson Intelligencer,* May 17, 1866. Ashmore letter, Hagood Papers, SCL.

11. W. M. Hawkins letter, February 2, 1867, Hagood Papers, SCL.

12. De Forest *Union Officer in Reconstruction,* 64; the behavior of many returning veterans is described in Avary, *Dixie after the War,* 156, 157.

13. "Communication," *Newberry Weekly Herald,* August 30, 1865; "Public Meeting," *Newberry Herald Weekly,* July 4, 1866.

14. Kantrowitz, *Ben Tillman,* 52.

15. "Public Meeting," *Keowee Courier,* August 11, 1866.

16. The idea of a "language of political exclusion" rather than a "language of class" is, of course, drawn from Gareth Stedman-Jones critique of the tendency to find class-consciousness in every social movement. See Stedman-Jones, *Languages of Class.* Like the Chartists discussed by Stedman-Jones, protests directed against the end of the Stay Law focused on "the changing character and policies of the state" and thus died out when those policies changed and other concerns emerged. See pp. 175–78.

17. Gaston, *New South Creed.* Gaston calls the Lost Cause a "myth" that "could perform in the service of the New South"; see pp. 160–77. See Hall, "Problem of Ideology," 40, 41. Hall challenges the idea of, as he puts it, "great, immovable class battalions heaving their ascribed ideological luggage about the field of struggle."

18. Bell, *Rebels in Grey,* 113, 123–24.

19. Foster notes that early memorial activities in Charleston drew from "the roster of the business and professional elite." *Ghosts of the Confederacy,* 44. He primarily examines the membership of the Ladies Memorial Association, which did have an elite membership, while failing to focus on the early veteran organizations. Foster does note that the leadership of organizations may have been elite but that popular involvement in memorial activities was high. Ayers uses largely impressionistic evidence to argue that their Lost Cause really celebrated middle-class values. *Promise of the New South,* 334–38.

20. Manuscript Census for Pickens District, 1860 and 1870, SCDAH; Pickens District of South Carolina Tax List, 1866, SCDAH.

21. Woodward has argued that South Carolina's heroes of the Lost Cause lent to middle-class values the legitimacy of "a glorious war record." Woodward shows that this phenomenon did occur in many parts of the South but ignores how Lost Cause values, the values of southern conservatism, could involve veterans in

debtor relief movements and other anticapitalist activities. See *Origins of the New South,* 21, 22, 172–74.

22. See Poole, "Wade Hampton," 920–23. Oddly, we have only one biography of this important Civil War, Reconstruction-era, and Redemption leader. Unfortunately, that work, Manly Wade Wellman's *Giant in Gray,* is an example of ancestral piety rather than scholarship.

23. Alfred Brockenbrough Williams, "Eyewitness Reporter . . . on Events of 1876 in South Carolina" Scrapbook, SCL. This scrapbook, assembled in 1926, contains newspaper articles that Williams wrote. Williams later published this material in a slightly altered form as *Hampton and His Red Shirts.* Hampton lost millions of dollars during the war and sold off family estates in South Carolina and Mississippi to pay his creditors. In 1876, the year he became governor, Hampton had to sell furniture and other personal possessions in order to remain financially viable. See Wellman, *Giant in Gray,* 195ff.

24. "Speech of General Wade Hampton," *Keowee Courier,* October 17, 1866. Interestingly, a later account of this event prepared by the Oconee County United Daughters of the Confederacy selectively chose quotes from Hampton's address that made the general sound remarkably conciliatory toward the North. See Bell, *Rebels in Grey.*

25. At least part of the point of the Black Codes seems to have been the certainty that the black race would die out without protective bounds and limitations of paternalism. Grace Brown Elmore wondered who would "worry over this lazy and self-indulgent race," since "they are no longer property." *Heritage of Woe,* 121.

26. Foster, *Ghosts of the Confederacy,* 50; "From Walhalla," *Anderson Intelligencer,* November 25, 1866.

27. Foster has done a thorough study of the Charleston Ladies Memorial Association, *Ghosts of the Confederacy,* 44; brief discussions of such upcountry organizations appear in Seigler, *Guide to Confederate Monuments,* 301–2.

28. Elizabeth Fox-Genovese has fully explored attitudes toward white women's labor in *Within a Plantation Household,* 166–91.

29. Apparently, Sloan, colonel of the Fourth, provided Reid with two hundred dollars to have his history of the regiment printed. Reid had worked as an operative in the small number of South Carolina cotton mills before the war. Reid letter, Sloan Papers, SCL.

30. De Forest, *Union Officer in Reconstruction,* 48, 49.

31. Seigler, *Guide to Confederate Monuments,* 301.

32. Mary Douglas, *Purity and Danger.* The irony of women's appearing as exemplars of the values of a patriarchal society is discussed by Marina Warner in *Monuments and Maidens,* xx. Warner suggests that "nymphs" often appear as defenders of a cause as if to substantiate its claims to righteousness, See pages 149–50. Kristeva argued that the Virgin Mary, and other Western female saints, could become symbolic representations only after her body had been "changed into an

innocent shell" and sexuality had been "brought down to the level of innuendo." Significantly, this section of Kristeva's essay is entitled "What Body?" See "*Stabat Mater,*" 160–86.

33. On the emergence and activities of the Ladies Memorial Association, see Foster, *Ghosts of the Confederacy,* 38–43; "Ladies Memorial Association," *Newberry Herald,* April 19, 1866.

34. Quoted in Allen, "Modern Conservatism," 589–92. Foster, *Ghosts of the Confederacy,* 44–46.

35. The text of Easley's speech appears in an undated file in the Easley Papers, SCL. The text can be dated from the *Keowee Courier,* April 21, 1866.

36. Material on McCord comes from O'Brien, *All Clever Men,* 337–56. Unfortunately, McCord wrote little after her husband's death, so none of her reflections on the Lost Cause are preserved for us. Except, of course, for her work with the South Carolina Memorial Association.

37. *South Carolina Monument Association,* 11–12.

38. Seigler, *Guide to Confederate Monuments,* 216–21; Foster, *Ghosts of the Confederacy,* 46.

39. *South Carolina Monument Association,* 15, 69–70.

40. The most important work on the subject is Boles, *Masters and Slaves in the House of the Lord.* A description of the break with white churches and the emergence of new religious forms appears in Tindall, *South Carolina Negros,* 186–91. The role of the black church throughout the southern states in the postbellum period receives a fine theoretical treatment in Brooks-Higginbotham, *Righteous Discontent.*

41. Minutes of Milford Baptist Church, Greenville District, 1856–66, microfilm, SCL; Avary, *Dixie after the War,* 205. Ironically, the response of white southern evangelicals seems to have been mirrored by the reaction of northern bourgeoisie black ministers. See Brown, *My Southern Home,* 239–43. The well-educated black clergyman called the revival meetings of southern blacks "injurious to both health and morals."

42. Material on the 1868 convention comes from Simkins and Woody, *South Carolina,* 90–111, and Thomas Holt, *Black over White,* 125 51.

43. A good review of the "black legend" of South Carolina Reconstruction appears in Macauley, "South Carolina Reconstruction Historiography." See Simkins and Woody for an evenhanded discussion of the constitutional convention. After describing the rather low moral character of a few of the leaders, Simkins and Woody conclude that the 1868 effort was "written in excellent English and embodied the best legal principles of the age." *South Carolina,* 93, 94. Of the Reconstruction regime in South Carolina, Eric Foner says it "compiled an unenviable record of malfeasance in office." See Foner, *Reconstruction,* 542.

44. Simkins and Woody, *South Carolina,* 100–104. Efforts on the part of the convention to reshape Carolina's conservative mores buttresses Peter Bardaglio's argument that the crisis of the antebellum household provided inroads for increas-

ing state intervention in private life, especially in the realm of marital relations. See *Reconstructing the Household,* 134ff, 226.

45. Carol Bleser tells the story of the land commission, and its Byzantine corruption, in *Promised Land;* Walter Edgar cites the statistics of land loss in South Carolina and notes the willingness of Republicans to use taxation as a weapon against the old order, shifting taxes away from merchants, banks, and railroads onto landowners. See *South Carolina,* 394–95.

46. Biographical File, 1809–1881, John S. Preston File, SCL; Democratic Party, [South Carolina] State Central Executive Committee, "Respectful Remonstrance on Behalf of the White People of South Carolina."

47. *Greenville Southern Enterprise* articles from May 19 and June 23, 1869, quoted in Batson, *History of the Upper Part of Greenville County.*

48. Quoted in Norton, "South Carolina Taxpayers Convention of 1871," 23.

49. *Proceedings of the 1871 Taxpayers Convention,* 16.

50. Speech of Martin W. Gary at the Taxpayers Convention of South Carolina, 19 February 1874, SCL; *Proceedings of the 1871 Taxpayers Convention,* 58.

51. Norton, "South Carolina Taxpayers Convention of 1871," 95. Simkins and Woody found the taxpayers conventions particularly impotent, and later historians have charged Matthew C. Butler and Martin Gary with being in the pay of New York capitalists who did not want conservatives to call for debt repudiation. See Simkins and Woody, *South Carolina,* 163. The not entirely proven charge against Gary and Butler appears in Williamson, *After Slavery,* 384, and is repeated in Edgar, *South Carolina,* 395. If the two former generals, both known for their utter hatred of all things northern, did engage in such behavior, the New York financial houses reneged on their end of the deal. Williamson admits that neither received any payment for their alleged services.

52. Kantrowitz's discussion of these organizations centers on racial politics. He is one of the few interpreters of the period to draw the important connections between these varying groups, including farmers' movements such as the Grange and, eventually, Tillmanism. See *Ben Tillman,* 56–57. The divisions among white Democrats regarding the meaning and the application of white rule are described in Cooper, *Conservative Regime,* 82ff.

CHAPTER FOUR. All the Natural Bonds of Society

1. Sermons, 1868, Frierson Papers, SCL.

2. Eaton, *Freedom of Thought in the Old South,* and Cash, *Mind of the South,* 94. The literature of southern intellectual history grows apace. See Singal, *War Within,* for a discussion of the struggles between modernism and Victorianism in southern letters. A study by Mark Malvasi, *Unregenerate South,* has set the Vanderbilt agrarians within a larger context of southern conservatism. C. Vann Woodward's description of intellectual life in the years following the war appears in *Origins of the New South,* 429–30.

3. Woodward, *Origins of the New South,* 173–74. Wilson's discussion of the "Lost Cause prophets" appears in *Baptized in Blood,* 79–99.

4. Faust, *Sacred Circle,* 2.

5. "Cause for Which They Fought," n.d., Easley Papers, SCL.

6. "Washington and Lee Address," Easley Papers, SCL. Much of the work of Eugene Genovese has centered on the contention that slavery linked the antebellum South to the modern world of finance capitalism and simultaneously prevented the capitalist ethos from subsuming its prebourgeois culture. See Genovese's *Slaveholder's Dilemma.*

7. "Cause for Which They Fought," n.d., Easley Papers, SCL; Speech of Martin W. Gary at the Taxpayers Convention of South Carolina, 19 February 1874, SCL.

8. Untitled speech, 1866, Easley Papers, folder 4, SCL. The ballad comes from the postbellum *Confederate Song Book,* 13.

9. Sermons, 1875, Frierson Papers, SCL.

10. Undated manuscript, Easley Papers, folder 17, SCL.

11. See Pocock, *The Machiavellian Moment;* see also Dickinson, *Liberty and Property.*

12. Keitt's connection to agrarian radicalism appears in Kantrowitz, *Ben Tillman,* 152–53; biographical material appears in a 1900 reminiscences by Keitt in the Keitt Papers, SCL.

13. Speech of the Honorable Ellison S. Keitt, October 9, 1881 before the Cleveland and Hendricks Campaign Club, SCL; "Speech of Ellison Keitt," *Newberry Herald,* October 14, 1868; "Thoughts on Aristotle by E. S. Keitt," n.d., Keitt Papers, SCL; untitled manuscript, Easley Papers, SCL.

14. "The Age of Democracy," *Anderson Intelligencer,* October 11, 1866.

15. Letter from Archivist, Lyle Papers, SCL; "Speech at Limestone Democratic Club," 1868, Lyle Papers, SCL.

16. Untitled manuscript, Easley Papers, folders 3 and 5, SCL; "The Growing Influence of Money," *Newberry Herald,* June 9, 1864. On the explication of ideas toward progress in nineteenth-century Victorian liberalism, see Briggs, *Age of Improvement.* Russell Kirk has discussed the conservative view of the meaning of "progress' in *Conservative Mind,* 9; Eugene Genovese has delineated its meaning in the southern context in *Slaveholder's Dilemma.*

17. The relationship between southern religious beliefs and belief's regarding the intractable nature of human evil are discussed in Wilson, *Judgment and Grace in Dixie,* 16–17. Easley evinced not only knowledge of the classics but also some familiarity with the history of the ancient Near East, knowledge he draws on for his discussion of historical change. Undated manuscript, Easley Papers, folder 4, SCL.

18. Literature on German romantic conservatism varies in its emphasis. The best work is Jerry Z. Muller's *Other God That Failed.* Noel O'Sullivan's investigation of the philosophical underpinnings of German conservative thought engages in so much theoretical speculation that it leaves behind the emphasis and political

concerns of individual thinkers and movements. See O'Sullivan, *Conservatism,* 58–81.

19. Jamieson Papers, SCL; Holmes, "Schlegel's Philosophy of History," 180. See also Gillespie, *Collapse of Orthodoxy,* and Faust, *Sacred Circle,* 76; "Cause for Which They Fought," n.d., Easley Papers, SCL.

20. The role of the past as a "prescriptive tradition" receives emphasis in Burke, who viewed the fusion of Classical, Christian, and Germanic feudatory practices as the root of a European Christian Commonwealth. See Stanlis, "Burke, Rousseau and Revolution"; "Speech of General Hampton," *Columbia Phoenix,* November 22, 1869; "Editorial," *Columbia Phoenix,* November 23, 1869.

21. "Speech of General Hampton," *Columbia Phoenix,* November 22, 1869; Clippings and Scrapbook, Youmans Papers, SCL.

22. "Yankee Schoolmarms," *Columbia Phoenix,* November 23, 1869, and "Speech of General Hampton," *Columbia Phoenix,* November 22, 1869.

23. Delacroix, "Varieties of Aesthetic Experience," 282.

24. Deference did last into this period, aided by the aesthetic of the Lost Cause, though it did not endure as long as Cash believes. On Tillman, see Kantrowitz, *Ben Tillman.*

25. Trachtenberg, *Incorporation of America,* 3, 4, 80–84. Trachtenberg argues that this new age created fashioned "new hierarchies of control," even as it used the language of equality and free labor. The "corporate form" even "altered basic concepts such as ownership." The economic effects of the newly powerful American nation-state are fully analyzed by economist Jeffrey Hummel in *Emancipating Slaves, Enslaving Free Men;* see especially 221–27, 313–60. Howard Zinn has rightly called Standard Oil, the Transcontinental Railroad, and U.S. Steel "the first beneficiaries of the welfare state." *People's History,* 251.

26. "Speech in Walhalla," 1866, Easley Papers, SCL; "Speech of Ellison Keitt," *Newberry Herald,* January 23, 1867.

27. The role of ritual in embodying cultural ideology has been explicated by Clifford Geertz in *Interpretation of Cultures.* A discussion of the evocative ritualistic setting of Lost Cause orations appears in Wilson, *Baptized in Blood,* 82.

28. Information on the Columbia monument comes from Seigler, *Guide to Confederate Monuments,* 216–22. Details of the celebration come from *South Carolina Monument Association,* 20, 21. Gaines Foster has suggested that the Confederate commemorative activities "helped create loyal workers" (*Ghosts of the Confederacy,* 130). Foster and Ayers have also stressed the nostalgic aspect of Lost Cause celebration, its role as ritual mourning, to underline its allegedly apolitical character. See Foster, *Ghosts of the Confederacy,* 46, and Ayers, *Promise of the New South,* 334–38.

29. *South Carolina Monument Association,* 20–21, 26.

30. Ibid., 27; Gaines Foster notes that "the ideal of true womanhood could have been affirmed by women of any age, yet the veterans chose young, usually pretty, unmarried women who were instructed to dress in white." He passes over

the importance of class position in this selection process. See *Ghosts of the Confederacy*, 137.

31. *South Carolina Monument Association*, 29.

32. Ibid., 33.

33. "General John S. Preston's Oration," May 13, 1879, John S. Preston File, SCL.

34. *South Carolina Monument Association*, 35.

35. Ibid., 38.

36. Ibid., 39.

37. "General John S. Preston's Oration," May 13, 1879, John S. Preston File, SCL.

CHAPTER FIVE. Killed by a Damned Rebel

1. The conservative whites of Newberry commemorated the Crozier incident on his tombstone. "Killing," *Anderson Intelligencer*, September 21, 1865. Also see Seigler, *Guide to Confederate Monuments*, 423–25.

2. Edwards, *Gendered Strife and Confusion*, xi.

3. Williamson, *After Slavery*, 262. Robert Scott organized the militia, even as violence declined in 1870. This had followed several years of white brutality.

4. Zuczek, *State of Rebellion*, 56, 65. Zuczek misunderstands Williamson. Though he argues that violence reached its height in the 1870s, in *After Slavery* he discusses white violence dating from the year following the war. See Williamson, *After Slavery*, 257ff. Williamson's more nuanced account recognizes black agency in its discussion of the relationship between the arming of freedman and the rise of the Klan.

5. Williamson discusses a number of these incidents. Rumors of rape and the church incident are recorded in Avary, *Dixie after the War*, 267. Account of Prince Rivers is in Vandiver, *Traditions and History of Anderson County*, 251. Black-on-white violence occurred with greater frequency in the low country. See Jenkins, *Seizing the New Day*, 133–52.

6. U.S. House, *Report of the Secretary of War*, 1867, 370–467; Vandiver, *Traditions and History of Anderson County*, 249.

7. Zuczek, *State of Rebellion*, 30.

8. "Further Arrests," *Newberry Herald*, April 11, 1866.

9. Meeting Minutes of the Liberty Hill Democratic Club, 1868, SCL.

10. Liberty Hill Democratic Club, Minutes, May 16 and June 6, SCL. Many interpreters have suggested that South Carolina never had a "national" Democratic Party, even in the antebellum period. See Ford, *Origins of Southern Radicalism*, 142–44.

11. "W. W. Russell Describes First Shot of Civil War to C. T. Martin," *Easley Progress*, April 16, 1924; Vandiver, *Traditions and History of Anderson County*, 251.

12. Hobsbawm, *Bandits*, 26. Hobsbawm has found examples of social banditry in a wide variety of historical and cultural contexts. Lacy K. Ford's master's thesis, "One Southern Profile," depicts the Klan as a response to forces of change that threatened to wrench apart southern republicanism. He does not use idea of conservatism to describe their resistance or make clear connections with the Lost Cause.

13. De Forest, *Union Officer in the Reconstruction, 14–15.*

14. *Anderson Intelligencer,* June 22, 1865; "Raiding," *Anderson Intelligencer,* May 24, 1865; "Outrages of the Military," May 3, 1866; McCully, "Letter from a Reconstruction Renegade," 38–40.

15. "Soldier's Aid Association," *Anderson Intelligencer,* August 23, 1866; De Forest, *Union Officer in the Reconstruction, 21.*

16. Miller, *Revenuers and Moonshiners,* 5, 70. Miller notes that students of Reconstruction have ignored for too long the role of Internal Revenue laws as an expansion of Federal power in the defeated South.

17. Jerry Hayne, "Once Upon a Time in Pickens County," unpublished manuscript, SCDAH.

18. "Stack (?) Case," n.d., Easley Papers, SCL. The attempt to enforce liquor laws coincided with efforts to crush other forms of white resistance. The 1871 Ku Klux Act not only struck at the Klan but also empowered revenue agents to summon "posses of troops to their aid." Miller, *Revenuers and Moonshiners,* 70.

19. "Once Upon a Time in Pickens County," 24.

20. Ibid., 44–45.

21. Ibid., 34.

22. Ibid., 56–57.

23. Miller, *Revenuers and Moonshiners,* 108–11; Elmore, *Heritage of Woe,* 180; "Once Upon a Time in Pickens County," 44, 45.

24. Trelease, *White Terror,* 362ff.

25. Klan organization appears in contemporary accounts such as Avary, *Dixie after the War.*

26. "Incidents in the Life of a Private Soldier," 145–48, Shand Papers, SCL.

27. Stagg, "Problem of Klan Violence," 303–38; Flynn, "Ancient Pedigree of Violent Repression," 192–93; Trelease, *White Terror,* xi.

28. Zuczek, *State of Rebellion,* combines the best of varying views. The Klan had a clearly stated purpose, whereas social banditry had a much more amorphous shape, even if we, rightly, see it as a reaction against modernization. The Klan also had different purposes than the agricultural clubs that emerged following the war.

29. *Proceedings in the Ku Klux Trials,* 178.

30. Zuczek, *State of Rebellion,* 78. Despite its effort to reach out to freedmen, the Union Reform Party had clear ties to the Klan. The Union Reform Party effort needs to receive more attention. Conservatives in South Carolina would make

calls for "reform" an essential part of their political efforts, including the 1876 Redemption campaign.

31. Ibid., 88.

32. Flynn, "Ancient Pedigree of Violent Repression," 192–93. E. P. Thompson discusses the "rough music" tradition in *Making of the English Working Class*, 62–78. Batson, *History of the Upper Part of Greenville County*, 590.

33. Avery, *Dixie after the War*, 269.

34. Foster has written that the Klan played little role in "shaping the Confederate tradition." He is correct that the klaverns "left the interpretation of the war to others," but their own participation in a violent campaign of postwar defiance suggests they had clear opinions on the matter. Moreover, Foster himself notes that Klan ritual and regalia "had fascinating ties to the southern celebration of the dead." *Ghosts of the Confederacy*, 48.

35. *Proceedings in the Ku Klux Trials*, 176.

36. Zuczek, *State of Rebellion*, 58.

37. *Proceedings in the Ku Klux Trials*, 175; Howe, *Ku Klux Uniform*, 27.

38. "Incidents in the Life of a Private Soldier," 142, 146, Shand Papers, SCL.

39. These and other horrid stories appear in Williams, *Great South Carolina Ku Klux Klan Trials*, 34–39. Williams believes that whites used the southern code of honor to justify such violence, a code that insisted on the defense of white male fraternal values, no matter what the cost. Patriarchal systems that foster an honor-shame dichotomy do rest on at least the threat of violence. However, reactions of many white conservative leaders to these Klan activities reveal that the most brutal of the Klansmen were operating outside the code of honor. Laura Edwards has argued that acts of sexual violence were essentially political, attempts to affirm "racial and class hierarchies." Such actions obviously cut across the southern class system, however, as conservative leaders like Shand and Lyle struggled to end the "outrages' and found their social subordinates in rebellion.

40. "Incidents in the Life of R. W. Shand, 1907–08," 145, Shand Papers, SCL; The rejection of hierarchical ideals in favor of racial violence suggests the growing power of doctrines of racial purity among yeoman whites and the rejection of traditional paternalistic ideals.

41. "Backward Glances," n.d., Lyle Papers, SCL.

42. Trelease, *White Terror*, 354.

43. Even organizers of local klaverns would later claim that they were horrified at the notion that they had been members of the organization. See the discussion of Matthew C. Butler in Martin, *Southern Hero*, 185–86, 190–91, both for evidence that Butler helped found the Edgefield Klan and as an example of how conservative defenders have attempted to gloss the Reconstruction behavior of Southern heroes; Klan arrests are calculated from Zuczek's figures in *State of Rebellion*, 99.

44. Zuczek, *State of Rebellion*, 138, 139.

45. Ibid.; Roll and By-Laws of the Richland County Rifle Club, SCL.

46. Miller, *Revenuers and Moonshiners*, 42.

47. Zuczek, *State of Rebellion*, 136. These figures are drawn from a report made by the Republican clerk of the South Carolina House of Representatives. Other items purchased by the legislature in these years included cigars, fine wines, clocks, furniture, and carriages.

48. In *State of Rebellion*, 142–58, Richard Zuczek has a complete discussion of the white conservative options in 1874–76.

CHAPTER SIX. Hampton or Hell!

1. "October '76, Critical for Carolina," Alfred Brockenbrough Williams's "Eyewitness Reporter . . . on Events of 1876 in South Carolina" scrapbook, SCL. The author would like to thank Charles Wilson, James Farmer, and Val Lumans for reading this chapter in its early stages. Special thanks also to Robin Copp and the staff of the South Caroliniana Library.

2. Good political histories of the Reconstruction era abound, including Gillette, *Retreat from Reconstruction*; Evans, *Ballots and Fence Rails*; and Stampp, *The Era of Reconstruction*. However, these important works ignore the role of culture and ideology. Foner has made use of religion and social history in his monumental account of the Reconstruction era, *Reconstruction*. Much of his thesis, though, turns on rather traditional political history combined with class analysis. See pp. 573–74 for his discussion of South Carolina and the Hampton campaign. Williamson, *After Slavery*, offers the best revisionist picture of Reconstruction in South Carolina. One very fine work that views itself as "post-revisionist" is Drago, *Hurrah for Hampton!* xi. Examining Hampton's African American supporters, Drago has dealt with some quite controversial material in a way that illuminates questions of agency and the complicated issue of "black conservatism." But any new revisionism, including that the present work, which focuses on cultural materials, should not obscure the level of violence endured by Afro-Carolinians during the Redemption contests. After the 1876 Ellenton riot, for example, whites executed between thirty and fifty black Republicans, including South Carolina state representative Simon P. Coker, of Barnwell County. Zuczek, *State of Rebellion*, 176, 178. Jenkins makes the important point that many low-country blacks actively and successfully resisted white violence in 1876. In a particularly sad irony, the only truly proactive measure taken by the Federal government during South Carolina's scurrilous election involved stationing troops to prevent African Americans from intimidating white voters in Charleston County. See *Seizing the New Day*, 150–52.

3. "Plan of Campaign," 1876, Gary Papers, SCL; also reprinted in Simkins and Woody, *South Carolina*, 566.

4. Simkins and Woody, *South Carolina*, 568;

5. Zuczek, *State of Rebellion*, 38–40, 47–63, 162, 166.

6. Zuczek, *State of Rebellion,* 30, 52–57, 125–27; Edgar, *South Carolina,* 402–3.

7. Gary had little newspaper support except for the *Carolina Spartan,* under the editorship of Hugh Farley. Unfortunately, the articles written in support of Gary no longer exist. See Cooper, *Conservative Regime,* 59.

8. Speech of Martin W. Gary at the Taxpayers Convention of South Carolina, 19 February 1874, SCL.

9. Constitution and Rules of the Richland Rifle Club of Columbia, S.C., with a Roll of Its Officers and Members, 1874, 3, in Records of the Richland Rifle Club, SCL. One inflated statistic had the numbers involved in the clubs as high as seventy-five thousand, more one thousand more than the number of white male voters in the state. Governor Chamberlain, who had no reason to minimize the tally of participants, told congressional investigators that approximately twenty thousand to thirty thousand had marched as Hampton supporters. See U.S. Senate, Subcommittee on Privileges and Elections, *South Carolina in 1876: Report,* 149, 459. Special thanks to Robin Copp at the South Caroliniana Library for helping me hunt down this source.

10. Jarrell, *Wade Hampton and the Negro,* 41–42. Surprisingly, very little worthwhile material on Hampton is available beyond standard military histories. Much else, like the Jarrell account, represents ancestor worship; Wellman, *Giant in Gray,* is one example.

11. Zuczek, *State of Rebellion,* 173.

12. "Hampton Campaign Opens at Anderson," in Alfred Brockenbrough Williams scrapbook, SCL; "Hurrah for Greenville!" *Greenville Southern Enterprise and Mountaineer,* September 13, 1876.

13. Faust has noted this basic tension within antebellum southern conservatism, especially in South Carolina. Faust, *James Henry Hammond and the Old South,* 40–43; Faust, *The Creation of Confederate Nationalism,* 38–40.

14. Kipling, *Enter the King,* 3.

15. Newman, *Parades and the Politics of the Street,* xi; Wilson, *Baptized in Blood;* Wyatt-Brown, *Southern Honor;* Greenberg, *Honor and Slavery.*

16. Interpreting the Lost Cause as primarily an aesthetic does not deny that religion or economic interest played a critical role in the movement. Aesthetic theory offers a way to consider the actual responses of listeners and spectators. More than a simple psychological interpretation, it provides historians with a tool to examine how affective sentiments are elicited through complex symbolism tied to larger political, religious, and economic contexts. White South Carolinians dramatized the Lost Cause as a set of meditative images that represented southern conservatism. See Delacroix, "Varieties of Aesthetic Experience," 279–85. A similar interpretation of the meaning of aesthetic experience appears in Scruton, "Recent Aesthetics in England and America," 3–13.

17. "The Seventh of September," *Greenville Southern Enterprise and Mountaineer,* September 6, 1876.

18. "Twelve Stirring Days in '76 Campaign" and "Spirit of Carolinians Indomitable," Williams scrapbook.

19. Drago, *Hurrah for Hampton!* 9–10; Ball, *State That Forgot,* 159. For more on the origin of the red shirts, see Oakley Park, the Martin W. Gary House and Red Shirt Shrine, in Edgefield, South Carolina, maintained by the United Daughters of the Confederacy.

20. "Hampton and Chamberlain Sketched," in Williams scrapbook; "Political Condition of South Carolina," by "A South Carolinian" [Townsend], 183.

21. "Speech of Gen. Wade Hampton," *Keowee Courier,* October 6, 1866; a full account appears in Louis Bell, *Rebels in Grey,* 113, 123–24. See also Thompson, *Ousting the Carpetbagger,* 26–27.

22. "Straight-Out Fight Gets Under Way," in Williams scrapbook; Richland County Democratic Club, Minutes and Scrapbook, March 1878, Richland County, S.C., SCL.

23. "A Grand Occasion," *Greenville Southern Enterprise and Mountaineer,* September 20, 1876.

24. U.S. Senate, Subcommittee on Privileges and Elections, *South Carolina in 1876: Report,* 260; Delacroix, "Varieties of Aesthetic Experience," 282.

25. Drago, *Hurrah for Hampton!* esp. 12; Ball, *State That Forgot,* 161; Zuczek, *State of Rebellion,* 93–108. Zuczek downplays the role of the Federal government in the elimination of the Klan and yet notes that "hundreds" of people were arrested (p. 108).

26. U.S. Senate, *Senate Miscellaneous Documents,* 44th Cong., 2nd sess., No. 48: *South Carolina in 1876: Testimony,* 1: 563, 965, 959. The testimony of Merriman Washington, Aaron Mitchell, Jonas Weeks, Asbury Green, and other African American Red Shirts is annotated and reprinted in full in Drago, *Hurrah for Hampton!* 57–94.

27. Thompson, *Ousting the Carpetbagger,* 26; Sheppard, *Red Shirts Remembered,* 102. Excerpts from several of the speeches made by Hampton to black audiences were compiled into a campaign pamphlet entitled *Free Men! Free Ballots!! Free Schools!!!,* 3, SLC. Kantrowitz notes that for most Conservative Democrats in 1876, "white government" did not mean "skin color as much as ideology," Kantrowitz, *Ben Tillman,* 73. A good discussion of Hampton and race appears in Cooper, *Conservative Regime,* 84–93.

28. Democratic Club of Liberty Hill, S.C., June 6, 1868, Meeting Minutes, SCL; Richland County Democratic Club, Minutes, September 7, 1876.

29. "October '76, Critical for Carolina," in Williams scrapbook; U.S. Senate, Subcommittee on Privileges and Elections, *South Carolina in 1876: Report,* 304.

30. Capers, *The Soldier-Bishop,* 120–21, 155; Wilson, *Baptized in Blood,* 55–57; "The Christian Patriots of South Carolina," *Working Christian,* November 16, 1876; [Townsend], "Political Condition of South Carolina," 186.

31. Wilson, *Baptized in Blood,* chap. 2; Wellman, *Giant in Gray,* 32–33.

32. A fuller discussion of this phenomenon appears in Thornton, *Politics and*

Power in a Slave Society, especially p. xviii; and Harris, *Plain Folk and Gentry in a Slave Society,* chap. 1.

33. Williamson has argued that the creation of an "organic society" in the Old South constituted the primary tenet of the southern conservative ethos. In such a society, "people would know their own places and functions." *Place* was "the vital word in the vocabulary of conservatism, and it applied to whites as well as to blacks." Williamson, *Rage for Order,* 17, 71.

34. Leland, *Voice from South Carolina,* 13, 91–97; "A Projected Raid on South Carolina," *Greenville Southern Enterprise and Mountaineer,* September 20, 1876.

35. [Townsend], "Political Condition of South Carolina," 180; Rhett, "Fears for Democracy," 311; "Speech of Ex-Gov. [Benjamin F.] Perry at Glassy Mountain Church," *Greenville Southern Enterprise and Mountaineer,* August 30, 1876. Evangelical religion's connection to republicanism gave a special moral impetus to critiques of political corruption. Historians of religion and the American Revolution have done the best job explicating this tendency. See, for example, Isaac, *Transformation of Virginia;* and Hatch, *Sacred Cause of Liberty.*

36. Zuczek, *State of Rebellion,* 177; "Governor Chamberlain Arming the Negroes," *Greenville Southern Enterprise and Mountaineer,* September 20, 1876; "Ellenton Riots Diffuse Dread and Horror," in Williams scrapbook.

37. McCurry, *Masters of Small Worlds,* 260.

38. "Opening of the Democratic Campaign in Edgefield County," *Edgefield Advertiser,* August 10, 1876; Leland, *Voice from South Carolina,* [iii], 13, 163.

39. Cash, *Mind of the South,* 86; Foster, *Ghosts of the Confederacy,* 28–29; Wilson, *Baptized in Blood,* 46; Whites, *Civil War.*

40. "Ellenton Riots Diffuse Dread and Horror," and "October '76, Critical for Carolina," both in Williams scrapbook.

41. "Hampton Receives Ovation in Yorkville," in Williams scrapbook. The notion of the Reconstruction struggle as a kind of "people's war" appears in Zuczek, *State of Rebellion,* 5. Unfortunately, this otherwise excellent study of South Carolina's Reconstruction era gives little attention to the role of the Lost Cause in its discussion of white conservatives. Edgar writes that the response of white South Carolinians to the tableaux "was something akin to religious ecstasy." Edgar, *South Carolina,* 403–4.

42. Silber, *Romance of Reunion,* 7. Anthropologists such as Victor Turner have stressed the role played by bodies and their attendant biological realities in stabilizing cultural values. Ritual, Turner has written, contains twin poles of meaning—at one pole reside "physiological phenomena (blood, sexual organs, coitus, birth, [and] death"; at the other reside "principles of organization: matriliny, patriliny, [and] kingship." The role of "ritual action" is to link these poles of meaning and to cause "an exchange . . . in which the normative referents are charged with emotional significance." The bodies of white southern women in the Lost Cause movement serve as an example of Turner's thesis: they grounded

the hierarchical order of the Old South, with its concern for a white male ordered liberty, in the allegedly stable realities of bodies and biology. Turner, *Dramas, Fields and Metaphors,* 55.

43. Zuczek, *State of Rebellion,* 178; "Edgefield Red Shirt Shot from Ambush," in Williams scrapbook.

44. Jarrell, *Wade Hampton and the Negro,* 123; "Edgefield Red Shirt Shot from Ambush," in Williams scrapbook. Williamson has described this phenomenon of the 1890s as the construction of the "black beast," the image that white southerners came to hold of a new generation of black men whose uncertain status within the southern social world rendered them threats to white male sexual and economic prerogatives. Williamson, *Rage for Order,* 186–91.

45. U.S. Senate, *Senate Miscellaneous Documents,* 44th Cong., 2nd sess., No. 48: *South Carolina in 1876: Testimony,* 1: 939 (Henderson), 560 (Weeks), 555–56 (Taylor); Drago, *Hurrah for Hampton!* 40–43; U.S. Senate, Subcommittee on Privileges and Elections, *South Carolina in 1876: Report,* 327.

46. "Straight-Out Fight Gets Under Way," in Williams scrapbook.

47. "Spirit of Carolina Indomitable"; "Radicals Close Ranks for '76 Campaign"; "Hampton Party Reaches Charleston"; all in Williams scrapbook.

48. Meynardie, *Amy Oakley,* 130–31.

49. The initial tally gave Hampton 92,261 votes to Chamberlain's 91,127. The extent that fraud produced this outcome becomes clear when we consider that in 1876 South Carolina had 74,199 eligible white voters and 110,744 eligible black voters. This result would have required that *every* white male voted (and voted Democratic), with an additional 18,062 black voters, whether through free will or intimidation, casting their ballots for Hampton. Notoriously, Edgefield, Aiken, and Laurens Counties had more votes cast for Hampton than eligible voters. U.S. Senate, Subcommittee on Privileges and Elections, *South Carolina in 1876: Report,* 224–92, 459–64; Edgar, *South Carolina,* 404; Cooper, *Conservative Regime,* 16. Cooper's study reveals how a cultural ideology like conservatism can encounter enormous difficulty when its adherents try to put its principles into practice in political arrangements and institutions.

50. "To The Baptists of South Carolina," *Working Christian,* November 16, 1876; Leland, *Voice from South Carolina,* 183, 152.

51. Leland, *Voice from South Carolina,* 16, 184.

52. Savage, *Standing Soldiers, Kneeling Slaves,* 155; Gaston, *New South Creed,* 186; Ayers, *Promise of the New South,* 334–38.

CHAPTER SEVEN. The Maintenance of Honor and Manhood

1. Letter from S. E. May, 1895, Warren Papers, SCL. The evidence is not conclusive, but considering his knowledge of Tillman, S. E. May is likely the same "S. (?). May" who served as secretary of the Edgefield Farmer's Alliance in

1893. See Farmer's Alliance of Edgefield County, Minutes and Roll Book, 1889–90, SCL.

2. Woodward, *Origins of the New South*, 263.

3. Ibid., 247; Goodwyn, *Populist Moment*, 33–35; Hahn, *Roots of Southern Populism*, 271, 274.

4. Hoftsader, *Age of Reform*; Woodward, "Populist Heritage and the Intellectual," 141–66.

5. Wilson, *Baptized in Blood*, 91. Wilson goes on to suggest that the populist critique of "New South materialism" centered on economics, and that the Lost Cause critique used the "moral and religious issue of virtue." Wilson seems to have revised his view in *Judgment and Grace in Dixie*, 12, 13; Foster, *Ghosts of the Confederacy*, 194–95.

6. Woodward, *Origins of the New South*, 249.

7. Cooper, *Conservative Regime*, 83.

8. Aiken, "Does Farming Pay in the South?"; McMath, *Populist Vanguard*. Kantrowitz, *Ben Tillman*, notes this connection between the Grange and the Redshirt challenge to republican rule. McMath briefly mentions that the "farmer's associations in the Carolinas did enter issue-oriented political action." Aiken's influence largely determined the political character of the Grange. See McMath, *Populist Vanguard*, 36.

9. Harold D. Woodman's contention that postbellum reformers told farmers that "they could persist by accepting a low standard of living, that is by eschewing modernization and accepting a marginal existence," bears no relationship to the South Carolina Grange movement's goals. Grangers inevitably argued that scientific agriculture promoted moderate affluence, independence, and all the social virtues that they believed accompanied these factors. See Woodman, "Class, Race, Politics and the Modernization of the Postbellum South," 17. John W. Ogilvie, "Stock Law of South Carolina Run through a Rhyming Mill and What Came Out," n.d., SCL.

10. Aiken, "What Is the Duty of the Hour?" 194; ibid., 197.

11. Ibid., 199.

12. Ibid.; *Rural Carolinian* 1 (1870): 362.

13. Ibid.

14. Aiken, *Grange*, 17.

15. "Johnson Hagood," *Rural Carolinian* 2 (May 1871): 434.

16. "Address of the Honorable B. F. Perry Delivered before the Pendleton Farmer's Society, October 9, 1884," *Keowee Courier*, November 13, 1884.

17. Kantrowitz has an excellent discussion on this oft-overlooked third-party effort in South Carolina. See Kantrowitz, *Ben Tillman*, 98–109.

18. A single thesis exists on the Greenback-Labor party in South Carolina. Much of my own interpretation rests on Stephen Kantrowitz's detailed discussion in his *Ben Tillman*, 98–109.

19. Cash, *Cash-Shannon Duel,* 4ff.

20. Kantrowitz, *Ben Tillman,* 92–94; Cash, *Cash-Shannon Duel,* 16–17.

21. Robert McMath notes the obscurity of the origins of the Farmer's Alliance, showing its roots in an "indigenous farmers' movement" in Lampasas during the mid-1870s. See McMath, *Populist Vanguard,* 3–11, 37–47.

22. Edgar, *South Carolina,* 431; State Farmer's Alliance Register, Folder 1, Special Collections, Clemson University, hereafter CUSC; Kantrowitz, *Ben Tillman,* 148–50; McMath, *Populist Vanguard,* 40.

23. Anderson County State Farmer's Alliance Minute Books, April 1889, SCDAH.

24. U.S. Senate, *Report of the Committee of Agriculture.* Lawrence Goodwyn has tabulated the amazing statistic that the city of Bridgeport, Connecticut, had a higher circulation of national bank currency than the states of South Carolina, Alabama, Texas, and North Carolina combined immediately following Appomattox. Goodwyn, *Populist Moment,* 22; Fite, "Agricultural Trap," 38–50. Edward Ayers suggests the relationship of rising consumerism to agrarian discontent in *Promise of the New South,* 213.

25. Aiken, *Grange,* 11.

26. Farmer's State Alliance, Minute Book, 1888–99, July 11, 1888, SCL; "Farmers Organize," *Lexington Dispatch,* July 1889.

27. "Rejections and Expulsions in Chesterfield County," State Farmer's Alliance, Register, Folders 67 and 76, CUSC; Harvey, *Redeeming the South,* 206–7.

28. State Farmer's Alliance, Register, Folder 76, CUSC; Constitutions, Folder 1, CUSC. Farmer's State Alliance, Minute Book, Third Annual Meeting, July 23, 1890, SCL.

29. Goodwyn, *Populist Moment,* 264ff.

30. Quoted from "Exposition and Protest," in Niven, *John C. Calhoun,* 160–61. Calhoun has been called "the Marx of the Master Class" for voicing such ideas eighteen years before the *Communist Manifesto.* Wilson, *Baptized in Blood,* 82ff.

31. Abner Perrin United Confederate Veterans Camp, Minutes and Roll Book, 1895–1897 and March 1897, SCL; Landrum, *History of Spartanburg County,* 439–41.

32. Dargan, *Parallelisms,* 4, 9, 14.

33. See *Cyclopedia of Eminent and Representative Men of the Carolinas,* 430–31.

34. Kershaw County Farmer's Alliance, Minutes, April 1889 to [1890?], SCL; Records of the Richard Kirkland Camp, Kershaw County, S.C., United Confederate Veterans of South Carolina, SCL. "Big Day in Lexington," *Lexington Dispatch,* August 22, 1888.

35. Kantrowitz, *Ben Tillman,* 153.

36. "Colonel E. T. Stackhouse," *Cotton Plant,* [1890?], CUSC.

37. State Farmer's Alliance, Minute Book, Fifth Annual Meeting, SCL.

38. Hampton continued to urge racial moderation, even as he proved unwilling to use the full weight of his influence to prevent his own party from disenfranchising black Carolinians in the 1880s. See Poole "Wade Hampton."

39. South Carolina State Board of Agriculture, *South Carolina*, SCL.

40. Edgar, *South Carolina*, 433.

41. Historians have heaped criticism on the bourbons with little investigation into their record. Frank Vandiver described the southern bourbons as creating "a shabby record of irresponsibility"; Woodward viewed them as firmly in the pocket of northern business interests. See Vandiver "Southerner as Extremist," 50, and Woodward, *Origins of the New South*, 50.

CHAPTER EIGHT. Headless Soldiers and Sham Duels

1. *South Carolina Monument Association*, 48, SCL.

2. "The South Carolina Monument," *Confederate Veteran* 7 (May 1899), 231, offprint, n.d., SCL; *South Carolina Monument Association*, 48, SCL.

3. *State*, November 8, 1859, quoted in Confederate Monuments Scrapbook, SCL. A contemporary description of the history and lore of Carolina Confederate monuments insists that "the face of the new statue is virtually the same." The state raised the new statue in 1884, further away from the iron dome of the capitol. See Seigler, *Guide to Confederate Monuments*, 220–21.

4. Sellers, *Market Revolution*, 237; Stuart Hall, following the Althuserians, has sought to complicate the base-superstructure dichotomy of traditional Marxism. Marx himself, Hall notes, oversimplified this paradigm because of his battles with Hegelian idealism, not because he ever clearly expressed how "social ideas" are born and operate. See Hall, "Problem of Ideology," 28–29, 32.

5. Catherine Hall and Leonore Davidoff argue that the bourgeoisie can be best understood as an ideology rather than as an economic configuration, an ideology entailing a transformation of gender roles, the growth of new institutions and the desire to represent "respectability." See Davidoff and Hall, *Family Fortunes*. The coming of bourgeois standards in the antebellum North has been best described in a local study by Mary P. Ryan, *Cradle of the Middle Class*.

6. Kantrowitz, *Ben Tillman*, 80; the condition of South Carolina farmers in the 1880s is amply discussed in Carleton, *Mill and Town in South Carolina*.

7. Stephen Kantrowitz notes that Tillman wished to be understood as a simple, crude figure, a construction of himself that "Masks the origins, intentions and achievements of Tillman's life and career." See Kantrowitz, *Ben Tillman*, 6; Werner, " 'New South' Carolina," 149–65.

8. "Statement of Edgefield Agricultural Society," *Edgefield Advertiser*, October 9, 1884.

9. Simkins, *Tillman Movement*, 47.

10. Hobsbawm, *Age of Revolution*, 277f.

11. Tillman's attitudes toward agricultural education are discussed in Kantrowtiz, *Ben Tillman,* 117–18, 127–28. Attitude toward the Bourbons receives full treatment in Cooper, *Conservative Regime,* 145–48.

12. Haynes, "Biographical Sketch" (Columbia, 1894), Pamphlets by and about Tillman and Tillmania in South Carolina, 1890–1918, SCL.

13. Foucault, *Care of the Self,* quoted in Stoler, *Race and the Education of Desire,* 80–88. Tillman's followers came from the rising bourgeois class. Cooper has noted that Tillman constructed as "farmers" all those who supported him. Though the Bourbon state legislature itself was made up largely of farmers, they could be nothing but political hacks according to Tillman's vocabulary. See Cooper, *Conservative Regime,* 154.

14. The surprising commitment to the education of both races did not last long and always evidenced a paternalist tinge. See Cooper, *Conservative Regime,* 112, and Edgar, *South Carolina,* 411. Black Carolinians remained a majority in the state, so funding per capita for black schools was slightly lower. Cooper notes that funding for public education crept up slowly until the first year of Tillman's governorship in 1890.

15. Quoted in Edgar, *South Carolina,* 464.

16. Kantrowitz, *Ben Tillman,* 218.

17. Allen Tullos notes that these new industrial experiments drew heavily on antebellum farming traditions, though he connects these traditions with the Protestant values of the backcountry rather than with the hierarchical civilization of the Old South that, in my view, shaped, and in turn was shaped by, those values. See Tullos, *Habits of Industry,* 1–15.

18. Ellis, "Model Factory Town," 62; Ely, "An American Industrial Experiment," 40–41.

19. Ely, "An American Industrial Experiment," 41, 43.

20. Tullos, *Habits of Industry,* 152–61. Marx himself would have likely noted that such actions provided "the discipline necessary for the wage system." See Marx, *Capital,* 372.

21. "Laying of the Cornerstone of Winthrop," May 12, 1994, Pamphlets by and about Tillman and Tillmania in South Carolina, 1890–1918, SCL.

22. *Piedmont Headlight,* November 4, 1895. Tillman quoted in Kantrowitz, *Ben Tillman,* 215.

23. "Inagaural Address," December 4, 1890, 41, Pamphlets by and about Tillman and Tillmania in South Carolina, 1890–1918, SCL; Foucault, *Madness and Civilization,* 63.

24. Link, *Paradox of Southern Progressivism,* 33–34, 104–6.

25. David Frierson, "Christianity and Women," sermon, n.d., Frierson Papers, SCL.

26. Chapin, *Fitz Hugh St. Clair,* 25, 53.

27. Ibid.

28. Ibid., 247.

29. Letter from Key, n.d., Cook Papers, box 2, 1880s and 1890s, Baptist Historical Collection, Furman University Archives; Harvey, *Redeeming the South,* 197ff. "Religious Reminiscences of Over Fifty Years Ago in Oconee County," *Keowee Courier,* July 3, 1884.

30. Wilson, *Code of Honor.*

31. Sims, *Story of My Life,* 100–102; on the antebellum role of South Carolina college as the cradle of the ruling class, see Cooper, *Conservative Regime,* 43–44.

32. Toole, *Ninety Years in Aiken County,* 40.

33. Wyatt-Brown, *Honor and Violence,* 26.

34. Kantrowitz, *Ben Tillman,* 120–22; Ute Frevert's study of European dueling finds that discourse about the practice changed as the absolutist state became more interested in expanding its regulatory power. See Frevert, *Men of Honour.* Tillman's evocation of the illegality of the duel resembles the complaint of the European middle class that private combat "undermined public order" (20).

35. Anne Stoler argues that this is why Foucault locates the emergence of "State racism" in the nineteenth century, when bourgeois nation-states directed violence against "internal enemies" and, by creating and at least symbolically destroying such enemies, made a new middle class. See Stoler, *Race and the Education of Desire,* 55–94.

36. Kantrowitz, *Ben Tillman,* 174ff.

37. Foucault, quoted in Stoler, *Race and the Education of Desire,* 61.

38. Kantrowitz notes that Tillman's white opponents "set the same limitations on black political aspirations"; however, the actual practice of white supremacy, as can be seen in attitudes toward education, lynching, and the meaning of citizenship, was very different. See Kantrowitz, *Ben Tillman,* 7, 8; Williamson, *Rage for Order,* 70–71. Williamson contrasts this departure sharply with the "organic society" shaped by slavery and conservative ideals in the antebellum period (see *Rage for Order,* 3–43).

39. Quoted in Williamson, *Origins of Segregation,* 67.

40. Lawrence J. Friedman concludes that these psychosexual fears, worsened by the experience of economic and social chaos, resulted in many southern whites' creating new institutions of control to prevent "black savagery." See Friedman, *White Savage,* 86–87.

41. Stephen Kantrowitz notes that even Tillman backed away from this extremity. Twentieth-century southern states have not been so wary. Kantrowitz notes that Mississippi's Sovereignty Commission practiced a similar surveillance of interracial sex in the 1950s and '60s. Kantrowitz, *Ben Tillman,* 197 and n. 95.

42. "Law to Be Enforced in Schools," *State,* January 25, 1903.

43. "The Latest Lynchings," *State,* June 4, 1894; "Cowardly Coyotes," *State,* June 28, 1895; Cauthen, *John J. Dargan,* 41–45.

44. Ellison Keitt, "The Alliance Responsible," *State,* June 9, 1892, Keitt Papers, SCL.

45. Letter to the editor, Keitt Papers, 1876 and 1890, SCL.

46. "A Trouncing of Tillman," *State*, June 9, 1892.

47. Vandiver, *Traditions and History of Anderson County*, 255.

48. Pamphlets by and about Tillman and Tillmania in South Carolina, 1890–1918, SCL.

49. Simkins, *Tillman Movement*, 193–96.

50. Quoted in Kantrowitz, *Ben Tillman*, 194–97.

51. "Strong Words from Edgefield," *Charleston News and Courier*, January 16, 1894.

52. George Tillman quoted in Simkins, *Tillman Movement*, 221; a full and incisive treatment of the 1895 proceedings appears in Kantrowitz, *Ben Tillman*, 198–242.

53. L. Q. C. Lamar letter, 1894, Youmans Papers, SCL.

54. "Nye at the Circus," *State*, November 3, 1895.

55. Kantrowitz, *Ben Tillman*, 302–5.

56. George Tillman quoted in Kantrowitz, *Ben Tillman*, 242; *State*, May 1895.

CHAPTER NINE. The Lost Cause We Cherished and Loved

1. "A Petrified Man," *State*, November 12, 1895.

2. "South Carolina Curiosity: The Petrified Man," 1895, Broadside, Buff Papers, SCL.

3. Foster, *Ghosts of the Confederacy*, 110–12, 152–53. A discussion of Gordon's New South interests appears in Woodward, *Origins of the New South*, 17, 156–58.

4. Letter to John D. Kennedy, September 28, 1893, Kennedy Papers, SCL; Foster, *Ghosts of the Confederacy*, 106–7.

5. Abner Perrin United Confederate Veterans Camp, Minutes and Roll Book, J——1899, SCL; Cunningham's running battle with Underwood, which eventually worked itself out in a series of lawsuits, became a major source of dissension in the turn-of-the-century UCV. Concern over status within the UCV likely played a role in this struggle, as did Cunningham's distaste for Underwood's conciliatory attitude. An excellent account of the Cunningham-Underwood controversy appears in Simpson, *S. A. Cunningham*, 120–45.

6. Address of Honorable J. L. M. Curry, Richmond, 1896, SCL; Hesseltine, *Confederate Leaders*, 91–92.

7. *Confederate Reunion at Charleston, 1899*, 494.

8. *Confederate Reunion at Charleston, 1899*, 490–91.

9. Ibid.; Vedder, "For What Did the South Fight in the War of 1861–65?," A. Burnet Rhett Camp United Confederate Veterans reunion, Charleston, November 17, 1901, SCL.

10. Snowden, *History of South Carolina*, 41.

11. J. W. Reid letter to J. B. E. Sloane, 1891, Sloane Papers, SCL; Reid, *History of the Fourth Regiment* (see especially pp. 8, 73, 105).

12. Perry, *Reminiscences of Public Men,* 75–76; S. E. May letter, 1895, Warren Papers, SCL.

13. Kantrowitz, *Ben Tillman,* 185; Cooper, *Conservative Regime,* 206. Cooper describes the veteran leaders as "stunned" by the rough treatment they received at the hands of Tillmanism. Their response was that they "simply clung to their banners; the defeat they met in 1890 was as final as that of 1865." Cooper, *Conservative Regime,* 207.

14. "Address Delivered to Confederate Survivors Association in Augusta, Georgia," April 26, 1893, SCL; Abner Perrin United Confederate Veterans Camp, Minutes and Roll Book, January 1895 and February 1897, SCL; *The Confederate Reunion at Charleston, 1899,* 476, 494.

15. J. W. Reid letter, [1891?], Sloane Papers, SCL.

16. Poppenheim et al., *History of the United Daughters of the Confederacy.*

17. Turner, *Courageous Caroline,* 34–35; Foster, *Ghosts of the Confederacy,* 171, 175. The UDC. remains a bastion of foolishness, maintaining a down-at-the-heels gentility and propagating a hoopskirt version of the Old South. See Horowitz, *Confederates in the Attic,* 244–45.

18. Brown, "Preservation of the Lost Cause," 25; "Augustine Thomas Smyth: In Memoriam," SCL.

19. Rosenburg, *Living Monuments,* 70–71.

20. Ibid., 140.

21. Seigler, *Guide to Confederate Monuments,* 358–61; "Confederate Memories: Address of Colonel James A. Hoyt at the Unveiling of the Confederate Monument, Greenville, S.C., Sept. 27, 1892," SCL.

22. Seigler, *Guide to Confederate Monuments,* 371; Waller Papers, SCL.

23. Seigler, *Guide to Confederate Monuments,* 340.

24. Foster, *Ghosts of the Confederacy,* 166–67. *Confederate Veteran,* April 1893; such advertisements increasingly filled the pages of the journal after 1900, including one offering stock options in something called the "Confederate Mining Company of Arizona," January 1903.

25. Cooper, *Conservative Regime,* 211. A little more than half in each demographic group gave their profession as "farmer or planter." Many, like Timmerman, described often as an "Edgefield planter," had their real interests in New South industry and commerce. See *Cyclopedia of Eminent and Representative Men of the Carolinas,* 310.

26. Edgar, *South Carolina,* 456.

27. Carlton, *Mill and Town in South Carolina.*

28. Edgar, *South Carolina,* 451.

29. Confederate Monuments Scrapbook, Camden, S.C., 1911, SCL; Siegler, *Guide to Confederate Monuments,* 94–95.

30. Wilson, *Baptized in Blood,* 161. Wilson makes clear that the Spanish-American conflict "was one stop on the road to reconciliation but not the final one," 163–64. However, certain classes in southern society, such as the bour-

geois membership of Greenville First Baptist, certainly seem to have been able to stomach a strong dose of American nationalism with barely a nod to Confederate virtue. See the *Greenville Mountaineer,* May 11, 1898.

31. *Gaffney Ledger* quoted in Oldfield, " 'Remembering the Maine,' " 48; *Greenville Mountaineer,* May 11, 1898.

32. "Richmond Reunion Incident," *Confederate Veteran,* September 1896; "Labor Question," *State,* January 17, 1903; Edgar, *South Carolina.*

33. "A Great Reunion," *State,* November 13, 1895; "Speech on Washington's Birthday," 1899, Youmans Papers, SCL.

34. Scrapbook, 1906, Youmans Papers, SCL.

35. Farmer's Institute clippings file, Series 37, CUSC.

36. Board of Trustees Minutes and Index, Clemson University, Record Book 1, June 6, 1904, CUSC.

37. Biographical file, R. W. Simpson, SCL; D. Keating Norris Memorial, Record Book I, *Board of Trustees Minutes and Index* 431, CUSC.

38. Norris and Thomson Family Papers, SCL.

39. "Captain Lake's Speech," *State,* November 20, 1895.

40. Lumpkin, *Making of a Southerner,* 115–16.

41. Ibid., 114.

CONCLUSION. The Great Train Robbery

1. Edgar, *South Carolina,* 544–45.

2. Cell, in *Highest Stage of White Supremacy,* makes the argument that segregation, rather than evidence of cultural lag, was a racism born of peculiarly modern conditions. See especially 13–20.

3. Cooper, *Conservative Regime,* 13, 207.

4. Gaston, *New South Creed,* 166. See Herberg's discussion of the liberal, democratic meanings of civil religion in *Protestant, Catholic, Jew.*

5. Guttmann, *Conservative Tradition in America,* 11. Writing in the late 1960s, Guttmann noted that a political party dominated by Burkean principles in the United States was "absolutely unthinkable," ibid. Faust, *Sacred Circle,* 42–44.

6. The foregoing may suggest to some that I am simply folding the meaning of "literary" and "aesthetic" together. The point is not to clearly define these terms, but rather to show that ideology can have an expression other than the merely political and to suggest that ideological constructions survive outside of politics.

7. Benet, *John Brown's Body,* 334.

8. Rossiter, *Conservatism in America,* 128–62; M. E. Bradford, in his *Reactionary Imperative,* has mounted the most incisive critique of the contemporary Right from the so-called paleoconservative perspective. See especially the chapters "On Being Conservative in a Post-Liberal Era" and "Undone by Victory: Political Success and the Subversion of Conservative Politics."

9. Crick, "Strange Quest for an American Conservatism," 361, 365.

10. Holden, "Is Our Love of Wade Hampton Foolishness?" 60–88.

11. Avelar, *Untimely Present*, 2. Special thanks to Beth Zeiss, assistant professor of foreign languages and literatures at the University of South Carolina-Aiken, for introducing me to Avelar's work.

12. Ibid.

13. Edgar, *South Carolina*, 473–75. A more substantive, and morally sensitive, account of the Bleasite years can be found in Simon, "Appeal of Cole Blease in South Carolina," 57–86.

14. Santayana, *Life of Reason*, 302.

15. James Farmer, "Whose Flag, Whose History?" *Polis* (University of South Carolina–Aiken History Department), spring 2000, 1–2.

16. Cooper is doubtful of finding a "single thread" of concern and definition in the bourbon movement. He himself notes, however, their undying devotion to the Lost Cause and, challenging Woodward, refuses to see him as a simple reactionary whose memory of the war intermingled with concern for personal economic gain. See *Conservative Regime*, 20.

17. "Flag Moved, Tempers Fly," *Greenville News*, July 2, 2000.

18. Information on this incident taken from account by reporter Lyn Riddle of the *Greenville News*. See "Flag Foes Confront One Another on the Streets of Columbia," *Greenville News*, July 2, 2000. The author also witnessed the incident.

BIBLIOGRAPHY

MANUSCRIPT COLLECTIONS AND PERSONAL PAPERS

Clemson University Special Collections, Clemson, S.C. (CUSC). Clemson University Board of Trustees, Minutes and Index, Record Book 1. Farmer's Institute, Clippings File, Series 37. State Farmer's Alliance Register.
Furman University Archives, Baptist Historical Collection. Harvey T. Cook Papers.
Hicks-Roach-Vandiver genealogical material. In author's possession.
Newberry College Archives, Newberry S.C. "Address on Education—Laying the Cornerstone at Newberry College."
South Carolina Department of Archives and History, Columbia, S.C. (SCDAH). Anderson County Farmer's Alliance, Minute Books. Hopewell A.R.P. Church, Records of the Session, 1832–97. Manuscript Census for Pickens District, 1860 and 1870.
University of South Carolina Libraries, South Caroliniana Library, Columbia, S.C. (SCL). Abner Perrin United Confederate Veterans Camp, Edgefield, S.C., Minutes and Roll Book. Big Creek Baptist Church of Williamston, S.C., Records, 1861–86. W. M. Buff Papers. Burns Family Papers. Ellison Capers Papers. Robert Means Davis Papers. William King Easley Papers. Farmer's Alliance of Edgefield County, Minutes and Roll Book, 1889–90. Farmer's Alliance of Kershaw County, Minutes and Roll Book. Farmer's State Alliance Meeting, Minutes, 1888–99. David E. Frierson Papers. Martin Witherspoon Gary Papers. Greenwood County Ladies Memorial Association File. James Earle Hagood Papers. David Flavel Jamieson Papers. Jefferies Family Papers. Jefferson Davis Memorial Association, Records and Minutes. Ellison Summerfield Keitt Papers. John Doby Kennedy Papers. Ladies Memorial Association, Camden, South Carolina, File. Liberty Hill Democratic Club, Minutes, 1868. J. Banks Lyle Papers. Milford Baptist Church of Greenville District, Minutes, 1856–66. Neals Creek Church of Anderson District, Minutes, 1866. Norris and Thomson Family Papers. Padgett's Creek Baptist Church, Minutes, 1864–67. Pamphlets by and about Tillman and Tillmania in South Carolina, 1890–1918. Pendleton Farmer's Society, Minutes, 1824–20. John S. Preston File. Richland Democratic Club, Minutes and Scrapbook, 1876–80. R. W. Shand Papers. J. B. E. Sloan Papers. United Confederate Veterans, Records of the Richard Kirkland Camp, Kershaw County, S.C. United Confederate Veterans of South Carolina File. C. A. C. Waller Papers. Thomas J. Warren Papers. Wilkinson Family Papers. Leroy W. Youmans Papers.

NEWSPAPERS AND MAGAZINES

Anderson Intelligencer
Carolina Spartan
Charleston News and Courier
Columbia Phoenix
Confederate Baptist
Confederate Veteran
Cotton Plant
Daily Register
Easley Progress
Edgefield Advertiser
Gaffney Ledger
Greenville News
Greenville Southern Enterprise and Mountaineer (also *Greenville Southern Enter-
     prise, Greenville Southern Patriot,* and *Greenville Enterprise and Mountaineer*)
Harper's Magazine
Keowee Courier
Lexington Dispatch
Newberry Weekly Herald (also *Triweekly Herald*)
Piedmont Headlight
Rural Carolinian
The State
Yorkville Enquirer
Working Christian

BOOKS, ARTICLES, DISSERTATIONS, AND THESES

Aiken, D. Wyatt. "Does Farming Pay in the South?" *Rural Carolinian* 2 (March
     1871): 323.
———. *The Grange: Its Origin, Progress and Educational Purpose.* Washington,
     D.C.: Department of Agriculture, Special Report 55, 1883.
———. "What Is the Duty of the Hour?" *Rural Carolinian* 2 (January 1871):
     194.
Allen, David Y. "Modern Conservatism: The Problem of Definition." *Review of
     Politics* 4 (1981): 582–603.
Avary, Myra Lockhart. *Dixie after the War.* New York: Doubleday and Page,
     1906.
Avelar, Idelbar. *The Untimely Present: Postdictatorial Latin American Fiction
     and the Task of Mourning.* Durham, N.C.: Duke University Press, 1999.
Ayers, Edward L. *The Promise of the New South: Life after Reconstruction.* New
     York: Oxford University Press, 1995.
Ball, William Watts. *The State That Forgot: South Carolina's Surrender to De-
     mocracy.* Indianapolis: Bobbs-Merrill, 1932.

Bardaglio, Peter. *Reconstructing the Household: Families, Sex, and the Law in the Nineteenth-Century South.* Chapel Hill: University of North Carolina Press, 1995.

Barrett, John G. *Sherman's March through the Carolinas.* Chapel Hill: University of North Carolina Press, 1956.

Batson, Mann. *History of the Upper Part of Greenville County.* Taylors, S.C.: Faith Printing Company, 1993.

Bell, Louis Matheson, ed. *Rebels in Grey: Soldiers from Pickens.* Seneca, S.C.: United Daughters of the Confederacy, 1984.

Bellah, Robert. *The Broken Covenant: American Civil Religion in a Time of Trial.* New York: Seabury, 1975.

Bellows, Barbara, and Thomas Connelly. *God and General Longstreet: The Lost Cause and the Southern Mind.* Baton Rouge: Louisiana State University Press, 1982.

Benet, Stephen Vincent. *John Brown's Body.* New York: Holt, Rinehart and Winston, 1962.

Berends, Kurt O. " 'Wholesome Reading Purifies and Elevates the Man': The Religious Military Press and the Confederacy." In *Religion and the American Civil War,* ed. Randall M. Miller, Harry S. Stout, and Charles Reagan Wilson. New York: Oxford University Press, 1998.

Berlin, Ira. *Many Thousands Gone: The First Two Centuries of Slavery in North America.* Cambridge: Harvard University Press, Belknap Press, 1998.

Berlin, Isaiah. "Joseph De Maistre and the Origins of Fascism." In *The Crooked Timber of Humanity: Chapters in the History of Ideas,* ed. Henry Hardy. Princeton: Princeton University Press, 1990.

Bernheim, G. D. *History of the German Settlements and of the Lutheran Church in North and South Carolina, from the Earliest Period of the Colonization of the Dutch, German and Swiss Settlers to the Close of the First Half of the Present Century.* 1872. Reprint, Spartanburg, S.C., 1972.

Bethell, Tom. *The Noblest Triumph: Property and Prosperity through the Ages.* New York: St. Martin's, 1998.

Blackbourne, David, and Geoffrey Eley. *The Peculiarities of German History: Bourgeois Society and Politics in Nineteenth-Century Germany.* Oxford: Oxford University Press, 1998.

Blakemore, Steven, ed. In *Burke and the French Revolution: Bicentennial Essays.* Athens: University of Georgia Press, 1992.

Bleser, Carol. "The Perrys of Greenville: A Nineteenth Century Marriage." In *The Web of Southern Social Relations: Women, Family, and Education,* ed. Walter J. Fraser Jr., R. Frank Saunders Jr., and Jon L. Wakelyn. Athens: University of Georgia Press, 1985.

———. *Promised Land: The History of the South Carolina Land Commission, 1869–1890.* Columbia: University of South Carolina Press, 1969.

Bloch, Marc. *French Rural History: An Essay on Its Basic Characteristics.* Berkeley: University of California Press, 1966.

Blum, Edward J. " 'Gilded Crosses': Postbellum Revivals and the Reforging of American Nationalism." *Journal of Presbyterian History* 79 (winter 2001): 277–92.

Blum, Jerome. *The End of the Old Order in Rural Europe.* Princeton: Princeton University Press, 1978.

Boles, John B., ed. *Masters and Slaves in the House of the Lord.* Lexington: University Press of Kentucky, 1988.

Bradford, M. E. *The Reactionary Imperative: Essays Literary and Political.* Peru, Ill.: Sherwood, 1990.

Braudel, Fernand. "History and Social Sciences: The Long Term." *Social Science Information* 9, no. 1 (February 1970): 145–74.

———. *A History of Civilizations.* New York: Penguin, 1993.

Briggs, Asa. *The Age of Improvement.* London: Longman and Green, 1989.

Brooks-Higginbotham, Evelyn. *Righteous Discontent: The Women's Movement in the Black Baptist Church, 1880–1920.* Cambridge: Harvard University Press, 1993.

Brown, Megan Josephine. "Preservation of the Lost Cause: The South Carolina United Daughters of the Confederacy as a Preservation Organization." Master's thesis, University of South Carolina, 1999.

Brown, William Wells. "My Southern Home or, The South and Its People." In *Afro-American Religious History: A Documentary Witness,* ed. Milton C. Sernett. Durham, N.C.: Duke University Press, 1985.

Burke, Edmund. *Reflections on the Revolution in France.* Oxford: Oxford University Press, 1993.

Burts, Robert Milton. *Richard Irving Manning and the Progressive Movement in South Carolina.* Columbia: University of South Carolina Press, 1997.

Capers, Walter B. *The Soldier-Bishop: Ellison Capers,* New York, 1912.

Carleton, David. *Mill and Town in South Carolina: 1880–1920.* Baton Rouge: Louisiana State University Press, 1982.

Cash, E. B. C. *The Cash-Shannon Duel.* Greenville, S.C.: Daily News Job Printing Office, 1881.

Cash, Wilbur J. *The Mind of the South.* New York: Vintage, 1991.

Cauthen, Henry F. *John J. Dargan: His Dares and His Deeds.* Columbia: University of South Carolina Press, 1975.

Cecil-Fronsman, Bill. *Common Whites.* Lexington: University Press of Kentucky, 1992.

Cell, John W. *The Highest Stage of White Supremacy: The Origins of Segregation in South Africa and the American South.* New York: Cambridge University Press, 1992.

Channing, Steven A. *Crisis of Fear: Secession in South Carolina.* New York: Oxford University Press, 1974.

Chapin, Sallie F. *Fitz Hugh St. Clair: The South Carolina Rebel Boy, or It Is No Crime to Be Born a Gentleman.* Philadelphia, 1873.

Chestnutt, David R., and Clyde N. Wilson, eds. *The Meaning of South Carolina History: Essays in Honor of George C. Rogers Jr.* Columbia: University of South Carolina Press, 1991.

Church, Joseph. "The Farmer's Alliance and the Populist Movement in South Carolina, 1887–1896." Master's thesis, University of South Carolina, 1953.

The Confederate Reunion at Charleston, 1899. Dixie Magazine, May 1899. Reprint, SCL.

Confederate Song Book. Greenwood, S.C.: Drinkard, 1898.

Confederate Sunday School Hymnbook. Superintendent of Greenville District, G. E. Elford Press, 1863.

Cooper, William J., Jr. *The Conservative Regime: South Carolina, 1877–1890.* Baltimore: Johns Hopkins University Press, 1968. Reprint, Baton Rouge: Louisiana State University Press, 1991.

Crick, Bernard. "The Strange Quest for an American Conservatism." *Review of Politics* 4 (October 1981): 361–71.

Cyclopedia of Eminent and Representative Men of the Carolinas. Spartanburg, S.C.: Reprint Company, 1972.

Dargan, John J. *Parallelisms of Negro Slavery and Protection in the United States.* Charleston, 1886. SCL.

Davidoff, Leonore, and Catherine Hall. *Family Fortunes: Men and Women in the English Middle Class, 1780–1850.* Chicago: University of Chicago Press, 1987.

De Forest, John William. *A Union Officer in the Reconstruction.* New Haven: Yale University Press, 1948.

de Grazia, Sebastian. *Machiavelli in Hell.* New York: Vintage, 1989.

Delacroix, Henri. "Varieties of Aesthetic Experience." In *The Problems of Aesthetics: A Book of Readings,* ed. Eliseo Vivas and Murray Krieger. New York: Holt, Rinehart and Winston, 1953.

DeSantis, Vincent P. "Rutherford B. Hayes and the Removal of Troops at the End of Reconstruction." In *Region, Race, and Reconstruction: Essays in Honor of C. Vann Woodward,* ed. J. Morgan Kousser and James M. McPherson. New York: Oxford University Press, 1982.

Dickinson, H. T. *Liberty and Property: Political Ideology in Eighteenth-Century Britain.* New York: Holmes and Meir, 1977.

Douglas, Mary. *Purity and Danger: An Analysis of Concepts of Pollution and Taboo.* Harmondsworth: Penguin, 1970.

Drago, Edward. *Hurrah for Hampton! Black Red-Shirts in South Carolina during Reconstruction.* Fayetteville: University of Arkansas Press, 1998.

Eaton, Clement. *Freedom of Thought in the Old South.* Durham, N.C.: Duke University Press, 1940.

Eatwell, Robert. "The Right as a Variety of Styles of Thought." In *The Nature of the Right: American and European Politics since 1789*, ed. Robert Eatwell and Noel O'Sullivan. Boston: Twayne, 1990.

Edgar, Walter. *South Carolina: A History.* Columbia: University of South Carolina Press, 1998.

Edwards, Laura F. *Gendered Strife and Confusion: The Political Culture of Reconstruction.* Urbana: University of Illinois Press, 1997.

Eliade, Mircea. *The Myth of the Eternal Return, or Cosmos and History.* Trans. Willard R. Trask. New York: Harper Mythos Books, 1991.

———. *The Sacred and the Profane: The Nature of Religion.* Trans. Willard R. Trask. New York: Harcourt Brace, 1959.

Ellis, L. B. "A Model Factory Town," *Forum,* September 1901, 62, SCL.

Elmore, Grace Brown. *A Heritage of Woe: The Civil War Diary of Grace Brown Elmore, 1861–1868.* Ed. Marli F. Weiner. Athens: University of Georgia Press, 1997.

Ely, R. J. "An American Industrial Experiment," *Harper's Magazine,* June 1902, 40–41.

Evans, W. McKee. *Ballots and Fence Rails: Reconstruction on the Lower Cape Fear.* Chapel Hill: University of North Carolina Press, 1966.

Farmer, James O. *The Metaphysical Confederacy: James Henly Thornwell and the Synthesis of Southern Values.* Macon, Ga.: Mercer University Press, 1986.

Faust, Drew G. *The Creation of Confederate Nationalism: Ideology and Identity in the Civil War South.* Baton Rouge: Louisiana State University Press, 1988.

———. *Ideology of Slavery: Proslavery Thought in the Antebellum South, 1830–1860.* Baton Rouge: Louisiana State University Press, 1981.

———. *James Henry Hammond and the Old South: A Design for Mastery.* Baton Rouge: Louisiana State University Press, 1982.

———. *A Sacred Circle: The Dilemma of the Intellectual in the Old South, 1840–1860.* Philadelphia: University of Pennsylvania Press, 1986.

Fields, Barbara J. "Ideology and Race in American History." In *Region, Race, and Reconstruction: Essays in Honor of C. Vann Woodward,* ed. J. Morgan Kousser and James M. McPherson. New York: Oxford University Press, 1982.

Fite, Gilbert C. "The Agricultural Trap." *Agricultural History* 51 (fall 1986): 38–50.

Flynn, Charles. "The Ancient Pedigree of Violent Repression: Georgia's Klan as a Folk Movement." In *The Southern Enigma: Essays in Race, Class and Folk Culture,* ed. Walter J. Fraser. New York: Greenwood, 1983.

Flynn, Jean Martin. *The Militia in Antebellum South Carolina Society.* Spartanburg, S.C.: Reprint Company, 1991.

Foner, Eric. *Reconstruction: America's Unfinished Revolution, 1863–1877.* New York: Harper and Row, 1998.

Ford, Lacy K. "One Southern Profile: Modernization and the Development of White Terror in York County." Master's thesis, University of South Carolina, 1976.

————. *Origins of Southern Radicalism: The South Carolina Upcountry, 1800–1860.* New York: Oxford University Press, 1988.

————. "Republics and Democracy: The Parameters of Political Citizenship in Antebellum South Carolina." In *The Meaning of South Carolina History: Essays in Honor of George C. Rogers Jr.,* ed. David R. Chestnutt and Clyde N. Wilson. Columbia: University of South Carolina Press, 1991.

Foster, Gaines M. *Ghosts of the Confederacy: Defeat, the Lost Cause and the Emergence of the New South.* Oxford: Oxford University Press, 1997.

Foucault, Michel. *The Care of the Self: History of Sexuality.* Vol. 3. New York: Random House, 1988.

————. *Madness and Civilization: A History of Insanity in the Age of Reason.* New York: Vintage, 1988.

Fox-Genovese, Elizabeth. *Within a Plantation Household: Black and White Women in the Old South.* Chapel Hill: University of North Carolina Press, 1988.

Franklin, John Hope. *The Militant South.* Boston: Beacon, 1961.

Fraser, Walter J., ed. *The Southern Enigma: Essays in Race, Class, and Folk Culture.* Westport, Conn.: Greenwood, 1983.

Fraser, Walter J., Jr., R. Frank Saunders Jr., and Jon L. Wakelyn, eds. *The Web of Southern Social Relations: Women, Family, and Education.* Athens: University of Georgia Press, 1985.

Freehling, William W. *Prelude to Civil War.* New York: Oxford University Press, 1992.

————. *The Road to Disunion: Secessionists at Bay, 1776–1854.* New York: Oxford University Press, 1990.

Free Men! Free Ballots!! Free Schools!!! The Pledges of Gen. Wade Hampton, Democratic Candidate for Governor, to the Colored People of South Carolina, 1865–1876. N.p., 1876.

Frevert, Ute. *Men of Honour: A Social and Cultural History of the Duel.* Trans. Anthony Williams. Cambridge: Cambridge University Press, 1995.

Friedman, Lawrence J. *The White Savage: Racial Fantasies in the Postbellum South.* Englewood Cliffs, N.J.: Prentice-Hall, 1970.

Furniss, Tom. "Stripping the Queen: Edmund Burke's Magic Lantern Show." In *Burke and the French Revolution: Bicentennial Essays,* ed. Steven Blakemore. Athens: University of Georgia Press, 1992.

Gallagher, Gary W., and Alan T. Nolan, eds. *The Myth of the Lost Cause and Civil War History.* Bloomington: Indiana University Press, 2000.

Gaston, Paul M. *The New South Creed: A Study in Southern Mythmaking.* New York: Knopf, 1970.

Gay, Peter. *The Pleasure Wars: The Bourgeois Experience.* New York: Norton, 1998.

Geertz, Clifford. *Interpretation of Cultures.* New York: Harper Collins, 1973.

————. *Negara: The Theatre State in Nineteenth-Century Bali.* Princeton: Princeton University Press, 1980.

Genovese, Eugene D. *A Consuming Fire: The Fall of the Confederacy in the Mind of the White Christian South*. Athens: University of Georgia Press, 1998.

―――. *The Slaveholder's Dilemma: Freedom and Progress in Southern Conservative Thought*. Columbia: University of South Carolina Press, 1991.

―――. "South Carolina's Contribution to the Doctrine of Slavery in the Abstract." In *The Meaning of South Carolina History: Essays in Honor of George C. Rogers Jr.*, ed. David R. Chestnutt and Clyde N. Wilson. Columbia, University of South Carolina Press, 1991.

―――. *The Southern Tradition*. Cambridge: Harvard University Press, 1994.

Genovese, Eugene, and Elizabeth Fox-Genovese. "M. E. Bradford's Historical Vision." In *Defender of Southern Conservatism*, ed. Clyde N. Wilson. Columbia: University of Missouri, 1999.

Gerster, Patrick, and Nicholas Cords, eds. *Myth and Southern History*, Urbana: University of Chicago Press, 1989.

Gettys, James Wylie. "Mobilization for Secession in Greenville District." Master's thesis, University of South Carolina, 1967.

Gillespie, Neal C. *The Collapse of Orthodoxy: The Intellectual Ordeal of George Fredrick Holmes*. Charlottesville: University Press of Virginia, 1972.

Gillette, William. *Retreat from Reconstruction, 1869–1879*. Baton Rouge: Louisiana State University Press, 1979.

Goodwyn, Lawrence. *Democratic Promise: The Populist Moment in America*. New York: Oxford University Press, 1976.

―――. *The Populist Moment: A Short History of the Agrarian Revolt in America*. New York: Oxford University Press, 1978.

Greenberg, Kenneth. *Honor and Slavery*. Princeton: Princeton University Press, 1996.

Guttmann, Allen. *The Conservative Tradition in America*. New York: Oxford University Press, 1967.

Hahn, Steven. *The Roots of Southern Populism: Yeoman Farmer and the Transformation of the Georgia Upcountry, 1850–1890*. New York: Oxford University Press, 1984.

Hale, Grace Elizabeth. *Making Whiteness: The Culture of Segregation in the South*. New York: Pantheon, 1998.

Hall, Stuart. "The Problem of Ideology: Marxism without Guarantees." In *Stuart Hall: Critical Dialogues in Cultural Studies*, ed. David Morley and Kuan-Hsing-Chen. London: Routledge, 1996.

Harris, J. William. *Plain Folk and Gentry in a Slave Society: White Liberty and Black Slavery in Augusta's Hinterlands*. Middletown, Conn.: Wesleyan University Press, 1985.

Harvey, Paul. *Redeeming the South: Religious Cultures and Racial Identities among Southern Baptists, 1865–1925*. Chapel Hill: University of North Carolina Press, 1997.

Hatch, Nathan O. *Sacred Cause of Liberty: Republican Thought and the Mil-*

lennium in Revolutionary New England. New Haven: Yale University Press, 1977.

Hatley, Thomas. *Dividing Paths: Cherokees and South Carolinians through the Revolutionary Era.* New York: Oxford University Press, 1995.

Heffer, Simon. *Moral Desperado: A Life of Thomas Carlyle.* London: Weidenfeld and Nicolson, 1995.

Hegel, G. W. F. *On Art, Religion and the History of Philosophy: Introductory Lectures.* Ed. J. Glenn Gray. Indianapolis: Hackett, 1997.

Herberg, Will, *Protestant, Catholic, Jew: An Essay in American Religious Sociology.* Garden City, N.Y.: Doubleday, 1960.

Herzog, Don. *Poisoning the Minds of the Lower Orders.* Princeton: Princeton University Press, 1998.

Hesseltine, William B. *Confederate Leaders in the New South.* Baton Rouge: Louisiana State University Press, 1949.

Heyrman, Christine Leigh. *Southern Cross: The Beginnings of the Bible Belt.* New York: Knopf, 1997.

Hill, Samuel. *Southern Churches in Crisis.* New York: Holt, Rinehart and Winston, 1967.

Hobsbawm, Eric. *Age of Capital: 1848–1875.* New York: Scribners, 1975.

———. *The Age of Revolution, 1789–1848.* New York: New American Library, 1964.

———. *Bandits.* New York: Pantheon, 1981.

Hoffman, Frederick L. *Race Traits and Tendencies of the American Negro.* New York: American Economic Association, Macmillan, 1896.

Hofstader, Richard. *The Age of Reform: From Bryan to FDR.* New York: Knopf, 1955.

Hogan, Edward. "South Carolina Today" *International Review,* vol. 8, 1880.

Holden, Charles J. "Is Our Love of Wade Hampton Foolishness? South Carolina and the Lost Cause." In *Myth of the Lost Cause and Civil War History,* ed. Gary W. Gallagher and Alan T. Nolan. Bloomington: Indiana University Press, 2000.

Holmes, George Frederick. "Schlegel's Philosophy of History." In *All Clever Men, Who Make Their Way: Critical Discourse in the Old South,* ed. Michael O'Brien. Fayetteville: University of Arkansas Press, 1982.

Holt, Thomas. *Black over White: Negro Political Leadership in South Carolina during Reconstruction.* Urbana: University of Illinois Press, 1977.

Horowitz, Tony. *Confederates in the Attic: Dispatches from the Unfinished Civil War.* New York: Pantheon, 1988.

Houghton, Walter E. *The Victorian Frame of Mind.* New Haven: Yale University Press, 1957.

Howe, Elizabeth M. *A Ku Klux Uniform.* Buffalo: Buffalo Historical Publications, 1921.

Hummel, Jeffrey Rogers. *Emancipating Slaves, Enslaving Free Men: A History of the American Civil War.* Chicago: Open Court, 1996.

Hunt, Lynn. *Politics, Culture, and Class in the French Revolution.* Berkeley: University of California Press, 1984.

Isaac, Rhys. *The Transformation of Virginia: 1740–1790.* Chapel Hill: University of North Carolina Press, 1982.

Jarrell, Hampton M. *Wade Hampton and the Negro: The Road Not Taken.* Columbia: University of South Carolina Press, 1949.

Jenkins, Wilbert L. *Seizing the New Day: African Americans in Post–Civil War Charleston.* Bloomington: Indiana University Press, 1998.

Johnson, Paul E. *A Shopkeeper's Millennium: Society and Revivals in Rochester, New York, 1815–1837.* New York: Hill and Wang, 1978.

Journal of the Convention of the People of South Carolina Held in 1860. Columbia, S.C.: R. W. Gibbes, 1860.

Kantrowitz, Stephen. *Ben Tillman and the Reconstruction of White Supremacy.* Chapel Hill: University of North Carolina Press, 2000.

King, Joe. *History of South Carolina Baptists.* Columbia: General Board of the South Carolina Baptist Convention, 1961.

Kipling, Gordon. *Enter the King: Theatre, Liturgy, and Ritual in the Medieval Civic Triumph.* Oxford: Oxford University Press, 1998.

Kirk, Russell. *The Conservative Mind: From Burke to Eliot.* 7th rev. ed. Washington, D.C.: Regnery, 1995.

Klein, Rachel N. *Unification of a Slave State: The Rise of the Planter Class in the South Carolina Backcountry, 1760–1808.* Chapel Hill: University of North Carolina Press, 1990.

Krick, Robert K. "Maxcy Gregg: Political Extremist and Confederate General." *Civil War History* 19, no. 14. Reprint, Kent, Ohio: Kent State, 1974.

Kristeva, Julie. "*Stabat Mater.*" In *The Kristeva Reader,* ed. Toril Moi. New York: Columbia University Press, 1986.

Kousser, J. Morgan, and James M. McPherson, eds. *Region, Race, and Reconstruction: Essays in Honor of C. Vann Woodward.* New York: Oxford University Press, 1982.

Landrum, J. B. O. *A History of Spartanburg County.* Atlanta: Franklin, 1900.

Langer, Susanne. *Philosophy in a New Key: A Study in the Symbolism of Reason, Rite, and Art.* 3rd ed. Cambridge: Harvard University Press, 1957.

Leconte, Emma. *When the World Ended: The Diary of Emma Leconte.* Ed. Earl Schienk Miers. New York: Oxford University Press, 1957.

Leland, John A. *A Voice from South Carolina.* Charleston: Walker, Evans and Cogswell, 1879.

Link, William A. *The Paradox of Southern Progressivism: 1880–1930.* Chapel Hill: University of North Carolina Press, 1992.

Logan, John Henry. *A History of the Upper Country of South Carolina.* Charleston, S.C.: Walker, Evans and Cogswell, 1859

Lumpkin, Katharine Du Pre. *The Making of a Southerner.* Athens: University of Georgia Press, 1991.

Macauley, Neil W. "South Carolina Reconstruction Historiography." *South Carolina Historical Magazine,* vol. 65, 1964.

Machiavelli, Niccolò. *Discourses on Livy.* Trans. Harvey C. Mansfield and Nathan Tarcov. Chicago: University of Chicago Press, 1996.

Malvasi, Mark. *The Unregenerate South.* Baton Rouge: Louisiana State University Press, 1996.

Mann, Golo. "Wat ist Konservative?" *Der Morat,* vol. 6, 1953–54.

Martin, Samuel J. *Southern Hero: Matthew Calbraith Butler.* Mechanicsburg, Pa.: Stackpole, 2001.

Marx, Karl. *Capital: An Abridged Edition.* Ed. David McLellan. Oxford: Oxford University Press, 1995.

Matthews, Donald. *Religion in the Old South.* Chapel Hill: University of North Carolina Press, 1982.

McCardell, John. *The Idea of a Southern Nation.* New York: Norton, 1979.

McCully, R. S. "Letter from a Reconstruction Renegade." *South Carolina Historical Magazine,* vol. 77, 1976.

McCurry, Stephanie. *Masters of Small Worlds: Yeoman Households, Gender Relations, and the Political Culture of the Antebellum South Carolina Low Country.* Oxford: Oxford University Press, 1995.

———. " 'Two Faces of Republicanism': Gender and Proslavery Politics in Antebellum South Carolina." *Journal of American History* 78 (March 1992), 1245–64.

McMath, Robert. *Populist Vanguard: A History of the Southern Farmer's Alliance.* Chapel Hill: University of North Carolina Press, 1975.

Meynardie, Florella. *Amy Oakley; or The Reign of the Carpet-Bagger.* Charleston: Walker, Evans and Cogswell, 1879.

Miller, Randall M., Harry S. Stout, and Charles Reagan Wilson, eds. *Religion and the American Civil War.* New York: Oxford University Press, 1998.

Miller, Wilbur R. *Revenuers and Moonshiners: Enforcing Federal Liquor Law in the Mountain South, 1865–1900.* Chapel Hill: University of North Carolina Press, 1991.

Moi, Toril, ed. *The Kristeva Reader.* New York: Columbia University Press, 1986.

Moore, Winifred B., Jr., Joseph Tripp, and Lyon G. Tyler. *Developing Dixie: Modernization in a Traditional Society.* Westport, Conn.: Greenwood, 1988.

Morley, David, and Kuan-Hsing-Chen. *Stuart Hall: Critical Dialogues in Cultural Studies.* London: Routledge, 1996.

Morris, Jane. *Pickens: The Town and the First Baptist Church.* Pickens, S.C.: South Carolina Department of Archives and History, 1971.

Morris, Michael P. *The Bringing of Wonder: Trade and the Indians of the Southeast, 1700–1783.* Westport, Conn.: Greenwood, 1999.

Muller, Jerry Z. *Conservatism.* Princeton: Princeton University Press, 1997.

———. *The Other God That Failed: Hans Freyer and the Deradicalization of German Conservatism.* Princeton: Princeton University Press, 1987.

Newman, Simon P. *Parade and Politics of the Street: Festive Culture in the Early American Republic.* Philadelphia: University of Pennsylvania Press, 1997.

Niven, John. *John C. Calhoun and the Price of Union: A Biography.* Baton Rouge: Louisiana State University Press, 1988.

Norton, Jerry William. "South Carolina Taxpayers Convention of 1871." Master's thesis, University of South Carolina, 1971.

Oakes, James. *The Ruling Race: A History of American Slaveholders.* New York: Norton, 1998.

———. *Slavery and Freedom: An Interpretation of the Old South.* New York: Norton, 1990.

O'Brien, Michael, ed. *All Clever Men Who Make Their Way: Critical Discourse in the Old South.* Fayetteville: University of Arkansas Press, 1982.

Oldfield, John. " 'Remembering the Maine': The United States, 1898, and Sectional Reconciliation." In *The Crisis of 1898: Colonial Redistribution and Nationalist Mobilization,* ed. Angel Smith and Emma Dávila Cox. New York: St. Martin's, 1999.

Osterweis, Rollin G. *The Myth of the Lost Cause, 1865–1900.* Hamden, Conn.: Archon Books, 1973.

———. *Romanticisms and Nationalism in the Old South.* New Haven: Yale University Press, 1949.

O'Sullivan, Noel. *Conservatism.* New York: St. Martin's, 1976.

Percy, Walker. "Metaphor as Mistake." In *The Message in the Bottle: How Queer Man Is, How Queer Language Is, and What One Has to Do with the Other.* New York: Farrar, Straus and Giroux, 1989.

———. "Stoicism in the South." In *Signposts in a Strange Land.* Ed. Patrick Samway. New York: Noonday, 1979.

Perry, Benjamin F. *Reminiscences of Public Men.* Greenville, S.C.: Shannon and Company, 1889.

Pocock, J. G. A. *The Machiavellian Moment: Florentine Political Thought and the Atlantic Republican Tradition.* Princeton: Princeton University Press, 1975.

"Political Condition of South Carolina." *Atlantic Monthly* 39 (February 1877).

Poole, W. Scott. "Wade Hampton." In *The Encyclopedia of the American Civil War,* ed. David and Jeanne Hediler. Santa Barbara: ABC-Clio, 2000.

Poppenheim, Mary B., Maude Merchant, and Ruth Lawton. *A History of the United Daughters of the Confederacy, 1894–1955.* N.p.: Richmond, Garrett, and Massie, 1938.

Pratt, Mary Louise. *Imperial Eyes: Travel Writing and Transculturation.* New York: Routledge, 1992.

Pritchard, Claudius Hornby. "Colonel Wyatt Aiken, South Carolina's Militant Agrarian, 1828–1887." Master's thesis, Longwood College, 1965.

Proceedings of the 1871 Taxpayers Convention. Charleston: Walker, Evans and Cogswell, 1872.

Proceedings in the Ku Klux Trials at Columbia, South Carolina, in U.S. Circuit Court, November 1871. New York: Negro Universities Press, 1969.

Rabinowitz, Howard. "The Origins of a Poststructural New South: A Review of Edward Ayers The Promise of the New South: Life after Reconstruction." *Journal of Southern History* 59 (1993): 505–15.

Racine, Phillip, ed. *Piedmont Farmer: The Journals of David Golightly Harris, 1855–1870.* Knoxville: University of Tennessee Press, 1990.

Ransom, John Crowe. *God without Thunder: An Unorthodox Defense of Orthodoxy.* Hamden, Conn.: Archon, 1965.

Reed, John Shelton. *Whistling Dixie: Dispatches from the South.* San Diego: Harcourt Brace Jovanovich, 1990.

Reid, J. W. *History of the Fourth Regiment of South Carolina Volunteers, from the Commencement of the War until Lee's Surrender.* 1892. Reprint, Dayton, Ohio: Morningside, 1975.

"Respectful Remonstrance on Behalf of the White People of South Carolina." Columbia, 1868.

Rhett, Robert Barnwell, Jr. "Fears for Democracy." *Southern Magazine* 17 (September 1875).

Robertson, Ben. *Red Hills and Cotton: An Upcountry Memory.* Columbia: University of South Carolina Press, 1960.

Rosenburg, R. B. *Living Monuments: Confederate Soldiers' Homes in the New South.* Chapel Hill: University of North Carolina Press, 1993.

Rossiter, Clinton. *Conservatism in America: The Thankless Persuasion.* New York: Knopf, 1968.

Ryan, Mary P. *Cradle of the Middle Class: The Family in Oneida County, New York, 1790–1865.* Cambridge: Cambridge University Press, 1981.

Samway, Patrick, ed. *Signposts in a Strange Land.* New York: Noonday, 1979.

Santayana, George. *The Life of Reason.* Amherst, N.Y.: Prometheus, 1998.

Savage, Kirk. *Standing Soldiers, Kneeling Slaves: Race, War, and Monument in Nineteenth-Century America.* Princeton: Princeton University Press, 1997.

Scruton, Roger. "Recent Aesthetics in England and America." In *The Aesthetic Understanding: Essays in the Philosophy of Art and Culture.* Manchester, Eng.: Carcanet, 1983.

Sease, Elberta. *Aunt Kate 100 Years Dear.* Lexington, S.C.: Privately Published, 1971.

Seigler, Robert S. *A Guide to Confederate Monuments in South Carolina: Passing the Silent Cup.* Columbia: South Carolina Department of Archives and History, 1997.

Sellers, Charles. *The Market Revolution: Jacksonian America, 1815–1846.* New York: Oxford University Press.

Sernett, Milton C., ed. *Afro-American Religious History: A Documentary Witness.* Durham: Duke University Press, 1985.

Sheppard, William Arthur. *Red Shirts Remembered: Southern Brigadiers of the Reconstruction Period.* Atlanta: Ruralist, 1940.

Shipp, Albert. *History of Methodism in South Carolina.* Nashville, Tenn.: Southern Methodist, 1883.

Silber, Nina. *The Romance of Reunion: Northerners and the South, 1865–1900.* Chapel Hill: University of North Carolina Press, 1993.

Simkins, Francis Butler. *The Tillman Movement in South Carolina.* 1926. Reprint, Gloucester, Mass.: Peter Smith, 1964.

Simkins, Francis Butler, and Robert H. Woody. *South Carolina during Reconstruction.* Gloucester, Mass.: Peter Smith, 1966.

Simms, William Gilmore. "Humiliation Spreads Its Ashes." In *The Confederate Reader,* ed. Richard B. Harwell. New York: Dover, 1989.

Simon, Bryant. "The Appeal of Cole Blease in South Carolina: Race, Class and Sex in the New South." *Journal of Southern History* 62 (1996): 57–86.

Simpson, John A. *S. A. Cunningham and the Confederate Heritage.* Athens: University of Georgia Press, 1994.

Simpson, R. W. *History of Old Pendleton District.* Anderson, S.C.: Oulla Printing and Binding, 1930.

Sims, J. Marion. *The Story of My Life.* 1882. Reprint, New York: Da Capo, 1968.

Singal, Daniel. *The War Within: From Victorian to Modernist Thought in the South, 1919–1945.* Chapel Hill: University of North Carolina Press, 1982.

Sinha, Manisha. *The Counterrevolution of Slavery: Politics and Ideology in Antebellum South Carolina.* Chapel Hill: University of North Carolina Press, 2000.

Snay, Mitchell. *Gospel of Disunion: Religion and Separatism in the Antebellum South.* Chapel Hill: University of North Carolina Press, 1997.

Snowden, Yates, ed. *History of South Carolina.* Vol. 4. Chicago: Lewis, 1920.

South Carolina Monument Association: Origins and History. Charleston: South Carolina Monument Association, News and Courier Book Press, 1879.

South Carolina State Board of Agriculture. *South Carolina: Resources, Population, Institutions, and Industry.* Charleston, 1883.

Sparks, Claude Ezell. *A History of Padgett's Creek Baptist Church.* Union, S.C.: privately published, 1967.

Stagg, J. C. A. "The Problem of Klan Violence in the South Carolina Upcountry, 1868–1871." *Journal of American Studies* 8 (December 1974): 303–38.

Stampp, Kenneth M. *The Era of Reconstruction, 1865–1877.* New York: Knopf, 1965.

Stanlis, Peter J. "Burke, Rousseau and Revolution." In *Burke and the French Revolution: Bicentennial Essays,* ed. Steven Blakemore. Athens: University of Georgia Press, 1992.

Stedman-Jones, Gareth. *Languages of Class: Studies in English Working Class History, 1832–1982.* Cambridge: Cambridge University Press, 1983.

Stoler, Anne Laura. *Race and the Education of Desire: Foucault's History of Sex-*

uality and the Colonial Order of Things. Durham N.C.: Duke University Press, 1995.

Stowe, Steven M. *Intimacy and Power in the Old South: Ritual in the Lives of Planters.* Baltimore: Johns Hopkins University Press, 1987.

Straka, Gerald. "The Influence of Thomas Carlyle in the Old South, 1848–1865." Master's thesis, University of Virginia, 1953.

Taylor, Mrs. Thomas, and Mrs. James Connor. *South Carolina Women in the Confederacy.* Columbia, S.C.: State Company, 1907.

Thompson, E. P. *The Making of the English Working Class.* New York: Vintage Books, 1966.

Thompson, F. M. L. *The Rise of Respectable Society: A Social History of Victorian Britain.* Cambridge: Harvard University Press, 1988.

Thompson, Henry Tazewell. *Ousting the Carpetbagger from South Carolina.* Columbia: R. L. Bryan, 1926.

Thornton, J. Mills, III. *Politics and Power in a Slave Society: Alabama, 1800– 1860.* Baton Rouge: Louisiana State University Press, 1978.

Tindall, George. "Mythology: A New Frontier in Southern History." In *Myth and Southern History,* ed. Patrick Gerster and Nicholas Cords. Urbana: University of Chicago Press, 1989.

———. *South Carolina Negroes, 1877–1900.* Columbia: University of South Carolina Press, 1952.

Toole, G. L. *Ninety Years in Aiken County: Memories of Aiken and Its People.* N.p., [1958?].

[Townsend, Belton O'Neall]. "The Political Condition of South Carolina." *Atlantic Monthly* 39 (February 1877), 183.

Trachtenberg, Alan. *The Incorporation of America.* New York: Hill and Wang, 1982.

Trelease, Allen. *White Terror: The Ku Klux Klan Conspiracy and Southern Reconstruction.* New York: Harper and Row, 1971.

Tullos, Allen. *The Habits of Industry: White Culture and the Transformation of the Carolina Piedmont.* Chapel Hill: University of North Carolina Press, 1989.

Turner, Josephine M. *Courageous Caroline: Founder of the U.D.C.* Montgomery, Ala.: privately published, 1928. Reprint, Montgomery, Ala.: n.p., 1965.

Turner, Victor. *Dramas, Fields and Metaphors: Symbolic Action in Human Society.* Ithaca: Cornell University Press, 1974.

U.S. House. *Report of the Secretary of War, 1867.* H. Exec. Doc. 1, part 1. 40th Cong., 2nd sess. Washington, D.C.: Government Printing Office, 1868.

U.S. Senate. *Report of the Committee of Agriculture and Forestry on the Condition of Cotton Growers.* 53rd Cong., 3rd sess., 1895.

———. *Senate Miscellaneous Documents,* 44th Cong., 2nd sess., No. 48: *South Carolina in 1876: Testimony as to the Denial of the Elective Franchise in South Carolina at the Elections of 1875 and 1876.* 3 vols. Serials 1727–29. Washington, D.C., 1877.

————. Subcommittee on Privileges and Elections. *South Carolina in 1876: Report on the Denial of the Elective Franchise in South Carolina at the State and National Election of 1876, to Accompany Senate Miscellaneous Document 48., 44th Cong., 2nd Sess.* Washington, D.C., 1877.

Van der Leuw, Gerardus. *Sacred and Profane Beauty: The Holy in Art.* Trans. David Green. Nashville: Abingdon, 1963.

Vandiver, Frank. "The Southerner as Extremist." In *The Idea of the South: Pursuit of a Central Theme,* ed. Frank E. Vandiver. Chicago: Published for William Marsh Rice University by the University of Chicago Press, 1964.

Vandiver, Louise Ayer. *Traditions and History of Anderson County.* Atlanta: Ruralist, 1928.

Vivas, Eliseo, and Murray Krieger, eds. *The Problems of Aesthetics: A Book of Readings.* New York: Holt, Rinehart and Winston, 1953.

Warner, Marina. *Monuments and Maidens: The Allegory of the Female Form.* New York: Athenaeum, 1985.

Weaver, Richard M. *The Southern Tradition at Bay: A History of Postbellum Thought.* Washington, D.C.: Regnery, 1989.

Weber, Max. *Sociology of Religion.* Boston: Beacon, 1963.

Weir, Robert M. *Colonial South Carolina: A History.* Columbia: University of South Carolina Press, 1997.

Wellman, Manly Wade. *Giant in Gray: A Biography of Wade Hampton of South Carolina.* New York: Scribners, 1949.

Wells, Edward L. *Hampton and Reconstruction.* Columbia, S.C.: State Company, 1907.

Werner, Randolph D. " 'New South' Carolina: Ben Tillman and the Rise of Bourgeois Politics, 1880–1893." In *Developing Dixie: Modernization in a Traditional Society,* ed. Winifred B. Moore Jr., Joseph Tripp, and Lyon G. Tyler. Westport, Conn.: Greenwood, 1988.

Whites, LeeAnn. *The Civil War as a Crisis in Gender: Augusta, Georgia, 1860–1890.* Athens: University of Georgia Press, 1995.

Williams, Alfred Brockenbrough. *Hampton and His Red Shirts: South Carolina's Deliverance in 1876.* Charleston: Walker, Evans and Cogswell, 1935.

Williams, Lou Falkner. *The Great South Carolina Ku Klux Klan Trials, 1871–1872.* Athens: University of Georgia Press, 1996.

Williamson, Joel. *After Slavery: The Negro in South Carolina during Reconstruction.* Hanover, N.H.: University Press of New England, 1990.

————. *The Origins of Segregation.* Boston: D. C. Heath, 1968.

————. *A Rage for Order: Black-White Relations in the American South since Emancipation.* New York: Oxford University Press, 1986.

Williamson, Gustauvus. "South Carolina Cotton Mills and the Tillman Movement." In *Proceedings of the South Carolina Historical Association.* Columbia: South Carolina Historical Association, 1949.

Wilson, Charles R. *Baptized in Blood: The Religion of the Lost Cause, 1865–1920.* Athens: University of Georgia Press, 1980.

———. *Judgment and Grace in Dixie: Southern Faiths from Faulkner to Elvis.* Athens: University of Georgia Press, 1995.

Wilson, Clyde N., ed. *Defender of Southern Conservatism.* Columbia: University of Missouri Press, 1999.

Wilson, John F. *Public Religion in American Culture.* Philadelphia: Temple University Press, 1979.

Wilson, John Lide. *The Code of Honor, or Rules for the Government of Principles and Seconds in Dueling.* Charleston: Walker, Evans and Cogswell, 1838.

———. *Exercise and Instructions of Field Artillery.* Charleston: Walker, Evans and Cogswell, 1834.

Woodman, Harold D. "Class, Race, Politics and the Modernization of the Postbellum South." *Journal of Southern History* 63 (February 1997): 3–22.

Woodmason, Charles. *The Carolina Backcountry on the Eve of the Revolution: The Journal and Other Writings of Charles Woodmason, Anglican Itinerant.* Ed. Richard J. Hooker. Chapel Hill: University of North Carolina Press, 1993.

Woodward, C. Vann. *The Burden of Southern History.* Baton Rouge: Louisiana State University Press, 1993.

———. *Origins of the New South, 1877–1913.* Baton Rouge: Louisiana State University Press, 1995.

———. "The Populist Heritage and the Intellectual." In *The Burden of Southern History.*

———. *Reunion and Reaction: The Compromise of 1877 and the End of Reconstruction.* Boston: Little, Brown, 1951.

Wyatt-Brown, Bertram. *Honor and Violence in the Old South.* New York: Oxford University Press, 1986.

———. *Southern Honor: Ethics and Behavior in the Old South.* Oxford: Oxford University Press, 1986.

Wyckoff, Mac. *A History of the Second South Carolina Infantry: 1861–65.* Fredricksburg, Va.: Sergeant Kirkland's Museum and Historical Society, 1994.

Young, Jeffrey Robert. *Domesticating Slavery: The Master Class in Georgia and South Carolina, 1670–1837.* Chapel Hill: University of North Carolina Press, 1999.

Zettler, B. M. *War Stories and School Day Incidents.* 1912. Reprint, Smyrna, Ga., 1993.

Zinn, Howard. *A People's History of the United States.* New York: Harper Perennial, 1995.

Zuczek, Richard. *State of Rebellion: Reconstruction in South Carolina.* Columbia, S.C.: University of South Carolina Press, 1996.

INDEX

Abbeville, 61, 143, 151
Abolitionists, 44–45, 50
Aesthetic(s), 17, 36, 64, 75, 81, 118; conflict of, with bourgeois ideology, 20–21, 157, 194, 201–2; and European tradition, 4–5; farmers movement and, 142, 149–50; as "game of ghosts," 91–92; and interpretation of the Lost Cause, 3–4, 48, 55–56, 198–99, 204; philosophical pessimism and, 56, 85; political tendencies of, 57–59, 115, 126; and ritual, 94–97, 121–22, 205; southern women and, 47–50, 58, 68–69, 128–35; and violence, 99, 111–12
African Americans, 40–41, 59–60, 161, 195, 197–98, 207; portrayal of, in 1876 campaign, 130–35; resistance of, to the conservative order, 61, 73–75, 101–2; in the twentieth century, 203; as viewed by white conservatives, 118–19, 124–25
Agricultural clubs, 78, 107, 158. *See also* Farmer's Alliance; Ku Klux Klan; Populism; Property
Aiken, 114, 128, 134, 158; violence in, 159
Aiken, D. Wyatt, 139–42, 148, 159, 183
Alcohol: church discipline and, 42–44; dispensary plan and, 174; evangelicalism and, 167; prohibition of, 162, 167. *See also* Evangelicalism; militia musters

Amy Oakley, 51–52, 133
Anderson County, 37, 42–43, 80, 86, 101, 150, 165, 173, 180, 193; Soldier's Aid Association in, 67; textile mills in, 161–62, 189; violence in, 101–2, 104–5
Augusta, Ga., 158

Bachman, John, 45, 60
Ball, William Watts, 122
Baptists, 15, 73, 125; individual congregations mentioned, 37, 39–41, 43, 46–47, 73, 101, 188, 191. *See also* Evangelicalism
Barnwell County, 169
Benedict College, 206
Black codes, 102
Blease, Coleman, 203–4
Bourbons, 138, 192, 201, 205; attacked by Tillman, 147, 153–54, 158, 162; and child labor, 191; interpretation of, 198–99
Bourgeoisie, 13, 19, 22, 40, 172–73, 176–77, 183; contrasted with southern conservatism, 157, 159, 194, 199–202; Lost Cause and, 179; relationship of, to the past, 202–3; violence and, 169. *See also* Capitalism; Property
Bradford, M. E., 33
Braudel, Fernand, 5
Brown, Texas, 104
Buff, W. M., 178–79
Burke, Edmund, 4, 17, 30, 87
Butler, A. P., 162
Butler, Matthew C., 114, 130, 144, 150, 152, 172